The Civil Justice Reforms One Year On

Freshfields assess their progress

THE CIVIL JUSTICE REFORMS ONE YEAR ON

FRESHFIELDS ASSESS THEIR PROGRESS

Authors

Michelle Bramley*

Anna Gouge*

Consultants

The Honourable Mr Justice Dyson, Technology and Construction Court, High Court

The Honourable Mr Justice Lightman, Chancery Division, High Court

The Honourable Mr Justice Langley, Commercial Court, High Court

Master Leslie, Queen's Bench Division, High Court

Harriet Kimbell, Member of the Civil Procedure Rule Committee

Paul Bowden, Freshfields

* Also authors of *The Woolf Reforms in Practice: Freshfields assess the changing landscape* (Butterworths, 1998)

BUTTERWORTHS
LONDON
2000

United Kingdom	Butterworths, a Division of Reed Elsevier (UK) Ltd, Halsbury House, 35 Chancery Lane, LONDON WC2A 1EL and 4 Hill Street, EDINBURGH EH2 3JZ
Australia	Butterworths, a Division of Reed International Books Australia Pty Ltd, CHATSWOOD, New South Wales
Canada	Butterworths Canada Ltd, MARKHAM, Ontario
Hong Kong	Butterworths Asia (Hong Kong), HONG KONG
India	Butterworths India, NEW DELHI
Ireland	Butterworth (Ireland) Ltd, DUBLIN
Malaysia	Malayan Law Journal Sdn Bhd, KUALA LUMPUR
New Zealand	Butterworths of New Zealand Ltd, WELLINGTON
Singapore	Butterworths Asia, SINGAPORE
South Africa	Butterworths Publishers (Pty) Ltd, DURBAN
USA	Lexis Law Publishing, CHARLOTTESVILLE, Virginia

© Reed Elsevier (UK) Ltd 2000

A CIP Catalogue record for this book is available from the British Library.

ISBN 0 406 93153 4

Printed and bound in Great Britain by
Butler & Tanner Ltd, Frome and London

Visit us at our website: http://www.butterworths.co.uk

CONTENTS

INTRODUCTION

'The message for all those involved in the civil justice system, judges, practitioners and court staff alike, is that the changes being introduced in April [1999] are as much changes of culture as they are changes in the Rules themselves. We have to be ready to be pro-active, not reactive. And we must see this as the beginning, not the end, of the process of change.' (Lord Irvine of Lairg, Foreword to the Civil Procedure Rules).

When we published a guide to the impending 'Woolf reforms' 18 months ago, the Civil Procedure Rules ('CPR') were still in draft form, and there was widespread uncertainty amongst commercial practitioners and their clients as to how the CPR would operate in practice. Since then, the litigation landscape has been transformed. The new rules and accompanying practice directions have come into force, pre-action protocols for personal injury and clinical negligence have been introduced (with the promise of many more to follow), and the specialist lists have published their own supplemental procedural guides and practice directions.

The pace of change has been fast, and shows little sign of slowing down. As the Lord Chancellor emphasised when the CPR were introduced, this is the beginning and not the end of the reform process. During the next twelve months new rules on many other aspects of civil procedure (including civil appeals) are to be implemented, the existing rules and practice directions will continue to be revised and amended where necessary, and proposals for further reform will be published for consultation. New legislation will also create further challenges, as the courts, practitioners and litigants adjust to the reform of the legal aid system under the Access to Justice Act 1999 and the implications of the introduction of the European Convention for the Protection of Human Rights and Fundamental Freedoms (the European Convention on Human Rights) into national law.

The speed and scope of the reforms have placed heavy demands on the judiciary, the court service and the legal professions. The busy commercial practitioner has not only had to master the rules, practice directions and protocols (and the variations applicable to each of the specialist lists) in short order, but also to adapt his working methods and office procedures in order to meet the challenges of the new regime. There is also an ongoing need to keep abreast of recent cases, to anticipate future developments in the interpretation and application of the rules, and at the same time to keep an eye on the 'big picture'. Whilst it is essential to master the detail, it is also important to have an overview of the impact of the changes on litigation practice as a whole, and the changes in culture they demand from law firms and their clients.

This guide aims to simplify that exercise by providing an overview of the progress of the CPR during the last twelve months by reference to recent cases and practical examples. It also considers how the reforms have affected the management of commercial litigation in practice; which aspects of the rules are working well and which areas may require further improvement; what effect the changes are having on litigants; the strategic and tactical considerations to take into account when acting for a claimant or a defendant; and how companies and their legal advisers can maximise their prospects of succeeding under the new regime.

The progress so far

The civil justice reform process led by Lord Woolf set itself ambitious aims. Lord Woolf's two reports together made over 300 separate recommendations to improve and streamline the civil litigation process, and his proposals went to the heart of the civil justice system. He proposed a complete overhaul of the system, and this is what the CPR delivered—an entirely new procedural code, which placed new demands on the judiciary, on parties to litigation and on their legal advisers, in order to achieve the overriding objective of 'dealing with cases justly'.

There were many predictions before the CPR were introduced that the court service, the judiciary and practitioners would not be ready in time, and that clients would not receive the improved, more efficient service they had been led to expect. In fact, initial reports from the courts and practitioners suggest that the changes have proved to be less disruptive than was feared and that despite some minor problems, the CPR are generally working well in practice.

There are obvious risks in attempting to form a view as to how the reforms are faring on the basis of only a year's practical experience of the new regime and relatively few decided cases. Such an assessment inevitably involves a degree of speculation as to how the rules will develop in practice. Conversely, this is precisely the time at which guidance is most needed by many practitioners. We have therefore offered in the chapters which follow some initial observations on how the reforms are progressing, based on our own experience and the experience of the consultants who have assisted with this project.

It appears that the antagonistic, adversarial culture deprecated by Lord Woolf is in decline and that in its place there is a new degree of cooperation between the parties. A new partnership is emerging between the parties, their advisers and the court. The new rules offer greater flexibility, and during the initial 'transitional phase' at least, the courts have in general been exercising their wide discretion with restraint. The new case management procedures are succeeding in defining the real issues earlier, and resulting in earlier settlements.

Further work still needs to be done on ironing out inconsistencies in the way in which the rules are applied in practice, and reducing the costs burden imposed by the new 'front-loaded' profile of litigation. Some practitioners have expressed concern that the reforms have so far failed to deliver simpler or more cost-effective procedures, or to provide greater access to justice to those who were disadvantaged under the previous regime. However, as the transitional phase draws to a close, with new cases started under the CPR outnumbering the remaining examples of poor case management under the old regime, the benefits of the new regime are likely to become more apparent. Case management procedures (which have placed a heavy administrative burden on the courts and on litigants) will become more predictable, streamlined and efficient. In the longer term, the introduction of improved IT systems, which are essential to the smooth running of a modern court service and civil justice system, should provide the opportunity to make pro-active case management by the courts achievable for all cases.

Among the greatest challenges facing those charged with the operation of the new regime in the next twelve months will be the introduction of the Human Rights Act 1998 in October 2000. While several provisions of the European Convention on Human Rights will be relevant to civil procedure (including the privacy rights in Article 8, the prohibition on discrimination in Article 14, and the protection of property in Article 1 of Protocol 1), most important among these will be the right to a fair trial enshrined in Article 6(1). The right to a fair trial is said to occupy a position of pre-eminence in the Convention and in the jurisprudence of the European Court of Human Rights. Indeed, more applications to Strasbourg concern the fair trial guarantees in Article 6 than any other provision, and most cases will nowadays relate, at least in part, to the fairness of court proceedings. Just as the Convention will inform the application of the CPR in coming months, so proceedings brought under the new regime will help to define and refine the implementation of the Human Rights Act.

The right to a fair trial under Article 6(1) applies to cases to be brought under the CPR and will be available not only to individuals, but to all private entities involved in litigation. Even commercial litigants will be able to have recourse to human rights arguments. The safeguards guaranteed by Article 6(1) must be observed in proceedings relating to quantum, as well as proceedings in which liability is to be determined, and in any subsequent appeals. Article 6(1) is open-ended and residual in nature, and can be thought of as establishing 'obligations of result'. Thus, national courts may follow such rules as they think fit, so long as their application results in a fair trial, and can be seen to do so, in the context of the proceedings taken as a whole. The overriding objective of the CPR appears to signal a similar conceptual approach, but the precise extent to which the two approaches coincide is open to debate and seems likely to generate considerable argument during the next twelve months.

One of the most important fair trial safeguards in the context of civil proceedings will be the principle of 'equality of arms', as developed by the European Court of Human Rights. The court has held[1] that in:

> 'litigation involving opposing private interests, "equality of arms" implies that each party must be afforded a reasonable opportunity to present his case—including his evidence—under conditions that do not place him at a substantial disadvantage vis-à-vis his opponent'.

1 *Dombo Beheer BV v Netherlands* (1993) 18 EHRR 213, ECtHR.

This principle is of obvious relevance to any judicial decision to restrict evidence in any way, and may become a prominent feature of case management conferences. However, the most important effect of the Human Rights Act may well be that it will require the English courts to think more in terms of substance and rights, and less in terms of form and remedies.

The scope of this guide

Whilst many of the worst abuses of the system which Lord Woolf identified did not arise in a commercial context, commercial litigation was not exempt from criticism nor from the impact of the proposed reforms. Anyone expecting 'business as usual' in commercial litigation will already have seen that this is not an option. The courts are making enthusiastic use of their new case management powers and expect litigants to participate actively in this new cooperative litigation environment. Even those specialist jurisdictions such as the Commercial Court and the Technology and Construction Court which have historically placed particular emphasis on active case management have introduced new practices.

The guide concentrates on the key provisions in the CPR in relation to multi-track cases, not only from the perspective of the commercial practitioner, but also from the perspective of the in-house lawyer and the lay business client (both of whom have increased roles and responsibilities in managing litigation under the new regime). We have not attempted to provide a comprehensive procedural guide to the rules and practice directions, since this is catered for elsewhere. The aim of the guide is to consider a number of key topics (including the critical area of pre-action tactics) and to bring together in relation to each topic the key rules, practice directions and protocols (and any variations applicable in the specialist lists), recent case law[2] and illustrations by reference to practical examples.

Finally, we should like to express our thanks to the individuals who have acted as consultants on this project, who despite the many other calls on their time have enabled us to supplement our own experience with their invaluable insight into how the reforms are working in practice.

Freshfields
April 2000

2   As at 17 March 2000.

1 PRE-ACTION TACTICS

A Introduction

In his Final Report Lord Woolf stated:

> 'My approach to civil justice is that disputes should, wherever possible, be resolved without litigation. Where litigation is unavoidable, it should be conducted with a view to encouraging settlement at the earliest possible stage'[1]

and that:

> 'Pre-action protocols will be an important part of the new system'.[2]

Lord Woolf's approach marks a fundamental shift in emphasis towards the pre-action stage of proceedings. Parties to a dispute are now expected to comply with any applicable pre-action protocol which relates to the dispute between the parties (discussed in detail below) and where none exists the parties are required in accordance with the overriding objective and the matters referred to in CPR 1.1(2)(a), (b) and (c)[3] to act reasonably in exchanging information and documents relevant to the claim and generally trying to avoid the necessity for the start of proceedings.[4]

Pursuant to the CPR, the court is specifically required to further the overriding objective by actively managing cases.[5] This includes:

- encouraging the parties to cooperate with each other in the cooperation of proceedings;
- identifying the issues at an early stage; and
- encouraging the parties to use an ADR procedure.

All of these themes are reflected in the practice direction to protocols and those pre-action protocols which have been published to date. They are also echoed in a number of pre-action protocols which are currently in draft or under development and which are discussed in detail in this chapter.

---

1 Final Report, Section III, Chapter 10, para 2
2 Final Report, Section III, Chapter 10, para 6.
3 In particular the parties are required to help the court in furthering the overriding objective of enabling the court to deal with cases justly and to have regard to the fact that dealing with a case justly includes, so far as is practicable:
   (a) ensuring that the parties are on an equal footing;
   (b) saving expense; and
   (c) dealing with the case in ways which are proportionate (i) to the amount of money involved; (ii) to the importance of the case; (iii) to the complexity of the issues; and (iv) to the financial position of each party.
4 Paragraph 4 of the practice direction to protocols.
5 CPR 1.4.

Twelve months after the implementation of the civil justice reforms it is clear that the pre-action period has increased significantly in importance. This chapter looks at the pre-action tactics which the parties should consider before commencing proceedings and at the court's approach to parties' pre-action conduct.

B   Pre-action protocols

The use of pre-action protocols to govern the conduct of parties as soon as a dispute emerges has been referred to by some as the cornerstone of the civil justice reforms. At present there are only two published pre-action protocols. These relate to personal injury claims and clinical medical negligence claims. The published pre-action protocols together with the practice direction to protocols are reproduced at Appendices C, D and E.

These pre-action protocols have a number of common features which are of general application to commercial litigation. For example, each pre-action protocol establishes a timetable for the exchange of information relating to the dispute and sets standards for the content of correspondence, enabling parties to make an informed judgment on the merits of their case at an early stage. This spirit should certainly be adhered to when complying with paragraph 4 of the practice direction to protocols. In particular the published pre-action protocols encourage the early identification of issues and the early disclosure of documentation relating to the claim. They also encourage the parties to enter into discussions and negotiations/alternative dispute resolution ('ADR') to settle the claim.

A further twenty protocols are also currently either in the development stage, in draft or under consultation. These protocols cover a whole host of disputes ranging from defamation and housing disrepair claims to professional negligence and Y2K claims. A full list of the protocols currently in development or in draft is at Appendix A and if all are implemented there is scope for considerable confusion with claims potentially being subject to a number of protocols, each adopting different procedures pre-action.

At present there is no general model protocol covering commercial disputes and in its absence the parties must comply with paragraph 4 of the practice direction to protocols. However both the draft protocol on professional negligence claims and the draft protocol on debt claims, if implemented, may have a major impact on the way in which a significant proportion of commercial disputes will be handled pre-action. At present the draft protocols differ greatly in their approach to pre-action conduct between the parties and are considered further below.

1   *Draft pre-action protocol on professional negligence claims*

The draft pre-action protocol on professional negligence claims is designed to apply to all claims against professionals (other than solicitors and healthcare providers which either have or are to have their own pre-action protocols). It is reproduced at Appendix B.

In summary the draft protocol sets out a framework for the provision of information between the parties, including the use of ADR to resolve the dispute without recourse to litigation.

The key features of the draft protocol are as follows:
- if a claimant is considering bringing a claim against a professional he should inform the professional in writing as soon as possible. The draft protocol states the information which this letter should contain and requires the professional to acknowledge receipt of the letter within 21 days;
- if the claimant decides that there are grounds for a claim against the professional he should send the professional a detailed letter of claim. Again the draft protocol states what this letter should contain and includes information such as a chronological summary (including key dates) of the facts on which the claim is based, copies of key documents, the allegations made against the professional and an estimate of how the alleged error has caused the loss claimed, an estimate of the financial loss suffered by the claimant together with supporting documents, confirmation of whether or not an expert has been appointed and if so the identity and discipline of the expert and the date of his appointment. Copies of any other letter of claim sent to other parties should also be included;
- the professional has 21 days within which to acknowledge receipt of the letter of claim and three months from sending this letter in which to investigate the claim although the claimant is expected to agree to any reasonable request for an extension of the three month period. Once investigations are complete the professional should send the claimant either a letter of response or a letter of settlement or both. Again the draft protocol specifies the information which the letter of response should contain, including whether the claim is admitted or denied in whole or part together with his version of the facts and his estimate of financial loss if the claimant's versions are disputed. The draft protocol also specifies what the letter of settlement should contain. This includes the settlement proposal or details of the further information required before the professional can formulate his proposal;
- if the letter of response denies the claim and makes no settlement proposals the claimant is free to commence proceedings;
- in any other circumstances the professional and claimant are to commence negotiations with the aim of concluding negotiations within six months of the date of the letter of acknowledgment;
- at any stage the parties can agree to take the dispute to ADR;
- if the claimant has not obtained expert evidence prior to sending the letter of claim the parties are encouraged to consider appointing a joint expert and to agree the expert's identity and terms of appointment; and
- the draft protocol states that the claimant should not commence proceedings (save for limitation purposes) until a letter of response denies the claim in its entirety and there is no letter of settlement or the end of the negotiation period or there has been an infringement (more than minor) by the professional of the time limits in this protocol.

2   Draft pre-action protocol on debt claims

A draft protocol on debt claims has been circulated for consultation. However, this is likely to be revised substantially to reflect comments made on the draft in the consultation phase. It is not yet known when a revised draft protocol will be available. The draft protocol was so widely drafted that it applied, in effect, to all claims for a specific sum of money, excluding only consumer credit and security transactions. It was also heavily weighted in favour of the claimant.

> **The key features of the draft protocol were as follows:**
> - the claimant was to send the proposed defendant a letter of claim. The draft protocol specified what the letter should contain and included details of the basis upon which the debt arose, the sum owing and a warning of the costs penalties if the letter was ignored;
> - the proposed defendant was to respond to the claimant's letter setting out details of the claim within a reasonable time and 'not less than seven days'[6] after the date of posting of the claimant's letter. If the defendant did not respond within this time the draft protocol stated that there would be no sanction against the claimant for commencing proceedings;
> - if the defendant disputed the claim and the claimant decided that disclosure was appropriate the draft protocol stated that the claimant should notify the proposed defendant that disclosure should be given by both parties; and
> - if the claimant considered that expert evidence was required the claimant had to give a list of one or more experts. The parties were to either agree a mutually acceptable expert within seven days or any objections were to be indicated. If all listed experts were objected to, each party could instruct an expert of his own choice. The court would subsequently decide if proceedings were issued whether the party who had objected had acted unreasonably.

3   Sanctions for non-compliance

The sanctions which the court may impose for failure to comply with an applicable pre-action protocol or paragraph 4 of the practice direction to protocols are severe. For example, pursuant to paragraph 2.1 of the practice direction to protocols the court may take into account compliance or non-compliance with an applicable protocol when giving directions for the management of the case.[7] Where a party has failed to comply with a pre-action protocol without good reason the court may order a party to pay a sum into court.[8] In addition, the extent to which a party has complied with an applicable pre-action protocol (or failed to do so) will be taken into account when the court considers any application for relief from sanctions as a result of a failure to comply with any rule, practice direction or order from the court.[9]

6   This was probably an error and should presumably have read 'within seven days'.
7   CPR 3.1(4).
8   CPR 3.1(5).
9   CPR 3.9(e).

To date there have been very few reported cases which indicate how the courts will exercise their powers set out above.[10] Indications from the courts are that the parties' pre-action conduct is being taken into account by the courts when giving directions at the case management stage. For example, the Commercial Court has been prepared to give a defendant more time to prepare his case where it considered that proceedings were commenced too early.

The court will also specifically take into account 'the conduct of the parties before, as well as during, the proceedings, and in particular the extent to which the parties followed any relevant pre-action protocol' when making orders for costs.[11] If the court considers that non-compliance with an applicable protocol has led to the unnecessary commencement of proceedings or has resulted in costs being unnecessarily incurred the court may order that the costs of the party at fault be reduced or that he is ordered to pay all or part of the costs of the proceedings of the other party or parties, possibly on an indemnity basis. If a claimant is at fault the court may order that he be deprived of interest on any award of damages made in his favour for a specified period or award interest at a lower rate than that which would otherwise have been ordered. If a defendant is at fault and is ordered to pay damages to the claimant the court may order the defendant to pay penalty interest for a specified period at a higher rate, not exceeding 10% above base rate.[12]

In exercising its powers the court's objective will be to ensure that the innocent party is placed in no worse position than he would have been in had the protocol been complied with. Examples are given in the practice direction to protocols as to the circumstances in which a claimant or defendant may be found to have failed to comply with a protocol. These include failure by the claimant to have provided sufficient information to the defendant or to comply with protocol procedure and, in the case of the defendant, failure to make a preliminary response to a letter of claim within the relevant time specified by a protocol.[13]

The Vice Chancellor, Sir Richard Scott, has emphasised the importance of pre-action protocols and has stressed that their spirit extends beyond specific practice areas. The courts are also demonstrating a willingness to make adverse costs orders where the spirit of the practice direction to protocols has not been observed.[14]

This approach has already been taken by the courts when assessing the effect of pre-action conduct on costs in *Mars UK Ltd v Teknowledge Ltd (No 2)*.[15] In

---

10 In the light of *Biguzzi v Rank Leisure plc* [1999] 4 All ER 934, [1999] 1 WLR 1926, CA, a case concerning strike out under CPR 3.4 it appears however that the court will use the widest possible range of sanctions available within the CPR.

11 CPR 44.3(5)(a). See also the comments of Lloyd J in *Sony Music Entertainment Inc v Prestige Records Ltd* (31 January 2000, unreported), Ch D.

12 Paragraph 2.3 of the practice direction to protocols.

13 Paragraphs 3.1 and 3.2 of the practice direction to protocols.

14 The Civil Procedure Rule Committee is currently considering introducing rules to deal specifically with the recoverability of costs incurred pre-action.

15 (1999) Times, 8 July, Ch D.

that case Mars brought claims against Teknowledge alleging infringement of copyright and breach of confidence. Mars' claim for infringement of copyright succeeded, however their claim for breach of confidence failed and they subsequently made an application for an interim payment of a substantial part of their legal costs pending detailed assessment. Although prepared to make an interim costs order, Mr Justice Jacob made it for significantly less than the amount which Mars sought and was highly critical of Mars' conduct pre-action. In particular, Mr Justice Jacob was critical of Mars' long and detailed letter before action which required a response within three days without any real justification for the tight deadline and that Teknowledge received no substantive response to their offer of a without prejudice meeting to resolve the dispute. Instead Mars commenced proceedings. Mr Justice Jacob also commented that Mars' pre-action behaviour would also be taken into account on a detailed assessment of costs.

In view of the increased importance which the courts now attach to the pre-action period, parties are strongly advised to adhere strictly to any relevant pre-action protocol and in their absence to generally comply with paragraph 4 of the practice direction to pre-action protocols. Failure to do so may result in severe sanctions being imposed on the defaulting party by the courts.

C   Front-loading

In order to comply with the spirit of pre-action protocols and the accompanying practice direction, parties to a dispute must now cooperate with each other prior to the commencement of proceedings by providing sufficient information to enable a claim to be properly evaluated and for attempts to be made to resolve the dispute without recourse to proceedings. This will involve the parties in significant front-loading of costs and time spent on a dispute as parties are required to analyse and exchange information relating to the key issues in dispute at a much earlier stage.

1   *Analysis of key issues*

A potential claimant will have to thoroughly research his case so that he is in a position to comply with any applicable pre-action protocol or paragraph 4 of the practice direction to protocols and cooperate with a potential defendant by exchanging information as to his claim before commencing proceedings. Potential defendants need to put themselves in a position to respond quickly with a similar exchange of information. In particular, the parties will need to:

- **Identify the relevant documents**

Potential claimants and defendants need to ensure that internal information retrieval and document management systems are in place so that relevant documents can be quickly identified and easily retrieved. These systems will enable the parties to collect the necessary documentary evidence to support their case in the event that a dispute arises. Parties can be expected to exchange at least some of this documentation in pre-action correspondence relating to the dispute. It will also assist them in requesting documentation from the other side and in responding to any applications for pre-action disclosure (discussed in detail below).

• Identify key factual evidence

Witness evidence must also be identified at an early stage so that each party knows the strengths and weaknesses of its case. Preliminary witness statements should be obtained to enable the parties to properly evaluate their case. These statements may be exchanged between the parties or at the very least, their contents used to substantiate letters of claim or response. The exchange of preliminary witness evidence is likely to be of particular importance where the parties are willing to try to resolve the dispute by ADR (discussed further below),[16] or where one party has made a pre-action offer to settle (also discussed further below).[17] Parties need to ensure that the necessary internal systems are in place to identify potential witnesses and to gather evidence from them promptly. Witnesses may also be in a better position than the party to the dispute to identify where information provided by the other party is insufficient or defective.

• Identify experts

Parties should consider whether or not it is necessary to obtain preliminary expert advice to assist them to evaluate their case and whether experts should be instructed to prepare preliminary reports with a view to them being exchanged between the parties. Contrary to the position when an expert is instructed to act as an expert witness in court proceedings, experts instructed pre-action will act as advisers to the party who instructs them and any instructions to them in relation to their advice or preliminary reports will be privileged.[18]

Consideration should also be given as to whether it is appropriate to appoint a single joint expert to give an opinion in relation to an issue in dispute. If one party suggests the use of a single joint expert and identifies the proposed expert he may be able to use this to gain a tactical advantage over the other party. Once a single joint expert approach is proposed it may be very difficult in view of the overriding objective, for the other party to come up with good reasons as to why that approach is inappropriate or to be able to object to the identity of the expert, unless of course the objection is based on the expert's lack of qualification or experience in relation to the issue in dispute. Many of the published and draft pre-action protocols propose the appointment of single joint experts to determine issues in dispute pre-action with the onus being on the party who objects to come up with reasons for not using them.

16   See also Chapter 2 on alternative dispute resolution.
17   See also Chapter 5 on Part 36 offers and payments.
18   See Chapter 9 on experts.

2   *Pre-action tactics for the claimant*

The claimant will need to prepare a letter of claim which contains details of the claim in full. As discussed above, the claimant will also need to consider including relevant key documents and possibly preliminary witness statements and experts' reports or suggest the appointment of a single joint expert if appropriate. In light of the comments of Mr Justice Jacob in *Mars UK Ltd v Teknowledge Ltd (No 2)*[19] the claimant will also need to set a reasonable time period for the potential defendant to respond.

3   *Pre-action tactics for the defendant*

The defendant should acknowledge the claimant's response as soon as possible. If required it may be coupled with a request for additional time for responding to the claimant's letter of claim. Given that once proceedings are commenced the defendant will be subject to the tight time limits imposed by the courts (exercising their powers of active case management) and that he is no longer able to serve a holding defence, the pre-action stage may be the defendant's best opportunity to prepare his case.

The defendant should prepare a letter of response which responds in detail to the claimant's letter and set out the defendant's version of events where different. The claimant should be requested to respond to the new points raised by the defendant within a specified time period. Key relevant documents, preliminary witness statements and experts reports may also be attached to the defendant's response. If not already proposed by the claimant the defendant may wish to consider suggesting the appointment of a single joint expert. The defendant should also consider whether the information supplied by the claimant in relation to the claim is inadequate or incomplete and advise the claimant accordingly. As well as gaining extra time for the defendant the additional information will be of particular importance where the defendant wishes to consider making a pre-action offer to settle. Finally, consideration should be given as to whether proposals for resolving the dispute by ADR should be included.

D   Pre-action disclosure and inspection of documents

Pre-action disclosure is now available in all types of cases.[20] Pursuant to CPR 31.16 the court will make an order for pre-action disclosure if it is satisfied that disclosure is desirable to dispose fairly of the anticipated proceedings, to assist the dispute to be resolved without proceedings or to save costs.[1]

---

19   (1999) Times, 8 July, Ch D.
20   Pursuant to the Supreme Court Act 1981, s 33 and the County Court Act 1984, s 52 as amended by the Civil Procedure (Modification of Enactments) Order 1998, SI 1998/2940.

The application must be made in accordance with CPR Pt 23 and be made against a party who is likely to be a party to subsequent proceedings and if proceedings had started the documents requested would fall within that party's standard disclosure obligations.[2] It must be supported by evidence.[3] If the court is satisfied that pre-action disclosure should be given the applicant will be required to specify the document or classes of documents which the respondent must disclose. The respondent when making disclosure will be required to specify any documents which are no longer in his control and which of the documents he claims a right or duty to withhold inspection.[4] The respondent may also be required to indicate what has happened to any documents which are no longer in his control and specify the time and place for disclosure.[5] The CPR do not specify the form in which pre-action disclosure is to be given, however as a matter of best practice a party should usually give disclosure by list.[6]

Pre-action disclosure has already been ordered in a construction case, *Burrells Wharf Freeholds Ltd v Galliard Homes Ltd* in the Technology and Construction Court.[7] In a dispute involving allegations of breaches of building regulations an application was made by Burrells, a company which had acquired the freehold of a property, for pre-action disclosure against Galliard, the developers. Dyson J held that the conditions for making an order for pre-action disclosure were satisfied in that case but that this 'did not indicate a relaxed approach to pre-action disclosure. An application would fail unless CPR 31.16 was fully satisfied'.[8]

Pre-action disclosure is a good tactical weapon. However before making the application it should be borne in mind that the costs of the application and the costs of complying with the request will usually be awarded in favour of the respondent.[9] As a result it may be better for a party to rely on an exchange of information pursuant to a pre-action protocol or paragraph 4 of the practice direction to protocols rather than apply for pre-action disclosure with the latter being made as a last resort. Evidence over the last twelve months suggests that potential claimants are not trying to use pre-action disclosure to mount 'fishing expeditions' and potential claimants

1   CPR 31.16(3)(d).
2   CPR 31.16(3)(a), (b) and (c).
3   CPR 31.16(2). Evidence may be in the form of an application notice verified by a statement of truth, a witness statement or affidavit. However if an affidavit is used the additional costs of making it may not be recovered unless the court orders accordingly.
4   CPR 31.16(4).
5   CPR 31.16(5).
6   See for example CPR Pt 31, practice direction, paras 3.1 and 3.2.
7   [1999] 33 EG 82.
8   See also *Wilma Elsie Hatcher v Plymouth Hospitals NHS Trust* (27 July 1999, unreported) in which District Judge Tromans held that the statements of two clinicians obtained by the hospital in the course of dealing with the claimant's complaint were not subject to legal professional privilege and were properly disclosable under CPR 31.16(3)(d) as they would probably assist in the just disposal of the case at an early stage.
9   CPR 48.1. However pursuant to CPR 48.1(3) the court may make a different order having regard to all the circumstances, including the extent to which it was reasonable for the person against whom the order was sought to oppose the application and whether the parties to the application complied with any relevant pre-action protocol.

should be extremely wary of trying to do so. Such applications are likely to be strongly condemned by the court.

However, potential defendants who wish to raise jurisdiction issues in proceedings should be extremely cautious when making or responding to an application for pre-action disclosure as it may be seen as a first step in prospective proceedings and as a submission to the jurisdiction.[10]

Finally, it is not possible at present to obtain pre-action disclosure against a party who is not intended to become a party to proceedings, that is a non-party unless the court may order it using some other power.[11] For example, under the *Norwich Pharmacal* principle[12] disclosure may be obtained against a non party in order to identify a wrongdoer. Disclosure can however be obtained against a non party once proceedings have commenced.[13] However, in accordance with the overriding objective it would appear that the arguments for obtaining pre-action disclosure between parties to proposed proceedings should apply equally to a non-party if it would assist the dispute to be resolved without commencing proceedings.

E   Pre-action offers to settle

Pre-action offers to settle may be made by either the claimant or the defendant at any time and may be in any form. However if the pre-action offer complies with the requirements set out in CPR 36.10 the court will take the offer into account when making any order as to costs in relation to proceedings which are subsequently commenced.

Pursuant to CPR 36.10 the pre-action offer must be expressed to be open for at least 21 days after the date it was made.[14] If it is made by a person who would be a defendant if proceedings were commenced it must also include an offer to pay the costs of the offeree incurred up to the date 21 days after the date it was made.[15] If proceedings are commenced at a later date and the offeror is a defendant to a money claim he must make a Pt 36 payment within 14 days of service of the claim form and the amount of the payment must not be less than the sum offered before the proceedings were begun.[16]

The court has complete discretion under CPR 36.10(1) as to how it will deal with costs where a pre-action offer is made. However, the cost consequences relating to Pt 36 offers and payments[17] are likely to influence the court when exercising its discretion.

---

10 Although decided under the old rules see *Caltex Trading Pte Ltd v Metro Trading International Inc* [2000] 1 All ER (Comm) 108, [1999] 2 Lloyd's Rep 724.
11 CPR 31.18 states that CPR 31.16 and 31.17 do not limit any other power which the court may have to order disclosure before proceedings have started or disclosure against a person who is not a party to proceedings.
12 *Norwich Pharmacal Co v Customs and Excise Comrs* [1974] AC 133, [1973] 2 All ER 943.
13 CPR 31.17. See Chapter 7 on disclosure.
14 CPR 36.10(2)(a).
15 CPR 36.10(2)(b).
16 CPR 36.10(3)(a) and (b).
17 See Chapter 5 on Part 36 offers and payments.

The cost consequences of rejecting an offer to settle may be severe, particularly for a defendant. For example, a defendant who has failed to beat a claimant's Pt 36 offer made once proceedings have been commenced may be ordered to pay interest on the whole or part of any sum of money awarded to the claimant at a rate not exceeding 10% above base rate. The defendant may also be ordered to pay the claimant's costs on an indemnity basis and interest on those costs at a rate not exceeding 10% above base rate.[18]

Pre-action offers are a great tactical weapon, especially for claimants. A potential claimant should consider making a pre-action offer in almost every case before commencing proceedings to put pressure on the potential defendant to resolve the dispute. If the defendant does not settle and subsequently fails to beat the claimant's pre-action offer at trial he risks potentially at least incurring interest and cost penalties.[19] However, the defendant is most likely to escape this if he can show that the claimant failed to supply him with the necessary information to properly evaluate the pre-action offer. As a result the claimant needs to ensure that sufficient information is provided with the pre-action offer and to respond promptly to any additional requests for information from the defendant relating to the pre-action offer.

A potential defendant should follow up a claimant's pre-action offer with a prompt request for any information which is necessary for him to evaluate the pre-action offer together with a request for a detailed analysis as to how the offer has been calculated.

He should also consider making a pre-action offer to settle if the potential claimant has not already done so or a counter-offer (if the potential claimant has) as soon as he is in a position to properly evaluate the potential claimant's claim. The threat of the claimant potentially being liable for the defendant's costs from the latest date that the pre-action offer could have been accepted if the claimant subsequently fails to beat the defendant's pre-action offer at trial should concentrate the potential claimant's mind on resolving the dispute sooner rather than later.[20] However the potential defendant will need to balance this against the fact that once proceedings have commenced, his pre-action offer will have to be backed up with a payment into court within 14 days if it relates to a money claim and that he may be deprived of funds for a long period. Evidence suggests that pre-action offers are being widely used by both potential claimants and potential defendants.

18 CPR 36.21.
19 In the context of a Pt 36 offer, if a claimant fails to beat his own offer at trial, he is unlikely to face any costs penalties unless his offer indicated bad faith or was otherwise in contravention of the overriding objective. Although unclear, the position is probably the same for a claimant who makes a pre-action offer. See Chapter 5 on Part 36 offers and payments.
20 See Chapter 5 on Part 36 offers and payments.

F   Early use of ADR

The parties may wish to consider using ADR[1] prior to commencing proceedings. They may soon be encouraged to do so in any event under relevant pre-action protocols. For example, the pre-action protocol on personal injury encourages the parties and their legal advisers to enter into negotiations/settlement prior to commencing proceedings and the pre-action protocol on clinical medical negligence disputes specifically suggests that ADR (in particular, mediation) be used. The draft pre-action protocol on professional negligence also encourages the early use of ADR/negotiation to try to settle the dispute prior to commencing proceedings.

In light of the overriding objective and paragraph 4 of the practice direction to protocols the party who suggests ADR at an early stage to try to resolve the dispute may find that it is more favourably looked on by the court than the party who expressed unwillingness to try it. Given that once proceedings commence the court will actively encourage the parties to use ADR as part of active case management in any event, parties should consider referring a dispute to ADR before commencing proceedings. If ADR works it will save time and costs. If it fails at least the parties can demonstrate to the court that they have given it a try and that they have complied with paragraph 4 of the practice direction to protocols.

1   See also Chapter 2 on alternative dispute resolution.

2 ALTERNATIVE DISPUTE RESOLUTION

A Introduction

There are many different forms of alternative dispute resolution ('ADR'), but all share the core characteristics of flexibility, confidentiality, speed and reduced cost. Above all, they offer a consensual, non-adversarial approach in tune with Lord Woolf's vision of a new, cooperative climate for dispute resolution. In his Final Report, Lord Woolf envisaged that ADR would have a central role in contributing to the reform of the dispute resolution process. Following the introduction of the CPR, ADR is now a relevant consideration in all disputes, whatever their size or complexity.

ADR is not of course a new concept. During the last five years it has become increasingly popular as a means of resolving disputes, or at least as an intermediate step before the parties commit themselves to a more formal legal process. Much of the credit for the significant increase in referrals to ADR in recent years must be given to the courts, which have increasingly directed that it should be considered as an option, and despite very limited resources have supported various ADR initiatives, including the Commercial Court Mediation Scheme, the Court of Appeal Mediation Scheme, the Central London County Court Mediation Scheme and the Patents County Court ADR Programme. The use of ADR has also been actively encouraged in the Technology and Construction Court.

However, until the introduction of the CPR, it was largely left to the parties themselves to decide whether to participate in some form of third party assisted settlement. Only those disputes where the parties had an ongoing business relationship which they were anxious to preserve tended to be referred to ADR at an early stage. Lord Woolf's aim was to build on these existing ADR initiatives, and to make ADR an integral part of the dispute resolution process from the outset for all but the most exceptional cases. The CPR have implemented this objective by introducing a variety of direct and indirect measures intended to encourage the parties to consider ADR both at the outset of a dispute, and at regular intervals during any subsequent litigation. Whilst commercial litigators and commercial litigants have often been hesitant to propose mediation or other forms of ADR in the past and have expressed reservations about the relevance of ADR to major commercial disputes, the CPR draw no such distinction, and the ADR provisions apply equally to all cases.

Twelve months on from the introduction of the CPR, ADR has already become a key feature of the new 'litigation landscape'. There is statistical and anecdotal evidence of increased referrals to the established ADR providers (including referrals of complex commercial disputes), and there appears to be a greater awareness generally amongst litigants of the potentially costly consequences of failing to consider ADR.

Most commercial practitioners will already be familiar with the various forms of ADR which are available[1] and how the process operates. This chapter therefore concentrates on the role of ADR under the CPR and how ADR has affected commercial disputes in practice since the new rules were introduced in April 1999. It also considers the role of the in-house and external lawyer in facilitating ADR and the practical steps which corporate litigants should be taking to ensure that they are well placed to manage the ADR process successfully.

B   The role of ADR under the CPR

Despite the emphasis placed on ADR by Lord Woolf, there are very few provisions in the CPR and accompanying practice directions which specifically address ADR. However, an awareness of and receptiveness to ADR are fundamental to the new cooperative climate envisaged in Lord Woolf's reports and the overriding objective set out in CPR 1.1. CPR 1.1 places a duty on the courts to further the overriding objective of 'dealing with cases justly' by actively managing cases, and places a duty on the parties to assist the court in doing so. The rule sets out twelve activities which are included in case management. One of these is to encourage the use of ADR if the court considers it appropriate and to facilitate its use. The suitability of a case for ADR will therefore have to be addressed both before proceedings are begun and at regular intervals during the litigation.

1   Pre-action conduct

As soon as the possibility of a dispute appears on the horizon, a potential claimant or defendant should consider whether the dispute may be appropriate for some form of ADR process. The new emphasis in the CPR on reasonable and proportionate pre-action conduct means that the parties cannot assume that the court will only scrutinise their behaviour from the date proceedings began. The parties' approach in the early stages of the dispute is likely to be influential in terms of how the court views their conduct later, and the extent to which they will recover their costs at the end of the case.[2]

---

1   See Appendix F for a summary of the principal ADR methods.
2   See Chapter 1 on pre-action tactics.

In particular, the parties will be expected to comply with the provisions of any relevant pre-action protocols. Ignoring them is likely to be regarded as unreasonable behaviour and to result in an adverse costs order. The protocol for personal injury claims does not refer to ADR, but the notes for guidance remind the parties that litigation should be a last resort and that claims should not be issued prematurely when a settlement is in reasonable prospect. The protocol for the resolution of clinical disputes states that the parties and their advisers should consider the full range of dispute resolution options and has a separate section on alternative approaches to settling disputes. A number of further protocols are in development and are likely to adopt a similar approach.

Even where no specific protocol applies, pre-action conduct may be taken into account by the court when exercising its discretion in relation to costs at the end of the action. The parties' approach to ADR both before and during the action is likely to be one of the factors taken into account when the court exercises its costs discretion under CPR 44.3(4).

The CPR provisions in relation to wider pre-action disclosure[3] will assist the parties in gathering the information they need in order to assess whether an attempt at ADR may be appropriate. Pre-action disclosure is no longer restricted only to personal injury cases and the courts are likely to be sympathetic to an application for documents which are genuinely required in order to clarify the issues and facilitate attempts at ADR, whether made before proceedings begin or at a later stage in the litigation.

Whilst ADR may not be appropriate at such an early stage in large commercial cases where the evidence gathering and disclosure processes are expected to take many months, it should not be dismissed out of hand, as it may be possible to identify and isolate particular issues which are suitable for referral, where the factual evidence is less extensive or can largely be agreed.

2 *During the proceedings*

Once proceedings have been commenced, there are a number of stages in a multi-track case at which the court has an opportunity to encourage the parties to consider ADR. These include the filing of the allocation questionnaire; the case management conference; any subsequent interlocutory hearings; the filing of the listing questionnaire; and the pre-trial review.

In addition, the financial pressures resulting from 'front-loaded' costs which will inevitably be felt by the parties from the start of the action are likely to encourage them to review at regular intervals whether ADR may be a more cost-effective method of resolving the dispute.

---

3   CPR 31.16.

• **Allocation**

Although the overriding objective provides that encouraging and facilitating the use of ADR forms part of case management, the only explicit reference to ADR in the general rules is at the allocation stage. The allocation questionnaire asks whether the parties wish there to be a one month stay to attempt to settle the case. If both parties consent, the court can then order a stay. If the court orders a stay, the parties will be expected to use the time to make real efforts to explore settlement.

The court may also order a stay of its own initiative under CPR 26.4(2)(b), although the extent to which this will prove to be productive is doubtful where neither party is minded to settle. The court's power to impose a stay of its own motion also raises the possibility of a challenge under Article 6 of the European Convention on Human Rights, on the basis that it restricts a right of access to court (a mediation not being a tribunal established by law). The counter argument is that a mediation merely delays rather than prevents access to court, since the case will revert to the court if mediation fails.

In those specialist lists where allocation is unnecessary, the court may nevertheless order a stay at any stage of the proceedings to enable the parties to attempt ADR in accordance with the overriding objective. The Commercial Court Guide expressly provides that the parties may apply for directions in relation to ADR at any stage, including before service of the defence and before the case management conference.[4]

Concern has been expressed that defendants may apply for a stay in order to buy time to prepare their defence, and may simply 'go through the motions' of attempting ADR without any genuine desire to resolve the case. The July 1998 report of the Commercial Court Committee ADR working party, which reviewed the working of the ADR jurisdiction, found that a complete suspension of the pre-trial timetable pending ADR often led to substantial delays, and warned that it was important to avoid ADR orders being used by defendants as a means of delaying justifiable claims. Whilst the courts are likely to be sympathetic to requests for a stay made by both parties or by the claimant, they may be more sceptical about a request for ADR made by the defendant alone (particularly if the defendant has been on notice of the claim but has not previously proposed ADR). In these circumstances the court may be minded to grant only a short stay, or to suggest that any attempt at ADR should be made in parallel with the ongoing litigation so that no time is lost should the ADR attempt fail.

The Commercial Court Guide provides[5] that where an adjournment is granted, the court will generally be prepared to agree to an extension of no more than four weeks, but will consider applications for further extensions. However, the parties are required to give careful consideration to fitting

---

4   Commercial Court Guide, Section G1.5.
5   Commercial Court Guide, Section D7.14.

ADR into any previously agreed pre-trial timetable 'without the need for any or much delay'. It is usually possible in Commercial Court proceedings to identify a period during which an attempt at ADR may be made without disruption to the existing timetable (for example, following disclosure and prior to the service of witness statements) and as a result the Commercial Court is not generally inclined to stay proceedings whilst the ADR attempt takes place. A stay may however be necessary in the majority of cases in the Queen's Bench Division, where the shorter timetables for trial preparation cannot accommodate an ADR attempt so easily, and it is undesirable to run up additional costs if the parties genuinely wish to settle the dispute.

What happens during the ADR process is confidential but the parties must make genuine efforts to resolve the dispute. There have not as yet been any reported cases of a party being accused of abusing the one month stay process (for example, to complete their own litigation preparations or to elicit information from the other party earlier than they would otherwise be able to do under the rules). If this were to arise, although a mediator is bound by confidentiality, it is possible that he might be required to report to the court as to whether, in his opinion, any party has deliberately abused the process. The court is unlikely in practice to wish to enquire into the reasons for the failure, but could in theory also ask the parties questions about the progress of ADR discussions, without inquiring into the privileged substance of those discussions. In a blatant case of non co-operation, the court may even exercise its discretion to make an order for indemnity costs for failure to comply with the spirit of the overriding objective.

- **Case management conference**

The parties will be expected to report on the suitability of the case for ADR at this stage and to report in general terms on any previous ADR attempts. In the Commercial Court, the parties are required to state in the case management information sheet submitted to the judge whether ADR has been discussed between the party, his solicitor and the advocate, and explored with the opposing parties. Similar information is required in the Technology and Construction Court's case management questionnaire. The initial case management conference occurs at a very early stage in the Commercial Court (usually within 6 weeks of close of pleadings) and is often adjourned for further information to be obtained, with any application for an ADR order being made at the restored hearing. If an adjournment for ADR is sought, an order in the terms set out in Appendix 7 to the Commercial Court Guide is likely to be made.

There will of course be some cases where ADR is inappropriate and there is no prospect of common ground. There are test cases where a precedent is required, or where a matter of principle has arisen which affects a particular field and where those practising in that field need clear guidance on the legal position. Occasionally, the ramifications of making any form of concession may be unacceptable (for example where a concession may lead to an adverse finding in related litigation before an overseas court, particularly if this involves litigation before a jury in the United States). Absent these factors, the court will need to be persuaded that there are no issues which can be identified as suitable for referral.

Where the court considers that the case is capable of settlement at this stage, it may require the parties themselves to attend in person in order to give them an opportunity to negotiate informally, or to explore the possibility of attempting ADR. Where a representative from the client attends the conference (or is ordered to do so by the court) the judge or Master may ask them whether ADR has been considered and if not, to give reasons. The client will need to be ready to explain what further information if any is needed from the other side before the merits of ADR can be assessed.

It should be noted that the provisions in relation to summary assessment of costs[6] enable the court to make an immediate costs order following interlocutory hearings of less than one day, including a case management conference. Neither party is likely to want to leave the case management conference with a finding by the court that they should be penalised in costs, payable within 14 days, for failing to comply with the spirit of the overriding objective in the way in which they have dealt with ADR.

- **Listing questionnaire/Listing hearing/Pre-trial review**

One of the directions which the court will give at the case management conference will be the date on which completed listing questionnaires must be returned to the court. The court will then take a view as to whether there are issues which need to be discussed at a listing hearing or pre-trial review— if a hearing is convened, the parties will normally be expected to report on the scope for ADR.

In the Commercial Court, following the progress monitoring date the parties are required to submit a pre-trial checklist which asks whether some form of ADR might resolve or narrow the issues in dispute. At first sight it might appear more difficult to resist ADR at this stage, as the case will have been prepared and the issues will be clear. However, if ADR is a realistic option in a Commercial Court case, it is likely to have been explored prior to the pre trial review, since this usually takes place only a few weeks before trial.

By the pre-trial review stage the parties will also have run up very substantial costs, and therefore the financial incentive for participating in ADR (ie to save costs) has largely been lost. The costs may have escalated beyond the sum in dispute and at this stage, neither side is likely to be prepared to pay the other's costs as part of a mediated settlement. This can create a major psychological as well as financial barrier to a sensible settlement. It is important that the parties and the judge or Master charged with case management should be able to identify cases which may lend themselves to mediation as early as possible in order to gain the maximum costs saving. This presents a particular problem where the trial judge has not had an opportunity to assess the suitability of the case for ADR previously at a case management hearing (in the Chancery Division for example, only cases estimated to last 10 days or more currently qualify for a pre-trial review before the trial judge).

---

6   See Chapter 10 on costs.

There are few reported cases so far involving orders for ADR. However, in *Dyson v Leeds City Council*,[7] the Court of Appeal, led by Lord Woolf, took the opportunity to remind the parties (in a case where damages had already been substantially agreed) of the suitability of the case for ADR. The parties were also warned of the court's powers to impose an order for indemnity costs or to award a higher rate of interest on any damages awarded if they rejected the court's recommendation to attempt ADR.

C   What effect have the ADR provisions had in practice?

The statistical information relating to the use of ADR which is available from the courts and leading commercial ADR providers suggests that there has been an increase in demand for and successful referral to mediation since the introduction of the CPR.

Although reliable figures are difficult to obtain, the Commercial Court, which has a well-established ADR scheme in place, reports that at least 100 ADR orders have been made by the court in the last two years. Of these, only approximately 5% have come back to be dealt with by the court. Of the cases which did not return to the litigation process, it appears that a number were resolved not by formal ADR procedures but by bilateral negotiation between the parties, apparently prompted by the direction from the court to consider ADR. The Commercial Court's annual report published in September 1999 comments that 'ADR orders have now become a regular, if not standard, feature of pre-trial directions'.

The Commercial Court's practice statement, which introduced the concept of ADR orders in 1996, emphasises that a judge in the Commercial Court may also offer to conduct an early neutral evaluation (ENE) where he thinks it likely to assist in the resolution of the dispute. This involves the judge giving his opinion as to the strengths and weaknesses of each party's case based on a summary of the evidence and oral argument. The parties can then use this as the basis for settlement or further negotiation. The judge takes no further part in the case, if it returns to court, unless the parties agree. ENE has only been used in a small number of cases in the Commercial Court (in the first two years following the introduction of ADR orders, there were only four ENE cases heard by a Commercial Court judge).[8] This may be because the parties take the view that a speedy trial which will finally determine the dispute is preferable to an interim ENE decision which, if not accepted by the unsuccessful party, will simply add to the costs of the litigation (and may delay the resolution of the case if a replacement judge is not immediately available).

---

7   (22 November 1999, unreported).
8   The procedure has also been used occasionally in the Technology and Construction Court.

Figures published in August 1999 by one of the leading ADR providers, the Centre for Dispute Resolution ('CEDR') show that mediations referred to it doubled in the second quarter of 1999 when compared with the same quarter in 1998. The largest percentages were in the construction and engineering/property sector (28%) and professional negligence sector (22%). The largest take up was for disputes in the £100,000–£1 million bracket, where the costs of litigating commercial claims, and particularly the cost of preparing detailed expert evidence, can frequently make the litigation process uneconomic. CEDR reports that court referrals overall rose from just 4% in the first quarter after the introduction of the CPR to 14% in the second quarter, and since then it has seen further substantial increases in referrals. It appears that cases which clearly lend themselves to resolution through mediation are being referred by the parties on their own initiative, pre-empting a referral through the court.

The expansion of ADR has led to the creation of new service providers, such as the Panel of Independent Mediators, which was launched in January 1999. There has also been a trend towards more focussed initiatives by the established ADR organisations, targeted at particular business sectors or types of dispute, including disputes arising from the 'millennium bug'. Insurers, particularly in the professional indemnity market, have also taken a lead in this area, after some initial reluctance to participate in mediation. In November 1998, the London Underwriting Centre launched the 'Market ADR Commitment' which is a written, but non-legally binding, undertaking by insurers to use mediation in preference to litigation. If mediation is not used, the parties that have signed up to the Commitment (and there are reported to be fourteen insurance company signatories) have to justify why ADR is not suitable. This initiative is working in the professional indemnity market but there is no reason to suppose that it will not extend to other areas of civil dispute. At least one large insurance company, convinced of the benefits of ADR in many cases, has circulated to its panel of legal advisers a 'league table' indicating the number of recommendations to mediate and attempts at mediation attributable to each firm, and reportedly seen a significant increase in ADR referrals across the board as a result.

D   The future of ADR

Despite these encouraging developments, the take up for ADR remains relatively low in comparison with the number of cases proceeding through the courts. In November 1999, the Lord Chancellor's Department published a consultation paper on the future of ADR[9] to explore the reasons for this and invite suggestions on how to promote wider acceptance and use of ADR. The concern behind the consultation paper is not primarily commercial disputes, but those disputes for which public funding is no longer available,

---

9   'ADR—a discussion paper'.

where ADR may offer the most realistic prospect of extending access to justice to those who could not otherwise afford it. However, any changes to the ADR process introduced as a result of this consultation process may also affect its use in resolving commercial disputes.

The wide ranging paper looks at what methods of ADR are being used and by whom; who provides them; their advantages and disadvantages; which cases ADR methods work best for; how to quantify benefits and savings, and any additional costs; how to raise awareness of ADR; ensuring quality control and how the procedures and rules for litigation should take account of ADR.

The key issues raised in relation to the operation of ADR which may have an impact on its use in the commercial arena include:

- The need for a consistent approach: the paper notes that it is desirable for court users to know what approach the courts will take towards ADR. At present, the extent to which the parties are encouraged to pursue ADR (for example, whether they are directed simply to consider ADR, or are actually ordered to attempt it) is largely dependent on the attitude towards ADR of the judge or Master responsible for managing the case. The degree of enthusiasm for mediation varies considerably between the specialist lists, and between individual members of the judiciary. The ADR Sub-Committee of the Civil Justice Council is concerned with monitoring the extent to which opportunities for ADR are being considered by the courts on a day to day basis, but no guidance has been issued so far as to how appropriate cases will be identified, and the circumstances in which sanctions for an 'unreasonable' refusal to participate in ADR may be imposed.
- Whether further specific references to the need to consider ADR should be introduced in the procedural rules. However, the report suggests that such references are likely to serve as a reminder of the parties' existing obligations under the overriding objective rather than introducing additional obligations.
- Whether some form of compulsion should be introduced (subject to the provisions of Article 6 of the European Convention on Human Rights which provides that in the determination of civil rights and obligations everyone is entitled to a fair and public hearing by an independent tribunal established by law). The paper acknowledges that the Commercial Court has successfully promoted the use of ADR without the need for compulsion, but notes that a Commercial Court judge's personal recommendation to attempt ADR has so far been given only in a relatively small number of cases, and carries considerable weight with the parties. The paper observes that it may be more difficult to achieve the same result in the wider variety of cases elsewhere in the High Court and county courts.

E   The role of ADR in commercial disputes

Lord Woolf's view was that the fact that a dispute is complex, for a very large sum or involves many parties should not necessarily be a barrier to an attempt at ADR and this has been borne out by some notable ADR successes in complex, high value commercial disputes which might not have been thought of as candidates for an ADR procedure a few years ago.

Even before the CPR were introduced, ADR had been used effectively in several large and complex disputes. Notable cases include:

- the settlement between the UK government and Arthur Andersen, after 12 years of litigation arising out of the De Lorean collapse, following an order made by the Commercial Court encouraging the parties to attempt ADR. Both parties protested (unsuccessfully) against the imposition of the order, but went on to reach settlement;
- the successful mediation between British & Commonwealth (B&C) and Atlantic Computers. The litigation concerned a claim by B&C for more than £850m, related to B&C's acquisition of Atlantic Computers in 1988 and the subsequent collapse of both companies in 1990. The proceedings commenced in 1994 and a trial had been fixed for May 2000, for 12–15 months. Following the largest ever European mediation conducted with the support of the CEDR the litigation was settled in January 1999; and
- the 'Reconstruction and Renewal' settlement between Lloyd's of London and the Lloyd's Names, which involved what was probably the largest mediation process ever to take place in the UK.

The confidential nature of the ADR process means that detailed information about its use in practice can be difficult to obtain. Freshfields' experience is that whilst commercial clients who regularly litigate have always been prepared to contemplate alternative methods of resolving disputes, ranging from mediation and expert determination to structured settlements, there has been an increase in the use of ADR (primarily but not exclusively through mediation) since the introduction of the CPR. It has been used successfully in disputes in the construction, energy, environmental, banking and insurance sectors. Many of these disputes involved complex issues and a large number of parties. There does not appear to be a particular pattern as to the type of case in which it succeeds, although in most large commercial cases, ADR is not attempted until after exchange of disclosure and witness statements. It is interesting to note that of those cases which failed to settle during the mediation itself, approximately half settled within a month of the mediation taking place.

In the past, commercial litigants have had a number of reservations about the suitability of proposing ADR in commercial disputes. The main concern was a fear that making the first approach would be construed as demonstrating weakness. However, the perceived disadvantage of being the first to propose ADR has largely receded under the CPR and indeed in some cases has been reversed, with the parties competing to be seen to demonstrate a cooperative approach by adopting a pro-ADR stance. Where the parties are still reluctant to make the first move but the case appears to lend itself to mediation, some judges will take the initiative and order mediation, and have found this course to be productive.

Complex commercial cases are usually managed by in-house counsel who are familiar with the litigation process and are experienced negotiators. It can be difficult to persuade an experienced negotiator that a third party neutral will add anything to the negotiation process, although the potential costs consequences of failing to attempt ADR must be considered. Once this hurdle has been overcome, some commercial litigants are finding that mediation or other forms of ADR are well suited to their considerable negotiating skills, and that routine claims can be disposed of quickly through ADR.

Whilst mediation is well suited to claims which fit a standard pattern (for example, it is being increasingly used to resolve smaller disputes in the retail banking sector) it has often been considered less appropriate for the sort of commercial disputes typically handled by City firms, which raise unique points and often involve a large number of parties in complex relationships. However, ADR practitioners and processes are becoming more sophisticated and mediation is now being used increasingly in multi-party and cross-border disputes. In a cross-border dispute, it enables the parties to sidestep the jurisdictional issues which would otherwise have to be dealt with at the start of an action and are costly, time consuming and do not advance the resolution of the central issues in dispute. If necessary, the mediation can be held at a neutral venue in a neutral country, before one or more neutral mediators. In these circumstances the mediation process is likely to prove expensive, but this needs to be balanced against the fact that if the dispute is resolved at an early stage the overall costs savings can be very substantial.

It remains the case that ADR is likely to be most successful where the parties are involved in an ongoing business relationship, which can be weighed against the particular issue or issues in dispute. In many large commercial disputes, this element is absent as the dispute relates to a one-off transaction and there may therefore be less incentive to participate in ADR, unless it offers substantial costs savings over litigation. However the increased financial pressures of litigating in a front-loaded environment, where timetables are shorter and there is the possibility of an adverse costs order for non cooperation, are persuading more commercial litigants to contemplate mediation.

F   The lawyer's role in ADR

Both the parties and their legal advisers have a duty under the overriding objective actively to consider ADR. A party's approach to ADR now forms an essential part of his strategy for the case, and will need to be developed in discussions between the company's management, in-house counsel and the external lawyers from the outset. The company's senior management representative will be expected to play a leading part in any mediation or other informal ADR process (although there is less scope for a direct contribution from the client in more formal processes such as ENE). A number of large corporations are already sophisticated users of ADR, with established systems for screening cases for their suitability for referral for expert determination, mediation or other ADR process. Other corporate litigants may be less familiar with the ways in which the recent extension of ADR affects their business and the way in which they handle disputes. In these circumstances, as set out below, there are a variety of ways in which in-house and external lawyers can assist in managing the process effectively.

1   At the outset

- **Consider including ADR clauses in contractual documentation**

Consideration should be given to using ADR clauses more frequently in commercial contracts in order to ensure that ADR is attempted as a first step in resolving disputes, where this is perceived to have potential commercial benefits, including saving legal costs. 'Stepped' dispute resolution clauses specifying negotiation, followed by ADR, followed by arbitration are becoming increasingly common. It is of course hard to anticipate at the time of contractual negotiations whether ADR will best protect the client when it comes to resolving all or any disputes which might arise later from a particular contract. There are classes of contract, particularly large supply contracts, and contracts in the construction sector, where the courts can be expected to show a strong interest in ADR when disputes arise. In these cases it is clearly in the client's interest to set the agenda by promoting ADR on its terms, rather than those of the other contracting party. In these circumstances, it is likely that debate over ADR clauses, in future, will become as much a feature of contract negotiations as the choice of arbitration clause.

- **ADR screening**

Since ADR will almost inevitably be raised by the court at an early stage, clients will need to carry out more assessment of cases at the outset to decide if they are suitable for ADR. Where ADR is a realistic option for a significant part of a litigation portfolio, the client may consider pursuing an in-house ADR screening programme (or its own ADR 'protocol') to identify which cases are particularly suitable for ADR (for example, where there is an ongoing commercial relationship with the potential opponent) and appoint an individual or team to manage the ADR process.

- **Managing expectations**

In order to make an early, informed judgment as to the key commercial objectives in a complex case, senior management, the in-house lawyer and external counsel will need to be involved in analysing the evidence and the strengths and weaknesses of the case during the first few weeks of its life.

This may mean a significant investment of management time in the case at an early stage. A senior management representative is also likely to be needed to attend the mediation in order to provide the necessary authority to settle. Any other interested parties whose consent will be needed (notably insurers) must also be fully involved in the process. Whilst a number of companies are already attempting mediation in large scale commercial disputes, significantly more management time is likely to have to be invested if ADR becomes much more common, if not routine.

- **Be well informed about the range of ADR options and individual mediators**

Before consulting an established ADR service provider, think about what you are looking for. The individual should certainly be a dispassionate neutral third party who has the confidence of the parties in the dispute. Beyond that, expertise in the subject matter may be valuable in a complex technical dispute—for example in the insurance sector—but it is not essential and indeed may to a degree prejudice that individual towards one particular opinion or outcome. Whilst specific training in mediation may be an advantage, experience in negotiation and the appropriate approach count for a great deal.

- **Advise on the timing of an ADR approach**

This will depend on various factors, including costs. Clearly, it is cheaper to attempt mediation before beginning proceedings at all, or in the very early stages of proceedings. When acting for a defendant who is on notice of a potential claim, particularly where aspects of the defence may be weak, offering mediation before the claim is issued may be the best option but it is important be realistic (in a fraud case, for example, ADR is unlikely to be a suitable option). The later the mediation takes place, the more entrenched views may be. However, there may be benefits to gained by starting proceedings and delaying any attempt at ADR—for example, do you want to see the other side's documents? Conversely, do you have any concerns about them seeing your documents? Disclosure and exchange of expert evidence are expensive procedures, but there are substantial risks in agreeing to proceed with ADR in their absence. Possible compromises include providing key disclosure documents only, together with an undertaking from both sides that they are not aware of any other documents which would materially affect the position of either party; or providing expert evidence on a 'without prejudice' basis.

2 *Preparing for the mediation*

- **Briefing the client**

The client needs to know precisely what to expect from the process itself. The lawyer should take the client through the questions the mediator is likely to ask, the strengths and weaknesses of the case, the client's underlying interests, and discuss settlement ranges, options and variables which might be included to reach a deal. Once the parties have started a mediation procedure it can be hard to exit, even where there is no realistic prospect of success, as the mediation can develop a momentum of its own. It is important to avoid running up costs in futile ADR discussions, and it is essential to stick to a previously agreed 'bottom line' to avoid the client feeling pressurised into accepting a deal which he is not satisfied with.

- **Preparation**

Once the mediation is underway, it is open to the mediator, and indeed to the other side, to ask questions about the parties' cases. It is essential to be prepared as much as if it were a trial—uncertainty or reluctance to deal with these points will create a poor impression and may affect your opponent's perception of your case, and even the mediator's perspective. Many mediators admit that, despite their ostensibly 'facilitative' approach, their strategy is to form an assessment of which side has the stronger case and to raise doubts about the strengths of a party's case. Creating a genuine impression of strength and confidence, through preparation, is therefore vital in caucus as well as joint sessions. It may be necessary to rehearse the presentations prior to the mediation session. If the mediation takes place when proceedings are well advanced, the degree of preparation required is even greater.

- **Preparing an ADR strategy**

An effective ADR strategy will need to be determined, including clear objectives for the ADR, and a fallback strategy if the ADR fails. This may include applying promptly to the court for directions (if proceedings have already been commenced), and dealing with any weaker issues which have been identified during the course of the ADR by making an offer to settle those issues. The ability to make well judged offers to settle (and counter offers where appropriate) under Pt 36 will be an effective way to exert pressure on a less well prepared opponent. The ADR process itself can be very expensive, and the client and his legal adviser need to be clear about their objectives—is the ADR a staging post to settlement, a chance to learn more about the other side's case and its commercial objectives, or a way of ensuring that the client's senior management focus on the issues in dispute?

- **Prepare the paperwork**

This will normally include preparing a mediation agreement, briefing papers for the mediator, and an opening statement. Full records should also be kept of all attempts to resolve the dispute through ADR, both prior to proceedings and at each subsequent key procedural stage. This material will then be readily available when the court asks for confirmation of the ADR position and the client's position can be protected in relation to costs by demonstrating that ADR has been fully considered.

- **Agree the format of the mediation**

Although the mediation session itself is relatively straightforward, it is important to set up a clear framework in advance so that the parties know exactly where they stand. A timetable will be needed for preparation and exchange of any written submissions, and for any formal opening submissions to the mediator. Provision should also be made for disclosure as appropriate and submissions of witness or expert evidence if these are to be included. Many ADR service providers produce standard guidelines which provide a helpful starting point for such a timetable. Finally, within the team itself, do not forget to agree who is to make the opening submissions—counsel, the solicitors, or the client?

3   At the mediation

The lawyer may give the opening statement on the client's behalf. During the mediation his role is to reassure the client, to take a positive approach and to advise on the alternatives to a mediated solution if agreement cannot be reached.

4   Concluding the mediation

• **If the mediation succeeds**

If the mediation lasts for several days, it is useful to draw up a summary of progress at the end of each day to avoid subsequent disputes. Once agreement has been achieved, a settlement document should be drawn up. As well as ensuring that the agreement accurately reflects the settlement, the lawyers should also ensure that it is final, binding and enforceable and affords the desired level of confidentiality (which should not be so absolute as to prevent enforcement, if necessary, of the agreement).

• **If the mediation fails**

Have a fallback position ready (for example, a Pt 36 offer or payment). If proceedings are already underway, it may be appropriate to apply to the court for directions straight away. Alternatively, there may be issues which have emerged as weaknesses in the other side's case (or indeed in your own case), and notwithstanding the 'without prejudice' nature of the negotiations, an offer to settle on those issues may be appropriate. Even if it does not succeed on the day, the process may narrow the issues and it may be appropriate to fix a 'follow up' settlement meeting. Many cases referred to mediation settle without proceeding to trial—statistics suggest as many as 80–90% of referrals—and whilst the evidence is necessarily anecdotal, it seems that the mediation process can be a productive exercise in focusing minds on the real issues and underlying interests and in resolving disputes earlier than would otherwise be the case.

3 FUNDING LITIGATION

A   Introduction

Any analysis of the Civil Procedure Rules 1998 and their impact in practice needs to take into account the context in which the procedural reforms were introduced. The procedural reforms are one aspect of a wider picture, being one of three strands of the government's civil justice reform programme. The other two strands are the reform of the legal aid system and the extension of conditional fee agreements (CFAs). The common aim of the proposals is to promote access to justice for the majority of the population, and clearly each strand is to some extent dependent on the success of the others. The procedural reforms introduce greater predictability and transparency in relation to legal costs—this should encourage wider use of CFAs, which in turn should reduce the demands on the overstretched legal aid budget.

A consistent theme throughout the government's reforming programme has been to encourage lawyers and clients to share the risks (and rewards) of litigation, particularly through the use of CFAs. The rationale is that CFAs will not only deliver savings in relation to legal aid, but will also provide an additional incentive to lawyers to 'buy into' the litigation and deliver a successful outcome.

Whilst the focus of funding reforms to date has been the reform of the legal aid system, the new funding regime as a whole applies to all cases, including commercial disputes. As Lord Woolf recognised in his Final Report, concerns about the cost of civil litigation in England are not limited to individuals who cannot afford to litigate—many commercial litigants, such as banks and other financial institutions, share these concerns. Multi-national corporations with experience of contingency fee deals in the US are increasingly looking to the new civil justice system in England to deliver not only faster, cheaper results but also more flexible ways of funding an action. In-house counsel and external lawyers need to be alive to these concerns and prepared to discuss a range of funding mechanisms to suit the particular needs of the client and the nature of the litigation.

CFAs were extended to all non-family civil matters in July 1998, creating the opportunity for major changes to litigation funding in future. Since the CPR were introduced in April 1999 there have been further major changes to the funding regime for civil cases, notably in the Access to Justice Act 1999 ('the AJA 1999'). The AJA 1999 introduces a new system for publicly funded cases (administered through the Legal Services Commission which replaces the Legal Aid Board) and makes further refinements to the operation of CFAs. This chapter provides an overview of the progress of the funding reform programme so far and looks at these developments in more detail. It also considers some of the practical issues likely to confront commercial litigants and commercial practitioners considering whether to adopt alternative funding arrangements.

B   The reform of legal aid

Whilst legal aid reform is clearly of greatest relevance to those claimants who may not be able to participate in the civil justice system without some form of financial assistance, it is also relevant to corporate defendants who may face claims from publicly funded claimants. Legally aided parties have been involved in some of the largest actions in the courts in recent years, including several major product liability and environmental cases, and the extent to which the proposed reforms will facilitate or impede the funding of such cases in future is an area which many corporate counsel will be monitoring closely.

The Lord Chancellor's Department's consultation paper 'Access to Justice with Conditional Fees'[1] stated that the principal objectives in relation to the reform of legal aid were to:
- promote access to justice for the majority of the population through the wider availability of CFAs;
- refocus legal aid by removing cases which can be financed in some other way and promoting access to justice for the needy by directing the legal aid budget to priority areas;
- deliver legal aid through contracts;
- remove weak cases from the legal aid system by toughening the legal merits test; and
- develop a way of supporting cases which have a significant wider public interest but which might not otherwise have been brought.

These aims have now been developed in the AJA 1999, which makes major changes to the award and administration of public funding for civil cases.

1   Key changes under the Access to Justice Act 1999

The AJA 1999 establishes a Community Legal Service operated by a new body, the Legal Services Commission ('the Commission').[2] One of the functions of the Commission will be to provide public funding for legal services, including legal advice and legal representation. This system replaces the legal aid scheme for civil cases under the Legal Aid Act 1988.

---

1   March 1998.
2   Effective from 1 April 2000.

The Commission may only award public funding to cases which are not excluded under Sch 2 to the Act. Sch 2 excludes personal injury claims (with the exception of clinical negligence claims), which will not be eligible for legal aid. However, the Lord Chancellor has proposed that certain categories of cases should be brought back within the scope of public funding, including cases with a wider public interest and personal injury claims with exceptionally high investigative or overall costs. The Lord Chancellor is also empowered under the AJA to authorise funding in other very exceptional individual cases 'where it is strongly in the interests of justice to do so'.

The Commission is responsible for preparing a 'Funding Code', setting out the criteria and procedures for deciding which cases should be funded, and to ensure that funding is directed to cases where the need is greatest. A draft Funding Code was published in October 1999 and following consultation and amendment was approved by the Lord Chancellor on 14 January 2000. The Code comes into force on 1 April 2000.

Various levels of financial assistance are available. These include:
- full representation;
- investigative help (legal representation which is limited to investigation of the strength of a proposed claim, including the issue and conduct of proceedings only so far as necessary to obtain disclosure of relevant information or to protect the client's position in relation to any urgent hearing or time limit for the issue of proceedings);
- support funding, limited to partial funding of proceedings which are otherwise being pursued privately, under or with a view to a CFA. Support funding may take the form of either 'investigative support' (limited to investigation of the strength of a proposed claim) or 'litigation support'.

In order to qualify for public funding, the case must have sufficient prospects of success. Different categories of prospects of success are defined as follows:
- 'Very good' means 80% or more;
- 'Good' means 60–80%;
- 'Moderate' means 50–60%;
- 'Borderline' means that the prospects of success are not poor, but because there are difficult disputes of fact, law or expert evidence, it is not possible to say that prospects of success are better than 50%;
- 'Poor' means clearly less than 50% so that the claim is likely to fail;
- 'Unclear' means the case cannot be put into any of the above categories because further investigation is needed.

The necessary level of likely success varies according to the type of case, but in general terms, full representation will be refused if:
- the prospects of success are unclear;
- the prospects of success are borderline and the case does not appear to have a 'significant wider public interest' (ie the potential of the proceedings to produce real benefits for individuals other than the client, other than benefits to the public at large which normally flow from proceedings of the type in question) or to be of overwhelming importance to the client; or
- the prospects of success are poor.

If the claim is primarily for damages and does not have a significant wider public interest, full representation will be refused unless certain cost benefit criteria are satisfied:

- if prospects of success are very good, likely damages must exceed likely costs;
- if prospects of success are good, likely damages must exceed likely costs by a ratio of 2:1;
- if prospects of success are moderate, likely damages must exceed likely costs by a ratio of 4:1.

If the claim is not primarily a claim for damages, and does not have a significant wider public interest, full representation will be refused unless the likely benefits to be gained from the proceedings justify the likely costs, such that 'a reasonable private paying client would be prepared to litigate, having regard to the prospects of success and all other circumstances'.

Subject to certain specified exceptions, funding will be refused or deferred unless it appears reasonable for it to be granted in the light of the resources available in the central budget, and the likely future demands on those resources.

Funding is available for ADR, and an application to fund litigation may be refused if there are complaints systems, ombudsman schemes or forms of ADR which should be tried before litigation is pursued. This will be particularly important to financial services organisations, given the wide ranging remit of the new Financial Services Ombudsman under the Financial Services and Markets Bill.

2   *The practical impact of the changes*

Until the Funding Code is in operation, it is difficult to anticipate precisely what effect the changes will have on commercial defendants facing, for example, product liability or environmental claims which may potentially be eligible for Commission funding. A number of issues remain unresolved, including:

- The definition of public interest cases is wide, and in theory a case with borderline prospects could qualify for funding. This raises the prospect of speculative litigation being funded, at least in its early investigative stages, without the claimant being required to submit to a rigorous merits test.
- How will the Commission respond when faced with a request for assistance in meeting investigative costs in a major product liability case which may run into many thousands of pounds? The fund is not open ended, and the Commission will face a difficult task in balancing competing claims to a limited fund.
- The Code envisages that large claims will be primarily be funded through a CFA, but the experience of firms which have attempted to finance major multi-party claims in this way, notably in the UK tobacco litigation, suggests that potential litigants may face difficulties in finding legal advisers able or willing to take on claims on this basis in the future, given the substantial financial risks involved in running lengthy litigation under a CFA.

C Conditional fee agreements

1 Why use a CFA?

Traditionally CFAs, also known as 'no win, no fee' agreements, have allowed solicitors to agree to take a case on the understanding that, if the case is lost, they will not charge their client for all or any of the work undertaken. In agreeing to this, the client also agrees that if the case is successful, the solicitor can charge a success fee on top of the normal fee, to compensate him for the risk he has run of not being paid all or some of his fees. That success fee is calculated as a percentage of the normal fee and the level at which the success fee is set will reflect the risk involved. The 'no fee' element relates to the solicitor's fees alone and does not cover the ancillary expenses of the case, such as experts' reports and counsel's fees.

The rationale for CFAs, (apart from alleviating the drain on legal aid and improving access to justice) is that lawyers are likely to be more concerned to ensure they do not take on cases where the chances of success are not sufficiently certain. If he does take on the case, the lawyer has an additional incentive to try to achieve a favourable outcome for the client, since the lawyer will then recover not only his normal fee but also the success fee. The extension of CFAs to all civil (non-family) cases in July 1998 was considered by the government to be a significant step towards removing the barrier of high cost which deters many people from starting legal proceedings. However the introduction of CFAs also raises important issues regarding potential conflicts of interest between the client and legal adviser which have not yet been resolved.

2 The introduction of CFAs

A CFA was defined in the Courts and Legal Services Act 1990, s 58 as an agreement between a person providing advocacy or litigation services and his client which 'provides for that person's fees and expenses, or any part of them, to be payable only in specified circumstances...'. Conditional fees were initially introduced in 1995 for certain categories of civil cases only: personal injury cases, insolvency cases and cases before the European Court of Human Rights. The Conditional Fee Agreements Order 1995[3] set out the parameters within which CFAs could operate. It provided that the maximum percentage by which normal fees could be increased in the event of a successful outcome in the case was 100% (ie the maximum a client could be charged if the case was won was double the normal fee). In addition, the Law Society issued guidance to the effect that the solicitor's success fee should represent no more than 25% of any damages recovered.

In July 1998, CFAs were extended to all types of civil cases (except family cases). The 100% 'cap' and the Law Society guidance remained in place.

---

3   SI 1995/1674.

However, the definition of a CFA in s 58 was limited, and did not encompass all situations where a legal representative might agree to act for his client at different rates to those which he would normally seek to recover from his client's opponent. In 1998, *Thai Trading v Taylor*[4] called into question the extent to which CFAs were permissible at common law, in circumstances where the s 58 statutory definition of a permitted CFA did not apply.

In *Thai Trading*, Mrs Taylor had employed her husband, who was a solicitor, to act for her on the understanding that she would not pay anything if she lost the case. In the event, she was successful. The issue which arose was whether the agreement between Mr and Mrs Taylor was valid and not contrary to public policy, in circumstances where the Solicitors' Practice Rules 1990 prohibited 'any arrangement to receive a contingency fee'. A contingency fee was defined as 'any sum (whether fixed or calculated, either as a percentage of proceeds or otherwise howsoever) payable only in the event of success in the prosecution of any action, suit or other contentious proceeding'. The 1990 Practice Rules made no distinction between the different types of contingency fees which might arise, varying from a US style 'contingency fee' where the lawyer receives a share of the winnings, to the type of 'conditional fee' agreement used in *Thai Trading*, ie to charge a normal fee if the case was won and no fee if it was lost.

Giving judgment in *Thai Trading*, Millett LJ observed that the prohibition on contingency fees at common law had been based on public policy considerations, but that 'public policy is not static'. Whilst it was understandable that a contingency fee which entitles the solicitor to a reward over and above his ordinary profit costs if he wins should be challenged, a contingency fee which entitles the solicitor to no more than his ordinary profit costs if he wins was another matter. He observed that he would regard a solicitor who entered into such an agreement 'not as charging a fee if he wins, rather as agreeing to forego his fee if he loses' and questioned 'whether this would be regarded as contrary to public policy today, if indeed it ever was'.

The Court of Appeal ruled that there was nothing unlawful in a solicitor agreeing to forgo all or part of his fee if he lost, provided that he did not seek to recover more than his ordinary profit costs and disbursements if he won. The prohibition on contingency fees under the Solicitors' Practice Rules was not regarded by the court as material, since 'the fact that a professional rule prohibits a particular practice does not of itself make the practice contrary to law'. The Solicitors' Practice Rules had been based on the perception of public policy applicable at the time they were drawn up, which was no longer appropriate.

The *Thai Trading* decision was regarded as a landmark judgment, and many solicitors entered into CFAs on the basis of the law as it was stated in that case. However, the situation was thrown into confusion by the decision in *Awwad v Geraghty & Co*.[5] In *Geraghty*, a solicitor agreed to charge a client her usual rate if the case was won, but a reduced rate if it was lost. This

4   [1998] QB 781, [1998] 3 All ER 65, CA.
5   (1999) Independent, 1 December.

arrangement was challenged by the client on the basis that it was contrary to the Solicitors' Practice Rules. The Court of Appeal agreed, disapproving *Thai Trading*, and ruled that such an agreement to accept a reduced fee was against public policy. The court held, based on the House of Lords' decision in *Swain v Law Society*[6] (which was not cited in *Thai Trading*) that the Solicitors' Practice Rules had the force of a statute, and disagreed with Millet LJ's observation that breach of a practice rule does not of itself make the practice contrary to law. The Court of Appeal also did not accept the *Thai Trading* premise that there was a distinction between an agreement to charge a fee or enhanced fee if the client won and an agreement to forgo some or all of the fee if he lost.

In the absence of a ruling from the House of Lords, it is unclear whether the decision in *Thai Trading* or *Geraghty* should be preferred. When s 27 of the AJA 1999 comes into force in April 2000, the position will be simplified, since the only enforceable CFAs will be those which satisfy the conditions set out in s 27, which includes all agreements to work for less than the normal fee. However, the AJA is not retrospective in effect. CFAs for personal injury cases made under the 1995 statutory instrument and CFAs made under the 30 July 1998 statutory instrument will be protected, but the validity of existing CFAs made outside the scope of the Courts and Legal Services Act 1990 remains unclear.

3   *The Access to Justice Act 1999*

The AJA, which received Royal Assent on 27 July 1999, introduces a number of refinements to the operation of CFAs, reflecting lessons learned since their introduction in 1995. The AJA itself only provides the framework for the new regime, and will be supplemented by secondary legislation, including regulations, new CPR, practice directions and protocols.

The provisions relating to CFAs and insurance premiums are contained in ss 27–31. The key changes relating to CFAs include:

- a new and clearer definition of CFAs, incorporating all agreements to work for less than normal fees. Section 27 provides that:
  - '(a) a conditional fee agreement is an agreement with a person providing advocacy or litigation services which provides for his fees and expenses or any part of them to be payable only in specified circumstances; and
  - (b) a conditional fee agreement provides for a success fee if it provides for the amount of any fees to which it applies to be increased, in specified circumstances, above the amount which would be payable if it were not payable only in specified circumstances';
- the winning party's success fee is potentially recoverable from the other side under an order for costs.[7] This change ensures there

---

6   [1983] 1 AC 598, [1982] 2 All ER 827, HL.
7   Section 27.

will be no ambiguity about whether the success fee is recoverable in principle, while retaining the court's general discretion as to the award of costs and determination of the amount of costs recoverable. The rationale for the change is that:

(a) in money cases, a successful claimant should be able to recover all the damages they were awarded, and

(b) CFAs should also be available to litigants in non-money cases, where there are no damages from which to pay a success fee.

This change effectively renders redundant the 25% cap recommended by the Law Society, since a successful claimant will no longer be responsible for meeting the success fee out of the damages he recovers;

- a party may be funded by a trade union, or other prescribed group, and such a trade union or group which takes responsibility for a party's liability may also recover the success fee from the opponent in recognition of this liability;[8]
- the costs of the winning party's 'after the event' insurance premium may be recoverable from the other side as a disbursement on assessment of costs, subject to the court's general discussion on assessment as to whether to allow a disbursement and at what level;[9]
- the Lord Chancellor may amend the indemnity principle which underlies costs, through rules of court;[10]
- regulations will prescribe requirements with which all CFAs must comply. These are likely to be similar in nature to the 1995 regulations. In addition, the Lord Chancellor may prescribe different requirements for different types of agreement or classes of case and define which CFAs will be eligible to incur a success fee and which will not.

In addition to the new statutory provisions set out in the AJA, the Lord Chancellor's Department issued a consultation paper[11] setting out more detailed proposals for the operation of CFAs in practice. Following consultation on the paper, the government published its proposals for extending and improving CFAs.[12] The proposals deal with the practical operation of the measures set out in the AJA in relation to CFAs, and sets out the areas which will be covered in forthcoming regulations and rules of court.

4   Regulations

In summary these will:
- specify that CFAs with success fees can be used in all civil non-family proceedings;

8   Section 28 and s 30.
9   Section 29.
10 Section 31.
11 'Conditional Fees: Sharing the Risks of Litigation' September 1999.
12 'Conditional Fees: Sharing the risks of litigation (Responses)' February 2000.

- set the maximum level of the success fee at 100% of the solicitor's normal costs, except in certain specialised cases. The 100% maximum will not apply to proceedings which would be brought in the Commercial Court, the Admiralty Court and the Technology and Construction Court, where the complexity of the cases and the sophistication of the users of those forums are considered to be 'such that a limit on the success fee appears neither to be desirable or necessary';
- require reasons for the level of the success fee to be included in the CFA. It will be for the solicitor to provide these reasons when he agrees to take the case on a conditional fee basis (subject to any requirements set out in regulations regarding client care). There will be no requirement in the regulations for counsel to produce written reasons to the client. The solicitor will have to distinguish the element of the success fee which relates to the risk of his not being paid any of his costs from the risk of having himself to meet other costs (such as disbursements) if the case is lost;
- prescribe the information that the client should receive from the legal representative both in writing and orally. This will include informing the client about alternatives to conditional fees (such as the possibility of Community Legal Service funding, 'before the event' insurance cover already purchased by the client, or funding through an employer, trade union or other membership organisation scheme);
- make provision for the Lord Chancellor to approve membership organisation schemes, and to approve them as bodies eligible to recover their self insurance costs in successful cases and set out the maximum amount recoverable for this self insurance element by membership organisations.

5   Rules of court

The AJA places the recovery of the success fee, any insurance premium and the self insurance costs of the membership organisation within the court's discretion when it is considering the question of costs. Additional rules of court will be introduced to provide detailed guidance to costs judges when making that assessment.

The rules will cover, in summary:
- the opponent's need for early notice that (a) a claim is being supported by a CFA (where this involves charging a success fee), (b) that there is an insurance policy, or (c) that the case is being run under a membership scheme. The opponent should be notified of the CFA when he is initially notified of the claim or within seven days of the CFA being concluded (if later). Notice of the existence of a CFA should also be provided in the particulars of claim or defence filed with the court. However, there is no requirement to disclose the amount of the success fee, pending detailed assessment

of costs at the end of the case (such a requirement might give grounds for a claim of prejudice to a fair trial under Art 6 of the European Convention on Human Rights);

- sanctions for non-disclosure of a CFA, making the success fee irrecoverable from the opposing party;

- rules to enable the losing opponent to challenge the success fee on final assessment on the basis that it was unreasonable given what the solicitor knew or reasonably ought to have known at the time the agreement was entered into. In these circumstances the client will not have to meet any shortfall, unless the solicitor can show there were exceptional circumstances which justified fixing a higher fee than it was reasonable to recover from the opponent. Whilst the ability of an opponent to challenge the uplift is intended to guard against excessive success fees, it seems likely that this provision will lead to considerable satellite litigation;

- on final assessment of costs, the court's need for details of the way the success fee has been calculated, the cover provided by an insurance policy and its price and how the self insurance in a case brought under a membership scheme has been calculated;

- the mechanism for assessment and recovery of costs in cases which settle before the commencement of proceedings, in order to avoid proceedings being issued just to resolve the issue of costs;

- where there is a dispute over an insurance premium, the paying party will be able to challenge it at final assessment by demonstrating (against relevant criteria) that the choice of insurance cover was unreasonable and generated excessive costs;

- where summary assessments take place in the course of proceedings, the assessment of any success fee element should be postponed until final assessment. An adjustment for the success fee element of the interim costs should take place at that final assessment.

6   Use of CFAs in commercial cases

Despite the extension of CFAs to all civil cases, they have largely been limited in practice to personal injury claims, where the risks inherent in the litigation can be predicted relatively easily. There have been several widely publicised initiatives to extend CFAs to other areas, including appeals from decisions of the Pensions Ombudsman (where the procedure is relatively straightforward) and defamation cases (where the non-availability of legal aid has excluded potential litigants). The demand from commercial clients for CFAs in large 'one off cases', which do not present the same opportunity to assess the fee by reference to similar cases, so far seems to have been low in practice, although an increasing number of clients are expressing interest in the possibility of a CFA in the future.

This reluctance on the part of commercial litigators and their clients to take advantage of the new system is not entirely surprising, since the CPR reforms notwithstanding, the risk assessment involved in budgeting for a major commercial action can be complex and involves many factors, not all of which will necessarily be clear from the outset. Whilst a detailed assessment of the merits of the case will of course be conducted in the early stages, it will not provide sufficient certainty to calculate an appropriate success fee. The initial risk analysis will need to be reassessed repeatedly throughout the case, since the prospects of success may fluctuate in a large case over a period of several years. Commercial practitioners are reluctant to commit to a success fee which may prove at a later date to have overestimated the prospects of success.

Equally, there are risks for a client who agrees to a CFA arrangement. Can he be sure that his interests will always prevail over those of the solicitor in the event of a conflict of interest? The client must be certain that he is receiving objective advice in relation to the appropriate level of success fee, and the merits of any settlement offered. A CFA in a large and complex case, where the inherent uncertainties justify a high success fee, may also prove to be very expensive if the client is successful. Whilst at least some part of the success fee will now be recoverable from the other side on assessment of costs it is unclear, pending the introduction of detailed guidance, what the courts will judge to be a 'reasonable' success fee, and therefore how much will be recoverable. Many clients are looking for certainty when budgeting for expensive long term litigation. In the absence of clear guidelines as to what amounts to a reasonable uplift, CFAs still include a substantial degree of uncertainty.

It seems likely that the introduction of CFAs in commercial cases will progress slowly, and be limited in the first instance to relatively routine and predictable procedures, or to a particular stage of a case. However, CFAs may affect the funding of commercial litigation more generally by raising awareness of the need to 'share the risk', encouraging commercial clients to look for flexibility and commitment from their legal advisers in terms of fixed fee arrangements, capped fees, discounts and other alternatives to standard hourly rates. In-house counsel should be exploring with their external lawyers the range of fee structures available, and working with them to ensure that they are tailored to meet their needs.

7 *Practical implications of CFAs*

Corporate claimants clearly stand to benefit more than corporate defendants from the changes to the CFA regime. If successful, they will not have to make any deductions in respect of costs from the damages they recover, and they will also recover their insurance premium. Corporate defendants generally have little to gain, and may face an increase in speculative claims from claimants, safe in the knowledge that the expense they face is minimal. This may put pressure on defendants to settle, in line with the emphasis in the CPR on early resolution of disputes, but it remains to be seen whether claimants will be prepared to negotiate now that the costs incentive to do so has been removed. There is an additional problem for defendants, which arises from the fact that where the claimant has a very good case, his uplift will be low, whereas on a 50/50 case his solicitor will seek an uplift of up to 100%, to reflect the increased risk he is taking on. As a result, a defendant with a reasonable defence will pay more if he loses, as the claimant's uplift will be higher, then a defendant with a very weak case, where the claimant's uplift will be lower.

The new provisions re-emphasise the need for law firms to have sophisticated budgeting tools and case management procedures in place, in order to predict the costs of litigation as accurately as possible. Successful use of CFAs is not just a question of accurate risk assessment—accurate costs prediction is equally important. This will enable a realistic assessment to be made as to whether a piece of litigation is suitable for a CFA, and if so, at what stage and for how long a CFA would be appropriate.

Many factors need to be taken into account when contemplating using a CFA. A number of key considerations are set out below.

- **Availability and cost of insurance**

This is a particularly important consideration for defendants contemplating a CFA. Whilst there are various 'after the event' insurance packages available, they are invariably tailored to the needs of claimants, particularly in personal injury actions. Coverage for contractual claims is extremely limited, and none of the major providers have so far targeted corporate defendants. Whilst individual defendant risks may be accepted on a case by case basis, the premium for any such cover, in the absence of detailed claims experience, is likely to be very high. Insurers may also demand a high price in terms of controlling the litigation, imposing unattractive exclusions and limitations, selecting the legal team and participating in settlement discussions. Provision may also need to be made against a situation where the insurer wishes to settle the action and threatens to withdraw cover unless the insured consents to the settlement.

- **Financing investigative costs**

In order to decide whether a case is appropriate for a CFA, extensive initial investigations will need to be carried out, including document reviews, and preparation of draft witness statements and experts reports. These investigative costs may be very high in commercial cases, and disbursements such as experts fees, which are not eligible for CFA funding, will have to be paid up front or covered by insurance (which may be very expensive). In a complex case it may also be appropriate for the client to receive independent legal advice on the terms of the CFA which he is proposing to enter into with his principal legal advisers, and this cost will also have to be met by the client upfront.

- **Will counsel agree to run the case on a CFA basis?**

Even if he will, there are a number of potential problems which need to be considered before entering into such an agreement. For example, what happens if he has to return the brief unexpectedly close to trial? Will his replacement agree to take the case on the same basis? What happens if the prospects of success are revised downwards close to or at trial, and counsel and the solicitor involved each hold the other responsible for this? At the moment these issues are unresolved, although the Commercial Bar

Association is currently working on a draft CFA agreement between solicitors and counsel which may provide guidance on some of these issues.

- **How is success defined?**

The definition will need to deal with the eventualities of settlement, ADR, change of circumstances, change in the client's commercial priorities and what happens if the client is awarded judgment in full, but for some reason cannot enforce that judgment? These are increasingly important issues in a climate where ADR, Pt 36 offers and counteroffers and early settlement are actively encouraged. Relatively few commercial cases proceed to trial, and this number may decrease further in the new era of active case management by the courts. Careful thought needs to be give to defining a range of successful outcomes, not limited to a successful result at trial.

- **Summary assessment of costs**

It is unclear what approach the court will take to applications for summary assessment of costs where the paying party is financing his case by means of a CFA, and whether it will look behind the CFA arrangement to establish whether the paying party is impecunious, or take the view that summary assessment is not appropriate in any case where a CFA applies, although it appears that the Civil Procedure Rule Committee favours the latter option. Otherwise, where the CFA funded party is backed by insurance, this may cover his liability in the event of an adverse interlocutory costs order, and the scope of such insurance cover will be a relevant factor in the exercise of the court's discretion.

4 STARTING AND DEFENDING A CLAIM

A Introduction

In his Final Report Lord Woolf criticised the complexity of the rules governing civil litigation which he considered could be seen as an obstacle to access to justice. In particular, he criticised the fact that under the old system there were four different ways of starting proceedings in the High Court and a further four in the county court. Within each of those categories there could be yet further variations. Lord Woolf made a number of proposals for the reform of the civil justice system which were aimed at simplifying the process by which a party might commence proceedings. In particular, he suggested that all claims should be started on a single claim form which could be used for every case, with variations according to the type of claim.[1]

He also recommended that the system of pleadings should be simplified. In particular, Lord Woolf commented that pleadings concentrated too much on causes of action and defences and not enough on the facts, and that failure to set out the facts clearly impeded the identification of issues. Defences in particular were drafted so as to keep all options open for as long as possible. In addition, they were too long-winded and were frequently superseded by later amendments and further and better particulars. Furthermore pleadings were not routinely subject to judicial scrutiny with the courts being reluctant to penalise the parties for late amendments to their case. This often resulted in delay and added inconvenience for the other party which was, in Lord Woolf's view, rarely adequately compensated for by an award of costs.[2]

In the light of these criticisms Lord Woolf recommended that the role of pleadings should be to set out the facts relied upon so that the court and the parties can ascertain what the dispute is about and the court can take appropriate decisions about the management of the case. He also proposed that pleadings be replaced by statements of case which should consist of a concise statement of the positive facts upon which the claimant or defendant relies in support of his case.

---

1 Interim Report, Section I, Chapter 3, para 44; Final Report, Section III, Chapter 12, paras 1–3.
2 Interim Report, Section V, Chapter 20, paras 4–5.

These recommendations[3] have in large part been implemented by the CPR and are discussed further in this chapter. This chapter also considers how the civil justice reforms in this area have been working in practice over the last twelve months.

B   Starting a claim

Proceedings will usually be commenced in the High Court or county court, by issuing a claim form under CPR Pt 7. There is also an alternative procedure for claims contained in CPR Pt 8 which should be used where the claim is unlikely to involve a substantial dispute as to fact. This is discussed later in this chapter. Although Lord Woolf's proposal that there should be one procedure for commencing a claim has been modified in to two it is still a significant improvement on the plethora of procedures available under the old system.

1   Issuing proceedings

Under the CPR a claimant may now use a single claim form to start all claims which can be conveniently disposed of in the same proceedings.[4] Proceedings are started when the court issues a claim form at the claimant's request. The claim form is issued on the date entered on the form by the court.[5]

Proceedings with which both the High Court and the county courts have jurisdiction to deal may be commenced in the High Court or in a county court. However, proceedings may only be commenced in the High Court where the claim is for damages or for a specified sum of money exceeding £15,000 (or £50,000 in personal injury claims) or if the claimant believes that the claim ought to be dealt with by a High Court judge by reason of the financial value of the claim and the amount in dispute and/or the complexity of the facts, legal issues, remedies or procedures involved and/or the importance of the outcome of the claim to the public in general.[6]

The CPR also make provision for the commencement and conduct of specialist proceedings and in particular for the allocation of a claim to a number of specialist lists within the High Court or certain county courts. Where a claim is the subject of specialist proceedings the top right hand corner of the claim form will normally be marked on issue indicating which

---

3   Interim Report, Section V, Chapter 20, para 3 and Final Report, Section III, Chapter 12, paras 11 and 16.

4   CPR 7.3. The alternative procedure for commencing proceedings contained in CPR Pt 8 is discussed further below.

5   CPR 7.2.

6   CPR Pt 7, practice direction, para 2.4. Paras 2.5 and 2.6 of the practice direction set out the jurisdiction of the High Court, Queen's Bench Division, Chancery Division and county court to deal with claims.

specialist list will deal with the claim.[7] Although the CPR will apply to claims brought under specialist proceedings, they will only do so to the extent that they are not inconsistent with the rules and practice directions which expressly apply to those claims.[8]

2 Contents of the claim form

A claimant should generally use practice form N1 to commence his claim, although where a claim is the subject of specialist proceedings a different practice form may have been approved in which case this should be used.[9]

In summary the claim form must contain the following:
- a concise statement of the nature of the claim;
- the remedy which the claimant seeks;
- where the claimant is making a claim for money, a statement of value (in the Commercial Court a claimant need only state the amount which he is claiming);[10]
- any other matters which are required by a practice direction;
- if particulars of claim are not contained in or served with the claim form, the claim form must state that they will follow;[11]
- state if the claimant is claiming in a representative capacity or the defendant is being sued in a representative capacity;[12]
- a verification by a statement of truth.[13]

---

3 Service of the claim form

After a claim form has been issued, it must generally be served on the defendant within four months after the date of issue, although where the

---

7 See CPR Pt 49, the practice directions thereto and the Commercial Court Guide, Chancery Guide, Patents Court Guide and the Mercantile Courts Guide. A claim which involves issues or questions which are technically complex, including for example, construction and engineering claims or claims relating to computers may be allocated to the Technology and Construction Court. Commercial claims issued in the Queen's Bench Division will be allocated to the Commercial List where they will be dealt with by the Commercial Court. Alternatively commercial claims may be issued in the Chancery Division of the High Court. Mercantile claims may be allocated to the Commercial Court, the Mercantile Court or the Business List of an authorised county court. Patents court business may be dealt with in the High Court, Chancery Division or the Patents County Court. Applications under the Companies Act 1985 or the Insurance Companies Act 1982 may be issued in the county court or the High Court, Chancery Division.
8 CPR Pt 7, practice direction, para 3.3.
9 In the Commercial Court the claimant must use practice form N1(CC).
10 See CPR 16.3 and Commercial Court Guide, Section B3.3.
11 The Commercial Court does not require the claim form to be accompanied by particulars of claim. See Commercial Court Guide, Section B3.4.
12 See CPR Pt 7, practice direction, paras 4.1–4.2 and r 16.2.
13 CPR 22.1, Pt 7, practice direction, paras 7.1–7.3 and Commercial Court Guide, Section B3.7.

defendant is outside the jurisdiction this period is extended to six months.[14] An application to extend time for service of the claim form may be made within the period in which the claim form is due to be served.[15] In certain circumstances the court will be prepared to extend time for service of the claim form notwithstanding that the period for service has expired.[16] Any application must be supported by evidence and may be made without notice.[17]

Unless the claimant notifies the court that he will serve the claim form it will be served by the court.[18] In the Commercial Court a claim form must be served by the parties and will be accompanied by forms for defending the claim, admitting the claim and acknowledging service.[19] Where the claimant serves the claim form he must also file a certificate of service with the court within seven days of service of the claim form.[20] If the claim form is served by the court it will send the claimant a notice specifying the deemed date of service.[1]

Under the CPR it is now possible for a defendant who knows that a claim form has been issued against him but not yet served on him to serve notice on the claimant requiring him to serve the claim form or discontinue the claim within the period specified by the notice (at least 14 days after service of the notice). If the claimant fails to comply with the notice, the defendant may apply to the court to have the claim dismissed.[2] This provision effectively prevents a claimant issuing proceedings on a general basis for protective purposes to avoid limitation issues.

C   Statements of case

Pleadings are now known as statements of case. CPR Pt 2 defines a statement of case as a claim form, particulars of claim (where they are not included on the claim form), defence, reply, Pt 20 claim and any additional information under CPR 18.1. Statements of case must consist of a concise statement of the positive facts upon which the claimant or defendant relies in support of their case. Their purpose is to:

> 'mark out the parameters of the case that is being advanced by each party. In particular they are still critical to identify the issues and the extent of the dispute between the parties…However no more than a concise statement of facts is required…'[3]

---

14   CPR 7.5. With effect from 2 May 2000, applications for permission to serve a claim form out of the jurisdiction will be governed by CPR Pt 6, Section III.
15   CPR 7.6.
16   CPR 7.6(3).
17   CPR 7.6(4).
18   CPR 6.3 and Chancery Guide, para 4.3.
19   See Commercial Court Guide, Sections B3.6 and B5.1 and CPR 7.8.
20   CPR 6.14 and Commercial Court Guide, Section B5.6. This is a prerequisite to obtaining judgment in default pursuant to CPR Pt 12. CPR 6.10 specifies what the certificate of service must state.
1   CPR 6.14(1).
2   CPR 7.7.
3   Per Lord Woolf MR in *McPhilemy v Times Newspapers Ltd* [1999] 3 All ER 775, [1999] EMLR 751, CA.

In the light of Lord Woolf's comments, statements of case should now be shorter and simpler and more issue focused and should be drafted having regard to the overriding objective contained in CPR 1.1. The preparation of statements of case will however involve no less work for the lawyer in investigating the facts and legal issues on which his client's case is based. In fact, more effort and costs may be incurred in preparing a statement of case than an old style pleading. The costs savings that are, at least in theory, to be delivered by complying with the overriding objective when preparing a statement of case are longer term. They lie in the identification, as the case is framed, of those issues which are not going to win or lose the case and which should not, therefore, merit investigation, pleading, evidential examination or further consideration by the court or the parties as the case proceeds.

Indications from the Queen's Bench Division and Commercial Court suggest that in practice, statements of case are more helpful to the courts than pleadings under the old system as the issues in dispute are, in general, more clearly stated. Statements of case have been described as less formalistic and more factually orientated with facts tending to be briefly stated. It also appears that counsels' involvement in the statement of case stage is diminishing as more solicitors take on the drafting exercise themselves.

All statements of case must be filed with the court and are subject to greater judicial scrutiny at a much earlier stage in proceedings.[4] In line with the courts' powers of case management, statements of case may be ordered to be dispensed with.[5] Alternatively, statements of case may be ordered in relation to particular issues only. For example, such orders have been made in the Technology and Construction Court. However, in exercising their power to dispense with or limit statements of case to particular issues, the courts need to be alive to potential human rights arguments being raised by the parties when the Human Rights Act 1998 is implemented in October 2000, as parties may seek to argue that their right to a fair trial under Art 6(1) of the European Convention on Human Rights has been infringed.

Claimant's statement of case

Unless otherwise ordered by the court, a claimant must serve particulars of claim with the claim form, alternatively within 14 days after service of the claim form.[6] In the Commercial Court this timescale is considered to be

---

4   For example, the court may now exercise its power under CPR 3.4 to strike out a statement of case on its own initiative. Strike-out is discussed in detail in Chapter 6 on case management.

5   CPR 16.8. See also CPR Pt 49, practice direction D, para 5 and Commercial Court Guide, Section B3.8.

6   Provided that the particulars of claim are served within four months (or six months) from issue of the claim form. See CPR 7.4(2), practice direction, para 6.1(2).

unrealistic and unless particulars of claim are served with the claim form they will be served 28 days after acknowledgement of service.[7]

Where particulars of claim are served separately from the claim form, the claimant must within seven days of service on the defendant, file a copy of the particulars together with a certificate of service.[8]

Particulars of claim must contain the following:

- a concise statement of the facts upon which the claimant relies;
- interest, if claimed and if so, upon what basis and at what rate;
- details of aggravated or exemplary or provisional damages if claimed;
- any other matters set out in a practice direction;[9]
- any particulars of fraud, illegality, misrepresentation, breach of trust, notice or knowledge of any fact, unsoundness of mind or undue influence, wilful default or mitigation;[10]
- they may also include details of any point of law relied upon;[11]
- where particulars of claim are not contained in a claim form, they must be verified by a statement of truth.[12]

Additional guidance on drafting statements of case in Commercial Court cases is given in Appendix 4 to the Commercial Court Guide, and in Chancery Division cases in Appendix 1 to the Chancery Guide. The Commercial Court also requires that case summaries be prepared where statements of case exceed 25 pages in length.[13]

Key documents supporting the claimant's case may be attached to the particulars of claim.[14] These may include copies of witness statements or

---

7   Commercial Court Guide, Section C2.4. The parties may also agree extensions of time for service of the particulars of claim. Any agreement must be evidenced in writing and notified to the Commercial Court. Extensions of time exceeding six weeks should also be accompanied by a brief statement of reasons and the Commercial Court may decide to request further information or convene a case management conference.
8   CPR 7.4(3). See also Commercial Court Guide, Section C2.5.
9   CPR 16.4. See also Pt 16, practice direction, paras 4–8 which set out the specific matters which must be included for certain types of claim.
10 CPR Pt 16, practice direction, para 9.2, Commercial Court Guide, Section C1.2 d and Chancery Guide, para 4.5.
11 CPR Pt 16, practice direction, para 14.3(1). See also Chancery Guide, para 4.5. The Commercial Court Guide, Section C1.2, paras e, f and g states that reliance on any statute and points of European Law or based on Human Rights legislation and allegations of foreign law must be stated.
12 CPR Pt 16, practice direction, para 3.4.
13 Commercial Court Guide, Section C1.3–1.5.
14 For example CPR Pt 16, practice direction, para 8.3 states that where a claim is based on a written agreement a copy of the contract recording the agreement should be attached to or served with the particulars of claim. In addition pursuant to para 14.3 a party may attach to or serve with his statement of case a copy of any document which he considers necessary to his claim (or his defence) or give the name of any witness he proposes to call. In Commercial Court cases the relevant pages of an agreement may be attached pursuant to the Commercial Court Guide, Section C1.2. See also Chancery Guide, Appendix 1.

experts' reports.[15] In practice it seems that whilst contractual documents (or extracts in the Commercial Court) are being attached to statements of case, there has been reluctance to attach preliminary witness statements or experts reports, although in personal injury cases experts reports will be attached. The Commercial Court positively discourages attaching an expert's report to a statement of case.[16]

As discussed in Chapter 1 on pre-action tactics, prior to commencing proceedings a claimant should analyse the key issues in dispute between the parties and identify relevant documents and key factual and expert evidence in order to be in a position to comply with any relevant pre-action protocol or, in its absence, paragraph 4 of the practice direction to protocols. This will involve significant front-loading of time and costs. However without this work, not only will the claimant face sanctions imposed by the court for his pre-action conduct, he will also be unable to properly plead his case in his particulars of claim. Given the court's powers of case management and the judicial scrutiny to which particulars of claim are now subject[17] it would be unwise for a claimant to commence proceedings without having undertaken this detailed case preparation.

D Defending a claim

1 Responding to the claim

Pursuant to CPR Pt 9 a defendant need not respond to a claim until particulars of claim have been served on him. The defendant may then file or serve an admission as to the whole or part of the claim[18] and/or a defence[19] or an acknowledgement of service.[20]

A defendant should now only file an acknowledgement of service[1] if he is unable to file a defence within the time prescribed under the CPR (generally 14 days after service of particulars of claim)[2] or if he wishes to dispute the court's jurisdiction under CPR Pt 11.[3] As a general rule, the acknowledgement of service should be filed 14 days after service of the claim form accompanied by particulars of claim or where a claim form states that particulars of claim are to follow, 14 days after service of the particulars of claim. However, in the Commercial Court the defendant should file an acknowledgement of

---

15 Evidence may now also be contained within the claimant's particulars of claim.
16 Commercial Court Guide, Section C1.2i.
17 See for example the court's power to strike out particulars of claim in CPR 3.4, practice direction, paras 1.4–1.5.
18 See CPR Pt 14 and Commercial Court Guide, Section B7.7.
19 See CPR Pt 15.
20 See CPR 10.5 and the practice direction to CPR Pt 10 as to the form and contents of the acknowledgment of service.
1 Practice form N9.
2 CPR 15.4.
3 CPR 10.1(3).

service[4] in every case 14 days after service of the claim form, regardless of whether or not particulars of claim accompanied the claim form.[5]

On receipt of the acknowledgement of service the court will notify the claimant in writing.[6]

Failure to file an acknowledgement of service and a defence or to serve or file an admission within the prescribed time period enables the claimant to apply for default judgment under CPR Pt 12.[7]

2   *The defendant's statement of case*

As a general rule, the defence should be filed 14 days after service of the particulars of claim or, where an acknowledgment of service has been filed, 28 days after service of the particulars of claim.[8] A copy of the defence must also be served on every other party to the proceedings.[9] The claimant and defendant may, however, agree one extension of time of 28 days for filing the defence and the court must be notified in writing of this.[10] In the Commercial Court it is possible to agree extensions of time for service of the defence in excess of 28 days and the Commercial Court must be notified in writing of this.[11] However, where an agreed extension exceeds six weeks the Commercial Court must also be informed of the reasons for the longer extension and the Commercial Court may request further information or convene a case management conference.[12]

The defence must contain the following:
- which of the allegations in the particulars of claim the defendant denies, including his reasons for doing so and his own version of events in so far as this differs from those of the claimant;
- which allegations the defendant is unable to admit or deny, but which he requires the claimant to prove;
- which allegations he admits;
- if the defendant disputes the claimant's statement of value his reasons for doing so and if he is able to do so, give his own statement of value of the claim; (this provision does not apply in Commercial Court cases);[13]
- if the defendant is defending in a representative capacity, state what that capacity is;

---

4   Form N9(CC).
5   See Commercial Court Guide, Section B7.2–7.3. The time period for filing the acknowledgement of service will be longer if the claim is served out of the jurisdiction or upon the agent of a principal who is overseas. See Commercial Court Guide, Section B7.4.
6   CPR 10.4.
7   CPR 10.2. See CPR Pt 12 and Commercial Court Guide, Section B7.6.
8   CPR 15.4 and Commercial Court Guide, Section C3.1.
9   CPR 15.6. It is not clear whether the defence should be served by the court although if an extra copy is sent to the court, it should serve it under CPR 6.3. In Commercial Court cases the defence is served by the party. See Commercial Court Guide, Section C3.1.
10   CPR 15.5.
11   Commercial Court Guide, Section C3.4.
12   Commercial Court Guide, Section C3.5.
13   Commercial Court Guide, Section C1.2.

- details of any limitation period relied upon;
- his address for service if he has not filed an acknowledgement of service; (this provision does not apply in Commercial Court cases);[14]
- it may also refer to any point of law on which the defence is based;[15]
- it may also include any defence of set-off, whether or not it is a Pt 20 claim;[16]
- the defence must be verified by a statement of truth.[17]

Additional guidance on the drafting of the defence is also given in Appendix 4 to the Commercial Court Guide and Appendix 1 to the Chancery Guide. Key documents supporting the defendant's case may be attached to the defence[18] and in practice it appears that this is being done. Although it is also possible to attach copies of witness statements or experts' reports to statements of case,[19] it appears that this practice has not been adopted, save in relation to expert reports in personal injury cases. The Commercial Court actively discourages attaching an expert's report to a statement of case.[20]

Given that the defendant must now state a positive case in his defence he will no longer be able to serve a holding defence and he risks immediate strike out by the court, either on its own initiative or upon application by another party to the proceedings, if he does so.[1] A defendant will need to gather documents and oral evidence in support of his defence as soon as he receives notification of the possibility of a claim being made against him. In particular, he will need to ensure that he has the necessary information retrieval systems in place in order to respond quickly to any claim made against him. Not only will this help him in his pre-action tactics, for example when considering or making any pre-action offers to settle, it will also ensure that he is able to comply with the tight timetable for filing his defence.

E   Part 20 claims

The aim of the Pt 20 claims procedure was to simplify the procedure for bringing counterclaims, claims for indemnity and contribution and third

---

14 CPR 16.5. See also practice direction, para 13 as to the matters which must be included in a defence in response to certain types of claims and Commercial Court Guide, Section C1.2 as to the contents of a defence in Commercial Court cases.

15 CPR Pt 16, practice direction, para 14.3(1). See also Chancery Guide, para 4.5. The Commercial Court Guide, Section C1.2, paras e, f and g require that reliance on any statute and points of European Law or based on Human Rights legislation and allegations of foreign law must be stated.

16 CPR 16.6.

17 CPR 22.1.

18 Pursuant to para 14.3 a party may attach to or serve with his statement of case a copy of any document which he considers necessary to his defence or give the name of any witness he proposes to call. In Commercial Court cases the relevant pages of an agreement may be attached pursuant to the Commercial Court Guide, Section C1.2. See also Chancery Guide, Appendix 1.

19 Evidence may now also be contained within the defendant's defence.

20 Commercial Court Guide, Section C1.2i.

1   CPR 3.4(2) and practice direction, paras 1.2 and 1.6.

party proceedings. In practice this has not been achieved. The Pt 20 claims procedure is both complex and confusing, covering a number of different types of claim.

As a general rule a Pt 20 claim is to be treated as a claim. However the rules relating to the time within which a claim form may be served, the requirement to include a statement of value where a claim is issued in the High Court and case management at the preliminary stage do not apply.[2]

Part 20 claims include:
- a counterclaim by a defendant against a claimant; or
- a counterclaim by a defendant against a claimant and another person;
- a claim by a defendant against any other person for contribution or indemnity or some other remedy; or
- where a Pt 20 claim has been made against a person who is not a party, any claim made by that person against any other person;[3]
- the contents of all Pt 20 claims must be verified by a statement of truth.[4]

1   Counterclaim against a claimant

A counterclaim can be made without the court's permission if filed with the defence and at any other time with the court's permission.[5] The defendant files and serves particulars of counterclaim[6] which normally follow on from the defence and are contained in one document.[7] There is no requirement to file a Pt 20 claim form.[8] Although, a claimant is not required to file an acknowledgement of service, given that a counterclaim is to be treated in other respects as if it were a claim, the claimant is required to file a defence to the counterclaim. The time period for serving a defence normally runs from filing the acknowledgement of service, however in the case of the defence to counterclaim no guidance is given in the CPR as to the time within which this should be done. If no defence to the counterclaim is filed, an application can be made for default judgment under CPR Pt 12.[9]

2   Counterclaim against a person who is not a party

Where a defendant wishes to make a counterclaim against a person who is not a party, an application must be made to the court for an order that the

---

2   CPR 20.3(1) and (2) and practice direction, para 3.
3   CPR 20.2.
4   CPR 22.1 and Pt 20, practice direction, para 4.1.
5   CPR 20.4. The application should be supported by evidence. See CPR Pt 20, practice direction, para 2.1.
6   CPR 20.4 and 20.8.
7   CPR Pt 15, practice direction, para 3.1 and Pt 20, practice direction, para 6.1.
8   CPR 20.7. However, there appears to be some confusion on this point as CPR 20.8(1)(a) refers to the service of a Pt 20 claim in the context of a counterclaim. This must be wrong in the light of CPR 20.4 and 20.7.
9   Civil Procedure (Amendment) Rules 2000, SI 2000/221; CPR 20.3(3) and 12.3(2).

person be added as a defendant to the counterclaim. Again, a Pt 20 claim form is not required. The application, which can be made without notice,[10] must be made pursuant to CPR Pt 23 and must be supported by evidence. If the court makes such an order it will also give directions for the management of the case at the same time.[11]

3   *Claim for contribution or indemnity from co-defendant*

Pursuant to CPR 20.6 a defendant may make a claim for contribution or indemnity against a co-defendant. The claim can be made once the defendant has filed an acknowledgment of service or a defence by filing a notice containing a statement as to the nature and grounds of the claim and serving the notice on the other defendant.

4   *Any other Part 20 claim*

Pursuant to CPR 20.7 a Pt 20 claim will be made in all other cases when the court issues a Pt 20 claim form. A defendant may make such a claim without the court's permission if the Pt 20 claim is issued before or at the same time as the defendant files his defence or at any other time with the court's permission.[12] Particulars of the Pt 20 claim must be contained in or served with the Pt 20 claim.[13] The Pt 20 claim must be served on the person against whom it is made within 14 days after the date on which the party making the Pt 20 claim files his defence.

Once a Pt 20 claim is served on a person, that person becomes a party to the proceedings.[14] Pursuant to CPR 20.11 it is possible to obtain default judgment against a party who has failed to file an acknowledgement of service or defence in response to the Pt 20 claim. However if a defence is filed in response to a Pt 20 claim, a case management conference will be convened to consider the future conduct of the case and give further directions.[15]

---

10 CPR 20.5(2).
11 CPR 20.5. See also CPR 20.8 as to the procedure for service of the Pt 20 claim.
12 CPR 20.7(3) and see practice direction, para 2.1.
13 CPR 20.7(4). If the court gives permission to make a Pt 20 claim it will also give directions for service: see CPR 20.8(3). CPR 20.12 sets out the requirements for service where the Pt 20 claim is to be served on a non-party.
14 CPR 20.10. Where the Pt 20 claim is served on an existing party to proceedings to enable the court to determine a point against that party, the party becomes a party in the capacity specified in the Pt 20 claim.
15 CPR 20.13 and practice direction, paras 5.1–5.4. For Commercial Court cases see Commercial Court Guide, Section D7.21–25. In Commercial Court cases a Pt 20 claim should whenever possible be made before the case management conference dealing with the main claim if permission is not required. Alternatively if permission is required this should be sought at the case management conference.

F   The claimant's reply

There is no requirement to file a reply[16] and a claimant who does not do so is not taken to have admitted the matters raised in the defence.[17] However if a claimant does wish to do so, the reply must be filed when the claimant files his allocation questionnaire.[18] The Chancery Guide suggests that if possible a claimant should serve any reply before filing the allocation questionnaire to enable other parties to consider it before filing their allocation questionnaires[19] and at the same time the claimant (and not the court) must serve a copy of his reply on the other parties.[1] In the Commercial Court, where there is no allocation questionnaire, a reply will usually be served 21 days after service of the defence although the Commercial Court recognises that for some commercial cases a longer time period may be necessary. Where this is likely to be the case, an application on paper should be made promptly after service of the defence for an extension of time for service of the reply and a postponement of the case management conference.[2]

Where a claimant files a reply and fails to deal with a matter raised in the defence the CPR state that the claimant shall be taken to require the matter to be proved.[3] The reply must not be inconsistent with or contradict the particulars of claim and must not introduce a new claim.[4] If a claimant wishes to introduce a new claim an application should be made instead to amend the claim form and particulars of claim. A reply must be verified by a statement of truth.[5]

Given that the defence will no longer be a series of denials and non-admissions but will be a positive statement by the defendant of his case, a claimant is now more likely to consider serving a reply to counter the new points raised in the defence.

It is not possible to file or serve any statement of case after the reply without the court's permission.[6]

G   Amendments to statements of case

A party may amend his statement of case at any time before it is served on any other party to the proceedings however, once the statement of case has

---

16   CPR 15.8.
17   CPR 16.7(1).
18   Pursuant to CPR 26.3(6) the reply and the completed allocation questionnaire must be filed no later than the date specified in it and which is at least 14 days after the date when it is deemed to be served on the other party in question.
19   Chancery Guide, para 4.9.
1   CPR 15.8(b) and Commercial Court Guide, Section C4.1 and C4.4.
2   Commercial Court Guide, Section C4.3 sets out the procedure for making the application.
3   CPR 16.7(2).
4   CPR Pt 16, practice direction, para 10.2. See also Commercial Court Guide, Section C1.1–C1.2 and Appendix 4 as to the contents of a reply in Commercial Court cases and Chancery Guide, paras 4.5–4.8 and Appendix 1 as to the contents of the reply in Chancery Division cases.
5   CPR Pt 22 and Commercial Court Guide, Section C1.7.
6   CPR 15.9.

been served, a party may only amend it with the written consent of all the other parties to the proceedings or with the permission of the court.[7] The Commercial Court proposes that where possible, questions of amendment and consequential amendment should be dealt with by consent and that a party should consent to an amendment unless he has substantial grounds for objecting.[8]

Where an application is made to the court to amend a statement of case this should be made by application notice filed at court together with a copy of the statement of case containing the proposed amendments. The application may be dealt with at a hearing or may be dealt with on paper.[9] Pursuant to CPR 1.4 the court has a duty to deal with an application without a hearing if it can do so.[10]

When giving permission to amend statements of case the court will usually give a direction that the amended statement of case is filed with the court within 14 days of the date of the order. Directions may also be given for consequential amendments to any other statements of case and for service of the amended statements of case.[11] Unless otherwise ordered by the court there is now no requirement to retain the superseded text in any statement of case[12] save in Commercial Court cases.[13]

Amendments made to a statement of case must be verified by a statement of truth unless the court orders otherwise.[14] However, there is some confusion as to whether there is a requirement to verify amendments to a statement of case in all cases, as appears from CPR Pt 22, or only where the substance of the statement of case has changed as a result of the amendment.[15] The Commercial Court Guide has removed this confusion in commercial cases by stating that amendments to statements of case should be verified in all cases.[16] It is submitted that the clear approach adopted by the Commercial Court should be followed in all cases.

In line with Lord Woolf's recommendation that there should be greater judicial scrutiny over statements of case, where a party has amended his statement of case without requiring the permission of the court, the court now has the power to disallow those amendments. A party may apply to the court for such an order to be made within 14 days of service upon him of the copy of the amended statement of case.[17] If it is claimed that the amendments are scurrilous or otherwise vexatious, the party may also apply for an order

---

7   CPR 17.1. See also CPR Pt 19 where the amendment includes the addition or substitution of parties.
8   Commercial Court Guide, Section C5.5.
9   CPR Pt 17, practice direction, para 1.1 and r 23.8.
10   CPR 1.4(2)(j).
11   CPR 17.3 and practice direction, para 1.3.
12   See CPR Pt 17, practice direction, paras 2.2–2.4 as to the procedure to be adopted where the court orders that the superseded text in an amended statement of case should be retained.
13   Commercial Court Guide, Section C5.3.
14   CPR 22.1(2).
15   CPR Part 17, practice direction, para 1.4.
16   Commercial Court Guide, Section C5.4.
17   CPR 17.2.

that the amendments be struck out pursuant to CPR 3.4 or apply for summary judgment under CPR Pt 24. The court's powers to make such orders are discussed in detail in Chapter 6 dealing with case management.

Under the old system applications to amend pleadings were generally refused only in exceptional circumstances. Under the CPR some recent cases suggest that the courts are now less willing to allow parties to amend their statements of case, particularly where the application to amend is made at a fairly late stage in the proceedings,[18] however the courts' position on this point is not entirely clear. For example, in *Elli Christofi v Barclays Bank plc*[19] the Court of Appeal (Stuart-Smith and Chadwick LJJ) refused the claimant's application to amend the statement of case on the basis that if the court were to allow an amendment at such a late stage (in this case after the claimant's action had already been struck out) it would not be acting in accordance with the overriding objective of CPR Pt 1 of dealing with cases justly.[20] However a late amendment was allowed by the Court of Appeal in *Cobbold v London Borough of Greenwich*[1] when Gibson LJ stated:

> 'The overriding objective is that the court should deal with cases justly. That includes, so far as practicable, ensuring that each case is dealt with not only expeditiously but also fairly. Amendments in general ought to be allowed so that the real dispute between the parties can be adjudicated upon provided that any prejudice to the other party or parties caused by the amendment can be compensated for in costs, and the public interest in the efficient administration of justice is not significantly harmed.'

Clarification as to the court's approach in this area is needed. In so far as the courts are willing to take a tough line to applications to amend statements of case, particularly late amendments, this approach reinforces the underlying philosophy of the civil justice reforms (and of Lord Woolf's recommendations) which require that parties identify at an early stage the issues in dispute with a view to trying to resolve them.

H   Part 8 Claims

CPR Pt 8[2] provides that a claimant may use the Pt 8 procedure where he seeks the court's decision on a question which is unlikely to involve a

---

18   The Commercial Court Guide warns at Section C5.6 that late amendments should be avoided and may be disallowed.

19   [1999] 4 All ER 437.

20   See also *Hussain v Cuddy Woods & Cochrane* (18 October 1999, unreported), QBD, in which Smedley J held that the claimant had no real prospect of success on the claim as originally drafted or as amended if the amendments were allowed to be made. Accordingly, leave to amend was refused. In *Chilton v Surrey County Council* (24 June 1999, unreported) the Court of Appeal did allow the late amendment of a schedule of damages in a personal injury case but this was on the basis that the claim which was the subject of the amendment had been foreshadowed at the outset.

1   (9 August 1999, unreported).

2   See also Chancery Guide, paras 4.10–4.15 and Commercial Court Guide, Section B4.

substantial dispute of fact or a rule or practice direction requires or permits the use of Pt 8.[3] For example, the Pt 8 procedure will be used where a party seeks a declaration as to the construction of a document or a question of law.[4]

1   Issuing the claim

A Pt 8 claim should be issued in accordance with the rules and directions contained in CPR Pt 7 and the accompanying practice direction in so far as appropriate.[5]

2   Contents of the claim form

Claim Form N208[6] must be used for Pt 8 claims.

> **The claim form must state that:**
> - Pt 8 applies;
> - the question which the court wants the court to decide or the remedy which the claimant is seeking and the legal basis for the claim to that remedy;
> - if the claim is being made under an enactment, what that enactment is;
> - if the claimant is claiming or the defendant is being sued in a representative capacity, what that representative capacity is.[7]

The claimant must file any written evidence (either in the form of a witness statement or an affidavit) on which he intends to rely with the claim form[8] which should be served in accordance with CPR 7.5 discussed above. Alternatively the evidence may be included within the claim form. In either case it must be verified by a statement of truth.[9] The claimant's evidence

---

3   CPR 8.1. A practice direction may modify or disapply any of the rules contained in Pt 8, in which case the relevant practice direction must be complied with.

4   See also CPR Pt 8, practice direction—Alternative Procedure for Claims, para 1.4, which sets out the type of claim for which the Pt 8 procedure may be used, and practice direction Pt 8, section A which sets out the claims for which the Pt 8 procedure must be used. Following the decision in *Financial Services Authority v Milward* (27 May 1999, unreported) an application under the Banking Act 1987, s 93 for injunctive relief against a defendant arising out of alleged breaches by him of the Act should be made under CPR Pt 7 and not Pt 8. Section A Table 1 of the practice direction—Pt 8 was erroneous.

5   CPR Pt 8, practice direction—Alternative Procedure for Claims.

6   In the Commercial Court practice form N208(CC) must be used.

7   CPR 8.2 and practice direction—Alternative Procedure for Claims, para 2.2. Where the Pt 8 procedure is being used by reason of any practice direction the claim form should also comply with that practice direction. See also Appendix 4 to the Commercial Court Guide which states that where applicable it should comply with the points contained in Appendix 4.

8   CPR 8.5.

9   CPR Pt 22 and r 8.5(7). The Commercial Court Guide, Section B4.3 requires that the claim form is verified by a statement of truth.

must also be served on the defendant[10] and must be accompanied by a form for acknowledging service.[11]

3   Responding to a Part 8 claim

A defendant who wishes to contest the proceedings or to take part in them may respond to a Pt 8 claim by filing an acknowledgement of service[12] not more than 14 days after the service of the claim form in which he states whether he contests the claim and if he seeks a different remedy from that set out in the claim form, what that remedy is.[13] In the Chancery Division, a defendant who acknowledges service but does not intend to file evidence must notify the court in writing of this when filing the acknowledgement of service.[14]

If the defendant does not file an acknowledgement of service within the time prescribed the defendant may still attend the hearing but may not take part in it unless the court gives the defendant permission to do so.[15] The provisions in relation to Pt 15 dealing with defence and reply do not apply to Pt 8 claims. Where a defendant wishes to rely on written evidence he must file this when he files his acknowledgement of service unless the parties have agreed in writing an extension of time for filing the evidence.[16] At the same time, copies must be served on any other party.[17]

If the defendant objects to the Pt 8 procedure being used, at the same time as filing his acknowledgment of service, he must give his reasons for objecting in writing. To the extent that evidence is included in his statement of reasons this must be verified by a statement of truth.[18]

Part 20 claims may also be made within the Pt 8 procedure, although not without the court's permission.[19]

4   The claimant's reply

Within 14 days of service of the defendant's evidence, the claimant may file written evidence in reply.[20] Again the parties can agree in writing to extend

---

10 CPR 8.5(2).
11 CPR 7.8(2).
12 In practice form N210, alternatively by letter. See CPR Pt 8, practice direction—Alternative Procedure for Claims, para 3.2.
13 CPR 8.3.
14 Chancery Guide, para 4.13.
15 CPR 8.4.
16 CPR 8.5(3). Pursuant to para 5.6(2) of practice direction—Alternative Procedure for Claims, the parties can not agree to extend time by more than 14 days after the defendant has filed his acknowledgment of service. In the Chancery Division if the parties agree that the defendant (or claimant in relation to his reply) should have a longer period in which to file written evidence the application should be made in writing and any agreement extending time should be filed. See Chancery Guide, para 4.12.
17 CPR 8.5(4).
18 CPR Pt 8, practice direction—Alternative Procedure for Claims, para 3.6.
19 CPR 8.7.
20 CPR 8.5(5).

the time for the claimant to file his evidence, however this cannot be extended to more than 28 days after service of the defendant's evidence on the claimant.[1] Within the same time limit a copy of the evidence must be served on the other parties.[2]

5   Managing the claim

All claims commenced under Pt 8 are treated as allocated to the multi-track.[3] The court may give directions either on the application of the claimant or on its own initiative immediately that the claim form is issued, including fixing a hearing date. Alternatively, the court will give directions for the disposal of the claim as soon as practicable after the defendant has acknowledged service of the claim form or the period for doing so has expired. The court may also convene a directions hearing before giving directions.[4] In the Commercial Court a case management conference will take place on the first available date six weeks after service and filing of the defendant's evidence when the court will make pre-trial directions.[5]

6   The hearing

Written evidence may not be relied upon at the hearing unless it complies with CPR 8.5 or the court has given permission. The court may require a party who has given written evidence to attend the hearing for cross-examination or may require or permit a party to give oral evidence at the hearing.[6]

I   Statements of truth

One of the major changes implemented by the civil justice reforms is the requirement that all statements of case contain a statement of truth.[7] It may be contained in the statement of case itself, alternatively it may be contained in a separate document.[8]

The statement of truth may be made by the party or his legal representative or his insurer (where the insurer has a financial interest in the result of the proceedings brought wholly or partly by or against that party) and should

---

1   CPR Pt 8, practice direction—Alternative Procedure for Claims, para 5.6(3). See Chancery Guide, para 4.12 as to the circumstances in which time may be extended in Chancery Division cases.
2   CPR 8.5(6).
3   CPR 8.9(c).
4   CPR 8.8(2) and practice direction—Alternative Procedure for Claims, paras 4.1–4.4.
5   Commercial Court Guide, Section D7.20.
6   CPR 8.6.
7   CPR 22.1.
8   CPR Pt 22, practice direction, para 2.3.

verify that the facts contained in the statement of case are true.[9] If there are multiple claimants or defendants to proceedings, each party must still sign a statement of truth.

Where the party to proceedings is a company or corporation only persons holding a senior position in the company or corporation[10] may sign a statement of truth on its behalf. A director, treasurer, secretary, chief executive, manager or other officer of the company or corporation may sign a statement of truth on behalf of a registered company or corporation. If a corporation is not a registered company, in addition to those set out above, the mayor, chairman, president or town clerk or other similar officer of the corporation may also sign the statement of truth. Further guidance has been given as to what is meant by the term 'manager'. Amendments to the practice direction to CPR Pt 22 now make clear that a manager signing a statement of truth should have a personal knowledge of the contents of the statement of case or be responsible for managing those who have knowledge of its contents. Where an insurer is to sign the statement of truth on behalf of an assured, the claims manager employed by the insurer responsible for handling the claim or managing the staff handling the claim may sign it.[11] However it is not actually necessary for the individual signing the statement of truth to have personal knowledge of all of the facts he is verifying. As an alternative, he may satisfy himself that a system of reporting to him is in place within his organisation which enables the 'truth' to be known with the result that the individual is able to sign the statement of truth knowing that the reporting system in place has given him the 'truth'.

In the Commercial Court where insurers have the conduct of a case involving multiple claimants or defendants, a senior individual with responsibility for the case at the lead insurer may sign the statement of truth rather than each of the parties. In these circumstances, the statement of truth will state that the lead insurer rather than the party believes that the facts stated are true. The Commercial Court also allows an application for permission to be made for someone other than a party to the proceedings to sign a statement of truth.[12] Neither of these options are available under the CPR.

The statement of truth may also be signed by the company's legal representative.[13] This does not include an in-house lawyer as the practice direction to CPR Pt 22 makes clear that an in-house lawyer is not a legal representative for the purposes of signing the statement of truth. However, the in-house lawyer may nonetheless be a manager within the company and

9   CPR Pt 22, practice direction, para 2.1 sets out the form of wording for the statement of truth.
10 CPR Pt 22, practice direction, para 3.5. Para 3.6 of the same practice direction states who may sign a statement of truth on behalf of a partnership.
11 CPR Pt 22, practice direction, para 3.11.
12 Commercial Court Guide, Section C1.8A. For example, permission may be given for a shipping agent to sign a statement of truth on behalf of a nameplate company.
13 The statement of truth will signed by the legal representative as an individual and not in the name of his firm. When signing he must state the capacity in which he signs and the name of the firm where appropriate. See CPR Pt 22, practice direction, paras 3.7 and 3.10.

therefore able to sign in that capacity.[14] Given that any statement of truth signed by a legal representative must refer to the client's belief and not his own, before signing a statement of truth the legal representative must ensure the following:

- obtain confirmation from his client that he believes that the facts stated in the document are true;
- obtain authorisation from his client to sign the statement on his behalf;
- inform the client of the possible consequences for him if it should later appear that the client did not have an honest belief in the truth of those facts; that is contempt of court proceedings may be brought against him.[15]

Where possible this should be recorded in writing.

At present it appears that statements of truth are being signed by clients and their legal representatives in approximately equal numbers (although in the Chancery Division, it appears that statements of truth have generally been signed by legal representatives). It is too soon to assess the extent to which statements of truth are now also being signed by insurers. However where it is intended that a client should sign a statement of truth, solicitors should bear in mind that applications for extensions of time for service of statements of case to enable clients to sign statements of truth are unlikely to be well received by the courts.

Solicitors should explain to their clients before proceedings are commenced the importance of the statement of truth and the need for the client to identify an appropriate person to take responsibility for its completion. It is also extremely important to emphasise to the party to the proceedings, and where this is a company or corporation, to the person making the statement of truth on behalf of that party, that he must have an honest belief in the truth of the facts which he is verifying. If a person makes or causes to be made a false statement without an honest belief in its truth contempt of court proceedings may be brought against him.[16] In the light of this, the same care must be taken with the preparation of statements of case as has traditionally been taken in relation to the preparation of affidavits.

The court has already considered an application by a claimant to commence committal proceedings in *Malgar Ltd v RE Leach (Engineering) Ltd*,[17] on the basis that the defendants had made false statements of truth. Although Sir Richard Scott V-C was not prepared to allow the claimant's application to bring contempt of court proceedings against the defendants he agreed with the claimant's argument that unless the parties approached verification of statements of case in a responsible manner then the benefits would be lost. He also agreed that where there was a flagrant breach of the obligation to be responsible and truthful in verifying statements of case contempt of court proceedings could be brought.[18]

---

14 CPR Pt 22, practice direction, para 3.11.
15 There is also a risk that a legal representative may be subject to contempt of court proceedings. See CPR 32.14.
16 CPR Pt 22, practice direction, para 3.8 and r 32.14.
17 (2000) Times, 17 February.
18 See Chapter 8 on witness evidence, where this case is discussed in detail.

Although failure by a party to verify his statement of case by a statement of truth will not render the statement of case ineffective until struck out, the party may not rely on the statement of case as evidence of the matters contained within it either in relation to any interlocutory application or at trial. He also runs the risk that the court may strike out the statement of case on its own initiative on the basis that it is has not been verified by a statement of truth[19] or that his opponent may apply for an order to strike out on this basis.[20] Alternatively, the court may make an order that the document be verified and an opponent may apply to the court for such an order to be made.[1] In practice, it is likely that both orders will be made at the same time in the form of an unless order. Whilst it will usually be possible therefore to delay verifying a statement of truth without having one's claim or defence struck out, it is likely to result in a cost penalty.[2]

The requirement to sign statements of truth and the basis upon which they are to be signed has been subject to criticism. Solicitors have complained about the administrative burden involved in explaining to clients what a statement of truth entails and the difficulty which a client may have in terms of identifying one individual with sufficient knowledge of the issues in dispute to be able to sign a statement of truth. There has also been some debate as to whether or not it is possible to sign a statement of truth where claims are made in the alternative based on inconsistent sets of facts. This point has not yet been resolved and guidance is needed from the courts on this. In addition there has been criticism as to the value of a statement of truth which is based upon multiple hearsay, for example a statement of case which refers to an expert's report which in turn is based upon documents and/or the evidence of others. In this situation it may be difficult for the party to the proceedings to realistically verify that *he believes* the facts to be true.

However, the requirement to complete a statement of truth in relation to one's statement of case does form an important part of the civil justice reforms. It reinforces the parties' need to consider at an early stage the merits of their case and to focus on the real issues in dispute. Parties will no longer be able to maintain claims or defences purely for tactical reasons, thereby saving time and costs.

J   Service of documents

As a general rule the court will serve any document which it has issued or prepared unless there is provision to the contrary or the party on whose behalf service is to be made wishes to do so himself.[3] Where a party prepares

---

19 See CPR 3.4 and practice direction thereto. Applications to strike out are discussed in detail in Chapter 6 on case management.
20 CPR 22.2 and practice direction, para 4.1–4.3.
1   CPR 22.4.
2   CPR Pt 22, practice direction, para 4.3.
3   CPR 6.3(1). See also Chancery Guide, para 4.3. CPR rr 6.13–6.16 contain special rules for service of a claim form. The Commercial Court Guide states that the claim form and all statements of case must be served by the party in Commercial Court cases. See Commercial Court Guide, Sections B5.1 and C1.9.

a document which is to be served by the court, the party must file a copy of the document for both the court and for each party to be served. The court will decide which method of service to use.[4]

The methods by which a document can be served have been expanded significantly and it is now possible to serve a document by any of the following:

- personal service;[5]
- first class post;
- leaving at an address for service;
- by DX;
- by fax or other means of electronic communication, for example, email.[6]

It is not possible to effect service by fax unless the party to be served has indicated his willingness to be served by this method. This can either be given expressly in writing or it can be inferred from the inclusion of a fax number in a document previously filed at court or from its appearance on notepaper. Service by other electronic means is only possible where both parties are legally represented, the legal representative has indicated that he is willing to accept service electronically and he has provided his email address. Where the court serves a document it will normally do so by first class post.[7] The court also has the power to order service to be effected by some other method than that prescribed in CPR 6.2 or to order that service be dispensed with.[8] CPR 6.7 sets out the deemed date of service for a document according to the method by which it has been served and CPR 6.5 sets out the address for service of a document where a party is not legally represented and has not given an address for service.

The increased flexibility in relation to service of documents is likely to be of great benefit to both the court and the parties, resulting in a saving of both time and expense.

---

4   CPR 6.3(2) and (3).
5   In accordance with CPR 6.4.
6   CPR 6.2 and practice direction thereto.
7   CPR Pt 6, practice direction, para 8.1.
8   See CPR 6.8 and 6.9. Any application to the court for such an order should be made under CPR Pt 23 and be supported by evidence.

5 PART 36 OFFERS AND PAYMENTS

A Introduction

Lord Woolf's Interim and Final Reports emphasised the importance of encouraging the settlement of disputes at an early stage, to reduce the costs and delays associated with litigation. In particular, Lord Woolf envisaged a greater role for offers to settle, supported by increased financial incentives for both parties to make realistic settlement offers early.

> **His principal recommendations on offers were:**
> - the system of payments into court should be replaced by a system of offers;
> - any party, the claimant as well as the defendant, should be able to make an offer to settle;
> - offers could be in respect of the whole case or individual issues (including liability) or claims;
> - offers could be made before the start of proceedings;
> - there should be financial incentives to encourage claimants, in particular, to make offers;
> - where an offer has been made, the court should exercise a wider discretion in respect of costs and interest than previously.[1]

Lord Woolf's recommendations have been reflected in Pt 36 of the CPR (with the exception of the proposed abolition of the system of payments into court, which was ultimately retained following consultation).

Part 36 restructures payments into court and introduces the new concept of a claimant's offer to settle. This chapter reviews the options available under Pt 36, the tactical issues and considerations they raise, and how the courts are approaching settlement issues generally under the CPR.

Part 36 is potentially one of the most significant aspects of the new CPR regime, providing for much greater flexibility and innovation in relation to offers to settle than under the previous rules. The introduction of Pt 36 is widely perceived by practitioners as having significantly shifted the 'balance of power' in favour of the claimant. Previously, faced by a defendant who was determined to delay the case coming to trial for as long as possible,

---

1 Final Report, Section III, Chapter 11, para 1.

there was little that a claimant could do. Whilst it was of course open to either party to make a settlement offer at any stage, willingness to initiate settlement discussions was often perceived by the parties as a sign of weakness. The new provisions offer claimants a powerful tactical advantage and a means of exerting considerable financial pressure on a defendant from the outset.

Whilst Pt 36 has only been in operation for 12 months, and there have as yet been relatively few reported decisions on the application of the new rule, the preliminary indications are that Pt 36 offers are being made in practice on a regular basis (particularly by claimants). In many cases this is leading to realistic settlements being achieved well in advance of trial (and in some instances, without the need for proceedings to be commenced). Claimants appear to have seized the opportunity to put the defendant on risk as to costs, and defendants are being forced to consider carefully from the outset whether their defence is sufficiently strong to continue.

The new provisions raise strategic and tactical issues for both claimants and defendants, whether they are making or receiving offers, counteroffers or payments into court, because of the significant costs consequences attaching to them. An understanding of these issues is essential in order to succeed under the new procedural regime. For commercial practitioners it is not only a question of keeping the client informed of the options at the outset of the case, but also ensuring that the situation is kept under review throughout the action, and any change in circumstances assessed to see whether a revised offer or payment should be made.

1   *Part 36 in context*

Part 36 does not of course operate in isolation—it needs to be seen in the context of the CPR as a whole, including in particular the provisions relating to pre-action conduct[2] and the overriding objective. Part 36 offers and payments can be valuable tactical measures, but they need to be used with caution, and within the spirit of the overriding objective, to obtain the maximum potential benefit in relation to costs.

Whilst the potential costs consequences of making a Pt 36 offer are clearly set out in the text of the rule, the court still retains a discretion in relation to costs. In particular, the costs consequences of a 'pre-action' offer to settle are dependant on the exercise of the court's discretion. The court will take into account not only the offer itself, but also the surrounding circumstances. This will include whether the offeror complied with any relevant pre-action protocols—for example, whether the offeree was given sufficient information to assess whether to accept the offer. If the offeror ignored a protocol, then the court may refuse to allow him any cost benefit.

2   *The scope of Part 36*

Part 36 provides a variety of settlement options. It covers both pre-action offers to settle, made by either party under CPR 36.10 (referred to below as

2   See Chapter 1 on pre-action tactics.

pre-action offers) and offers made after the commencement of proceedings, in accordance with the formal requirements set out in Pt 36 (referred to below as a Pt 36 offer when made by a claimant and a Pt 36 payment when made by a defendant). It is important to distinguish between pre-action offers and Pt 36 offers. Whilst both are contained in Pt 36, as set out below a formal Pt 36 offer has much more serious potential costs consequences for a defendant than a pre-action offer to settle.

The options available under Pt 36, and some of the issues which they raise in practice are outlined below. It is essential to ensure that the client is made aware of the potential effects of a Pt 36 offer or payment from the outset. When making an offer or payment under Pt 36 careful reference should be made to the detailed requirements set out in full in the text of the rule and accompanying practice direction, to ensure that the appropriate costs protection is obtained.

B   Pre-action offers to settle

Either a claimant or a defendant (or both) may make a pre-action offer to settle.

Under CPR 36.10 the offer must:

- be expressed to be open for at least 21 days after the date it was made, otherwise it will be a valid settlement offer but does not have Pt 36 automatic costs consequences. (In a particularly urgent case, a claimant need not necessarily wait for 21 days before issuing proceedings, since there is no express prohibition against doing so under Pt 36. However, he will need to be able to satisfy the court that the issuing of proceedings within a shorter timeframe was reasonable and that he was not in a position to make the offer earlier.);
- if made by a person who would be a defendant were proceedings commenced, include an offer to pay the costs of the offeree incurred up to the date 21 days after the date it was made. (Under the new frontloaded regime, these costs may be very substantial, including the costs of reviewing documents, compiling initial witness statements and expert evidence and producing draft particulars of claim);
- otherwise comply with Pt 36;
- where the offeror is a defendant to a money claim, be backed up by making a Pt 36 payment into court within 14 days of service of the claim form. The amount of the payment must be not less than the sum offered before proceedings began. (This provision applies notwithstanding that the claim form may not contain detailed particulars of the claim, as these may be served separately later. A defendant making a payment in must therefore be sure to satisfy himself beforehand that he has all the relevant details in relation to the claim.)

Provided the pre-action offer complies with the stated requirements, the court will take it into account when making any order as to costs.[3] There have not as yet been any reported cases on how the court will exercise this discretion, but it would be open to the court to award a party all or a portion of their costs from the date the offer was made. In practice, there may often be subsequent offers or payments which supersede the pre-action offer as the issues in the case become more clearly defined, and which more accurately reflect the likely outcome at trial, so that the original offer is no longer relevant by the time the court is asked to determine the costs liability.

A pre-action offer to settle is not stated to have any effect on the way in which the court awards interest at the end of the action, so the defendant who receives a pre-action offer is not expressly at risk regarding penalty interest on any damages awarded. However, under the Supreme Court Act 1981, s 35A any interest award is in the discretion of the court and it is possible that a well-judged pre-action offer to settle might be taken into account by the court when determining the appropriate rate or period of interest.

The claimant generally has little to lose by making a pre-action offer to settle, particularly where he is in a position to support it with a draft statement of case and documentary evidence.

The defendant will have to think more carefully before making an offer when he receives notice of a claim, or responding to the claimant's offer with a counteroffer. Whereas an initial pre-action offer may be worthwhile in order to dispose of the litigation, once proceedings have started he will have to back up the offer (in the case of a money claim) by making a payment into court within 14 days in order to maintain the offer and his credibility. This may deprive the defendant of funds for a long period, and once a payment in has been made, the defendant is effectively locked into the litigation. If he requires additional time in which to raise the funds, then this should be made clear at the time the pre-action offer is made.

The defendant also needs to be satisfied that he has sufficient information on which to judge the appropriate level of offer and payment in. Where particulars of the claim have been served, the defendant may have sufficient information. Otherwise it may be preferable to wait and issue requests for further information.

C   Part 36 offers by claimants

A claimant may make a Pt 36 offer after proceedings have commenced. The formal requirements are set out in full in CPR 36.5. In particular:
- a Pt 36 offer must be in writing;
- it may relate to the whole claim or to part of it or to any issue that arises in it;

---

3   CPR 35.10.

- it must:
  - (a) state whether it relates to the whole of the claim or to part of it or to an issue that arises in it and if so to which part or issue;
  - (b) state whether it takes into account any counterclaim; and
  - (c) if it is expressed to be inclusive of interest, give the details relating to interest set out in CPR 36.22(2).

CPR 36.5(2) allows for an offer or payment to be made in respect of the whole claim or part of it, or to an issue that arises under it[4]. In a complex case, where there may be a large number of issues and sub-issues, counterclaims and Pt 20 claims, it is essential to make it clear exactly which issues the offer relates to, which it excludes, and how any interest total has been reached, so that it is clear at trial whether or not the offer has been beaten. Where an offeree considers that a Pt 36 offer is ambiguous or unclear he should immediately seek clarification of the offer under CPR 36.9.

If the defendant accepts the claimant's offer, the claimant is entitled to receive 'his costs of the proceedings'.[5] There is no specific reference in Pt 36 to the claimant's pre-action costs, which may be substantial. CPR 44.3(6) generally enables the court to make an order in relation to costs incurred before proceedings are begun. However, where very substantial costs are likely to be incurred in attempting to settle the dispute (for example, in compiling evidence and documentation) it may be advisable to apply to the court for an order making the position clear when the offer is made.

If the claimant fails to beat his offer at trial, he is unlikely to face any costs penalty. The original wording of CPR 36.20 suggested that a claimant who failed to beat his own offer would have to pay the defendant's costs from 21 days after the date of the offer. This ambiguity has now been corrected, and it is only in the case of an offer from the claimant which indicated bad faith or was otherwise in contravention of the overriding objective that the court might be minded to impose an adverse costs order.

If, however, the claimant subsequently beats his offer at trial, the defendant faces potentially serious costs consequences.[6] The court may order:
- interest on the whole or part of any sum of money (excluding interest) awarded to the claimant at a rate not exceeding 10% above base rate for some or all of the period starting with the latest date on which the defendant could have accepted the offer without needing the permission of the court;
- that the claimant is entitled to his costs on an indemnity basis from the latest date on which the defendant could have accepted the offer without needing the permission of the court; and
- interest on those costs at a rate not exceeding 10% above base rate.

The court will make these orders 'unless it considers it unjust to do so', the presumption therefore being that they will be made and that the court has a

---

4   See also *Stock v London Underground Ltd* (1999) Times, 12 August, CA.
5   CPR 36.14.
6   CPR 36.21.

narrower discretion in this area than elsewhere under the CPR.[7] A defendant who seeks to challenge the imposition of costs and interest penalties will have to make out a strong case to avoid them being imposed. CPR 36.21 provides that the court will take into account all the circumstances of the case, including:

- the terms of any Pt 36 offer (this might include, for example, a situation where the claimant has only narrowly beaten his offer);
- the stage in the proceedings when the offer or payment was made (for example, the offer may have been made at a late stage in the proceedings when the defendant had already incurred most of his costs in bringing the action to trial);
- the information available to the parties at the time when the offer or payment was made. In *Ford v GKR Construction Ltd*,[8] the Court of Appeal awarded the claimant the costs of her personal injury claim against the defendants, notwithstanding that the defendant had made a Pt 36 payment in excess of the damages awarded at trial. The court decided that video surveillance evidence on which the defendant based its offer should have been disclosed to the claimant earlier to enable her to take an informed view of the merits of the offer;
- the conduct of the parties with regard to the giving or refusing to give information for the purposes of enabling the offer or payment into court to be made or evaluated.

Another possible ground of challenge arises under Art 6 of the European Convention on Human Rights, which entitles litigants to a fair and public hearing. One aspect of the fair hearing guarantee is that litigants should enjoy 'equality of arms'. In large scale litigation where both sides make offers, the potential penalty for the defendant is much heavier than for the claimant, and it may be argued that for an impecunious defendant the consequences of misjudging whether to accept an offer are potentially so disastrous that he has no option but to concede to a high claimant's offer. The counter-argument is that the court's residual discretion on costs is sufficient to enable it to correct any imbalance (and indeed, one aspect of the overriding objective is to seek to achieve a 'level playing field' between the parties). However, it would be a brave defendant who would run the risk of waiting until the final costs determination is made if the consequence of losing would be insolvency.

A particular problem arises where it is a matter of chance as to who becomes the claimant and who becomes the defendant in a piece of litigation, enabling the 'first past the post' to benefit from the advantages available to a claimant. This might also be a relevant factor for the court to take into account when exercising its discretion. In this situation it would also be advisable for the defendant to seek his own declaratory relief, so that he is also in effect a claimant in the action.

Given the potentially disastrous effects for the defendant of a claimant narrowly beating his Pt 36 offer at trial, it seems likely that defendants will

---

7   See *Little v George Little Sebire & Co* (1999) Times, 17 November.
8   (1999) Times, 5 November, CA.

attempt to challenge costs and interest awards on these and other grounds, and will look for increasingly inventive ways to avoid the potential penalties.

D Part 36 payments by defendants

In relation to a money claim, a defendant who makes an offer to settle must make a payment into court within fourteen days of service of the claim form in order to receive Pt 36 costs protection. For non-money claims, the defendant should make an offer to settle in accordance with the requirements of Pt 36. Where a claim combines a money and non-money element, the defendant should make a Pt 36 payment together with an offer in relation to the non-money element in accordance with CPR 36.4.

In relation to both money and non-money claims, if the claimant fails to beat the offer or payment at trial, the defendant will be entitled to his costs from the last date the offer could have been accepted) on a standard basis, unless the court considers it would be unjust. There is no provision for the claimant to meet the defendant's costs on an indemnity basis. This has led to criticism from defendants that the rules unduly favour claimants, and that they are vulnerable to abuse by a claimant who over inflates his claim.

E Principal differences between pre-action offers and Part 36 offers

- A Pt 36 offer is deemed to be 'without prejudice save as to costs', whether or not it is expressly marked as such. However there is no such presumption in relation to a pre-action offer, which can be made on an open basis if the offeror so chooses.
- In relation to a pre-action offer, the court will take the offer into account when making any order as to costs. There is no provision for dealing with interest, in contrast to a Pt 36 offer.
- Under a pre-action offer, the court has a wide-ranging discretion as to how it takes costs into account. For a Pt 36 offer, the Pt 36 cost consequences must apply 'unless it is unjust to do so'.
- A pre-action offer can be taken into account at any costs hearing (including interlocutory hearings).
- A Pt 36 offer provides for a formal clarification process of the terms of a Pt 36 offer or payment to a tight timetable. This is not available for a pre-action offer, although it is of course open to the offeree to seek clarification through correspondence.

F   Settlement offers outside the scope of Part 36

A payment which fails to observe the strict procedural requirements of Pt 36 is still a valid settlement offer, and can be taken into account when the court exercises its general discretion as to costs. CPR 44.3(4)(c) contemplates two situations in which the court would take into account the payment into court or an admissible offer which did not comply with the formal requirements of Pt 36.

First, if a claimant only narrowly beats a Pt 36 payment or offer, or narrowly fails to beat his own offer, he may ask the court to take the offer/payment into account in any event. The court may be willing to exercise its discretion under this rule, particularly if substantial costs have been incurred in achieving a small increase on the offer that has been made.

Second, in circumstances where the defendant finds it difficult to make a Pt 36 payment because of lack of resources, he may only be able to afford to make an order by way of instalments. The court might be prepared to take such an offer into account notwithstanding that it should normally have been backed up by a Pt 36 payment into court.

It remains to be seen what latitude the courts will give to the Pt 36 costs provisions when interpreting them in order to achieve the overriding objective of doing justice between the parties, and to what extent the courts will be prepared to look behind an offer to the parties' own circumstances.

G   Part 36 offers and payments: tactical issues

1   Preparation

Thorough preparation of the case at the outset will put the offeree in the best possible position when assessing the other party's early offer. This is particularly important for defendants, who may find themselves having to respond to an offer within days of receiving notice of the claim, and will need to ensure that the relevant documents and individuals are available in short order to enable the claim to be investigated.

2   Who should make the first move?

Where the possible range of outcomes is relatively clear, then it may make little difference who goes first. All claimants should consider making a Pt 36 offer 21 days before commencing a claim. Whilst some claimants may be concerned that taking the initiative will be seen as a sign of weakness, the potential costs benefits are likely to outweigh these concerns unless the defendant has a very strong case on liability. Where neither side can make an accurate judgment as to the strength of the other side's case, offers are likely to be pitched very high by the claimant and very low by a defendant. In this situation, it may be better to wait for a more realistic assessment to be made once further evidence and documents have been exchanged. If the offers are some way apart but there is a genuine spirit of compromise then an attempt at ADR may be appropriate to try to narrow the middle ground.

3 At what level should the offer be pitched?

In order to achieve a settlement, an offer must be realistic, but a party's opening offer is unlikely to reflect its true 'bottom line'. Each party will want to leave some leeway in case the offer is rejected and the case proceeds to litigation or ADR. When making a pre-action offer the claimant may be disinclined to compromise and offer any significant discount on the total sum claimed. However, the court is likely to expect the offer to take into account the financial and other benefits to the claimant of an early resolution of the dispute (such as accelerated receipt of the funds, risk avoidance, avoiding the distraction of the litigation process). The amount of the discount is likely to be a relevant factor under CPR 36.21, especially in relation to a liquidated claim. A claimant who simply offers to accept exactly what he believes the claim to be worth runs the risk that he will be awarded that amount at trial, in which case he will not be able to take advantage of the Pt 36 costs and interest penalties which only come into play if the claimant beats rather than matches his offer. In relation to an unliquidated claim it is perhaps arguable that the fact that the claimant has made an offer at all may be sufficient to entitle it to the full costs and interests benefits available under Pt 36, but in applying the overriding objective the court will be looking for evidence of a real desire to settle rather than a purely tactical use of Pt 36.

4 Seeking further information

A defendant will often be under great time pressure at the early stages of an action, particularly where the claimant has had many months to compile the evidence and documents to support his claim, and may be at risk of compromising his case without knowing the true strength of his defence. It may simply not be possible to respond to the offer within 21 days, either because further information is required, or because aspects of the offer and how it relates to particular issues are unclear. A defendant should make clear any reasons why he is unable to respond, as this may be relevant to the issue of costs later, and if further information is required, this should be set out in a detailed request for particulars. This will gain time for the offer to be properly considered. The defendant may also decide to suggest ADR as a way of clarifying the issues more quickly than through the normal litigation process.

5 Giving reasons for the offer

Under the previous rules no reasons had to be given by a defendant to support a payment in. The payment might be due to an extraneous reason (for example, where the defendant's disclosure obligation would require him to reveal damaging information to the other side). The power to order an amendment to a notice of payment in was limited and the offeree was effectively obliged to take or leave the payment as it stood. At first sight the clarification procedure under CPR 36.9 appears to offer more scope for seeking further information about the offer or payment. There is considerable scope for disagreement between the parties as to what information is reasonably required in order to reach a decision on the offer, and it seems likely that the courts will need to provide guidance in this area. In the event that the offeror is required to give full particulars of the reasoning behind the offer, then he must be careful to ensure that in doing so he complies with his duty actively to assist the court, and to ensure that any statements of truth he has given remain accurate.

6   The position if the 21 day period elapses

Normally after this period an offer can only be accepted if the parties agree on costs liability or the court gives permission. This may give rise to uncertainty as to exactly what the cost position should be, and it is therefore preferable to set out in the offer itself that it is expressly conditional on full payment of costs on the indemnity basis.

7   Costs estimates

Whilst the final decision as to whether to make or accept an offer will be for the company's senior management to decide based on the company's commercial objectives, an important element of the decision will be the amount of costs they stand to pay or to receive if the case continues, and how this will fluctuate give the various ways in which the litigation may develop. The solicitor's ability to accurately forecast his own and the other side's likely costs is key—it may make the difference between whether to accept or reject a Pt 36 offer. This is a complicated exercise, even in an era of more predictable costs, and law firms need sophisticated budgeting systems to enable them to monitor and predict costs with a much greater degree of precision than before.

8   Multiple offers

CPR 36.5(8) states that if a Pt 36 offer is withdrawn, it will no longer have Pt 36 consequences in relation to costs. What happens if a Pt 36 offer is made, but then withdrawn in order to be replaced with a new (possibly upwardly revised) offer? Does the offeror gain any costs benefit from having been prepared to settle at an earlier stage, albeit for a different figure? Part 36 does not specifically deal with this situation, but it is likely that the court would exercise its discretion, in accordance with the overriding objective and its aim of doing justice between the parties, so that the original offer would be taken into account when a costs order is being made, where it was for a lesser sum than the amount awarded at trial. For example, the claimant may initially offer to accept £70k in a £100k claim, but later revise the offer upwards to £90k. If the claimant subsequently wins £80k, he would recover indemnity costs up to the time the £90k offer was made, but standard costs thereafter. Alternatively, the claimant may offer to accept £90k in a £100k claim, but later revise this down to £70k. If he is awarded £80k at trial, he would receive costs on a standard basis up to the time the £70k offer was made, and indemnity costs from that date.

9 Complex offers

In practice, it is likely that there will be a series of offers (increasing offers from the defendant, reducing offers from a claimant) as the litigation progresses. In complex cases there is potential for very sophisticated offers, linked to each stage of proof of each cause of action or head of damage, possibly on a sliding scale, taking into account individual issues, contributory negligence, potential counterclaims and so on. The time involved in calculating a series of complex offers should not be underestimated. Experience so far has been that calculating and responding to offers in complex cases can be a very time consuming and expensive process, which can place a heavy demand on senior management time.

10 Relationship with ADR

A Pt 36 offer from a claimant coupled with an invitation to attempt ADR is likely to be welcomed by a defendant in order to minimise his potential costs exposure if the case proceeds further. Even if it fails, ADR will usually leave both sides much better informed about their prospects in the litigation, and may lead to a revised and more realistic Pt 36 offer or payment.

6   CASE MANAGEMENT

A   Introduction

The central theme of Lord Woolf's recommendations on case management was that there should be a fundamental transfer in the responsibility for management of civil litigation from litigants and their legal advisers to the courts. He observed that:

> 'without effective judicial control…the adversarial process is likely to encourage an adversarial culture and to degenerate into an environment in which the litigation process is too often seen as a battlefield where no rules apply'.[1]

Lord Woolf was anxious to bring to an end a procedural regime under which the parties could take advantage of a variety of measures to delay the proceedings or to make their opponent's life difficult and costly, often secure in the knowledge that any costs sanction which the court might impose would be of little practical assistance to their opponent. Case management was of course not a new concept, and had already been used with considerable success in the Commercial Court and the Technology and Construction Court in particular. Lord Woolf recommended that the courts should take over responsibility for effective and efficient case management in all cases, in order to ensure that cases proceeded according to strict court-imposed timetables and that the costs generated by the litigation were proportionate to the issues and the amount involved.

These themes were adopted and expanded in the CPR, which developed active case management by the courts as a core theme of the new procedural landscape. Under CPR 1.4(1) the court *must* further the overriding objective by actively managing cases. Twelve features of active case management are set out in CPR 1.4(2), including encouraging the parties to cooperate with each other; identifying the issues at an early stage; encouraging the parties to use ADR and to settle the case; fixing timetables; and considering whether the likely benefits of taking a particular step justify the cost of taking it. These general criteria are supplemented by more detailed case management provisions for each track, set out in Pts 26–29 and the accompanying practice directions, and by the applicable provisions in the specialist lists.

The application of the rules in practice inevitably depends on the facts of each case, and as a result the degree to which the courts would embrace

---

1   Final Report, Section II, Chapter 3.

their 'active case management' role was one of the greatest areas of uncertainty in the run up to the introduction of the CPR. Whilst the aim of the changes was to introduce greater certainty and predictability into the course of litigation in the longer term, in the absence of any authorities or detailed guidance on the new rules, opinions were divided amongst commentators as to how far existing practices would change. In addition, those specialist lists which had already developed their own detailed case management procedures, tailored to the needs of their own users, had to reconcile the new regime with their existing practices, and supplemented the CPR where necessary with their own procedural guidelines.[2] This added to the initial confusion amongst practitioners as to how the case management concepts would be applied in practice.

Twelve months on from the introduction of the CPR, virtually all cases have now been through at least one case management conference or other case management hearing (and any which have not are at imminent risk of being stayed).[3] An initial view at least can be taken on whether cases are now better managed, settling earlier, and more focussed on the key issues as a result of the active case management principles. This chapter considers how the courts are exercising their case management powers in practice, what demands the new case management requirements are making on law firms and their commercial clients, and how best to respond to them.

B   Case management steps in a multi-track case

The court may exercise its case management powers at any stage in a case (see Appendices G and H for flowcharts of key steps in multi-track and Commercial Court cases respectively). On the multi track, the court's likely approach to the management of the case needs to be considered by both parties as soon as the possibility of a dispute arises, as this will influence the type of directions sought pre- and post-issue. The case will be subject to particular scrutiny at the case management conference, and at the pre-trial review (subject to any alternative case management requirements applicable in any relevant specialist list). Whilst it may not be necessary to hold a case management conference or pre-trial review in all cases, experience to date suggests that they are likely to be required in most multi-track cases.

The key stages at which the court is likely to exercise its case management powers are considered below. In addition, the courts have given some general guidance as to what they expect in terms of efficient case management. In *McPhilemy v Times Newspapers Ltd*,[4] the Court of Appeal was asked to consider whether the first instance judge was correct to allow extensive late re-

---

2   See Commercial Court Guide, Section D; Chancery Guide, Section A, Chapter 5; Technology and Construction Court practice direction; Mercantile Courts Guide, paras 2–4; and Patents Court Guide, para 17.
3   See CPR 51, practice direction, para 19.
4   [1999] 3 All ER 775, [1999] EMLR 751, CA.

amendments to be made to the defendant's pleading. The Court of Appeal upheld the first instance decision on the basis that the amendments were potentially central to a legitimate defence. Lord Woolf also took the opportunity to emphasise broader issues relating to case management under the CPR. He noted that in this case, commenced under the old rules, there had been a number of 'skirmishes' involving 'sterile argument' about the particulars of the pleadings, and that 'the distinct impression was given by the parties that both sides were engaged in a battle of tactics'. He stated that proper case management requires a consolidated case management conference at which the issues to be decided at trial can be identified, and a decision is taken as to what evidence would be appropriate for this purpose.

On the question of proportionality (which had been invoked by the claimant who argued that the trial should be limited to essential issues as he was without funds and could not obtain legal aid) Lord Woolf was again critical of the parties' behaviour, observing that if the claimant had wanted to limit expense he could have focused his complaint more narrowly from the outset ('if a party because of his or her personal circumstances wishes the court to restrain the activities of another party with the object of achieving greater equality, then that party must behave in a way which demonstrates a desire to limit the expense as far as practical'). Clearly, the courts will be alert to prevent the parties from using the CPR for tactical benefit at the expense of the principles underlying the rules.

An early ruling on the importance of case management was also given in the Chancery Division in *St Albans Court Ltd v Daldorch Estates Ltd.*[5] In this action for breach of company directors' duties, Mrs Justice Arden identified a number of unsatisfactory features in the claimant's skeleton argument and the general pre-trial preparation of the case. This included the claimant's failure to include a summary of the case in its skeleton argument, an attempt to refer to issues in the skeleton which had not been pleaded, the absence of a core bundle, and the extension of the original time estimate by two days without explanation. The judge exercised her powers under the CPR to set a trial timetable by identifying the provisional issues, directing that the CPR applied to the case subject to a direction to the contrary, and ordering that the witness statements should stand as evidence in chief and the experts should meet to agree the relevant issues as soon as possible.

1 Pre-action conduct

Lord Woolf considered that effective case management starts even before proceedings are issued, and this is reflected in the CPR which provide that as part of its case management role the court can take pre-action conduct into account when deciding how to award costs. The court can revisit

5   [2000] 07 LS Gaz R 39.

pre-action conduct on costs issues, and is likely to penalise an uncooperative or ill prepared approach.[6]

The parties need to consider at the outset how the case is likely to develop, what the strategic options are, and how best to present the issues to the court. It may be appropriate for example to apply for pre-action disclosure, to make a pre-action offer, to determine specific issues by way of a preliminary issue hearing or to suggest that the dispute be referred to ADR. It is not always possible to predict at an early stage exactly how the case will develop, and how the court will wish to manage it, but it will certainly help to create the right impression with the court from the start if a party is well prepared, and has a view of the 'big picture' and the various paths the litigation might follow.

2   Allocation

Following the issue of proceedings, case management will first be considered when the parties complete their allocation questionnaire (outside the Commercial Court, the Technology and Construction Court and the Patents Court, where allocation to the multi-track is automatic). The parties need to have an outline case strategy in place by this stage as they are asked to identify the number of experts and witnesses they will need and to give a global estimate of the costs to trial.

It appears that allocation hearings are rarely proving necessary in the High Court. Where they do arise, it is generally in order to clarify or oppose preliminary directions for case management given by the court on the basis of the parties' allocation questionnaires (any disputes regarding the appropriateness of the multi-track being largely dealt with by the county court). Where there are likely to be disputes between the parties as to the appropriate directions, the court may consider it more appropriate to postpone giving directions on some or all issues until the case management conference.

3   Case management conference

The case management conference ('CMC') plays a key role under the CPR. The CMC will usually take place after exchange of statements of case, although it can be requested earlier where necessary (eg where there is a dispute as to the appropriate jurisdiction).

In the Commercial Court, the initial CMC takes place approximately six weeks after close of statements of case, which may be too early to make substantive directions in many large cases. The CMC may therefore be adjourned for several weeks, with substantive directions being given at the restored hearing. Alternatively the court may schedule one or more preliminary CMCs to deal with urgent matters such as jurisdiction issues.

---

6   *Mars UK Ltd v Teknowledge Ltd (No 2)* (1999) Times, 8 July.

For example, in a major oil and gas case involving five sets of consolidated proceedings and more than 30 potential parties, the court ordered a series of preliminary CMCs prior to the service of statements of case. At the first CMC the court directed the parties to provide 'bullet point' statements of case to enable the issues to be identified, notwithstanding that some of the parties contested the jurisdiction of the court, and fixed a timetable for further progress reports to the court. This enabled progress to be made regarding the identification of the main issues in dispute whilst the parties awaited the outcome on the jurisdiction question.

It appears that CMCs are being convened in most commercial cases, and in virtually all cases in the Commercial Court. This was to be expected in the early days of the new rules, particularly where it was necessary to determine how existing cases should be transferred to the new regime. In future, where there is general agreement between the parties as to the appropriate directions, the courts may be willing to grant directions by consent without the need for a hearing, provided they are proportionate and set out a speedy timetable.

The approach to CMCs has varied widely, although as expected they are generally longer than directions hearings under the old rules. In complex cases, they may take several days, ranging across a wide variety of issues, and sometimes including substantive applications (eg for summary judgment). The parties are expected to be well prepared, not only to argue for their proposed directions but also to deal with alternative case management suggestions from the court (eg the disposal of some issues by means of a preliminary issue hearing).

In general, the parties are proving to be well prepared for case management hearings. Whilst the case management issues discussed at the CMC are largely similar to those raised under the old directions procedure, the courts report that there is evidence of a greater willingness by the parties to focus on the issues in advance (further encouraged in the Commercial Court by the requirement to submit skeleton arguments) and to agree directions, particularly regarding timetables and the scope of disclosure. The use of preliminary issues, and the scope of expert evidence remain more contentious areas.

- **Materials for the CMC**

The documentation differs between the various specialist lists. The practice direction to Pt 29 provides that the parties must provide at the hearing all the documents which the court is likely to ask to see, including witness statements and experts' reports where these have been prepared.[7] In addition, the parties must provide a case summary of not more than 500 words, including a brief chronology.[8] In the Technology and Construction Court the parties must complete a case management questionnaire and case management directions form prior to the hearing, and exchange them in

---

7 CPR Pt 29, practice direction, para 5.6.
8 CPR Pt 29, practice direction, para 5.7.

order to try to reach agreement on the directions sought.[9] In the Commercial Court, the parties must provide a 'case management bundle' containing the claim form and statements of case; a case memorandum containing a short description of the case and its material procedural history; an agreed list of issues; the pre-trial timetable or case management information sheet; the principal orders made and any written agreement in relation to the scope of disclosure.[10] In complex cases, these may be fairly lengthy documents even though their purpose is only to provide an overview of the case. A skeleton argument will also be needed in relation to any issues which are not agreed.[11]

Considerable time and cost is now involved in preparing the various documents required for the CMC. In practice it can prove difficult to get the degree of cooperation between the parties needed to draw up an agreed statement of issues, notwithstanding the cooperative approach required under the overriding objective. Where such difficulties are anticipated, it may be appropriate to seek permission from the court to provide 'bullet point' lists of issues, or for one party to draw up the statement, with the other party submitting a list of points on which it disagrees. The court can then give further directions if it considers that a more detailed briefing document is required.

The additional paperwork has created a heavier burden for the courts in terms of pre-reading for CMCs, particularly in the Queen's Bench Division where each Master may be dealing with a large number of CMCs each week, involving consideration of witness statements and experts reports as well as the parties' statements of case. In the Chancery Division and Queen's Bench Division, in all matters where a bundle of documents is required, the bundle must now be accompanied by a reading list and a time estimate for the length of reading time required as well as an estimate of the length of the hearing.[12] In the Commercial Court, substantial reading time has to be built in to the timetable when scheduling a 'heavy' CMC. However, the Commercial Court reports[13] that on balance the new documents included in the case management bundle 'have greatly assisted the court'.

• Costs estimates

A costs estimate must be provided in the allocation questionnaire, but there is no requirement in Part 29 for a case budget or costs estimate to be provided at the CMC.[14] To date, consideration of costs estimates at CMCs appears to have been the exception rather than the general practice, particularly in cases where the parties are represented by City firms. However, it is advisable to have prepared one in order to demonstrate in the event of a dispute over

---

9   Technology and Construction Court Practice Direction, para 5.
10 Commercial Court Guide, Section D6.
11 The Commercial Court Guide is silent on this point, but the assumption that a skeleton argument would be required was confirmed by Rix J at the Commercial Court CPR surgery on 25 June 1999.
12 See practice direction of 17 December 1999 issued by the Vice-Chancellor.
13 See Commercial Court Annual Report, September 1999.
14 Other than in the Technology and Construction Court where a costs estimate must be provided in the case management questionnaire.

directions that the directions you are seeking are proportionate, particularly where the financial resources of the parties are unequal.[15] Where the costs appear to be disproportionately high, the court may require the parties to submit alternative proposals, or may limit the amount of costs recoverable in relation to a particular expense (eg an expert's fee). However, in *Maltez v Lewis*,[16] Neuberger J held that the claimant was not entitled to an order preventing the defendant from instructing more experienced counsel in order to put the parties on an equal footing. He held that the parties were free to instruct the legal advisers of their choice but that any costs payable by the other side could be restricted if the expense incurred was unreasonable. He did suggest however that the court might give some leeway to one side, bearing in mind the resources at its disposal and the experience of its advisers, and might, for example, order that the party with fewer reasons should have longer to prepare or that the wealthier party should meet the cost of preparing court bundles.

This is an important consideration for corporate litigants to take into account when budgeting for the costs of litigation against a financially weaker opponent, although it does not necessarily follow that a less wealthy litigant will be able to dictate the cost of the case. In the judicial review case of *R v Hammersmith and Fulham London Borough Council, ex p CPRE London Branch (No 2)*, the CPRE sought an order that pursuant to the overriding objective and so that the case was dealt with proportionately to the financial position of each party, neither party should have to pay more than ten percent of its annual turnover to the successful party by way of costs. Richards J declined to make the order. He held that whilst the case could be regarded as being of general public importance the perceived merits of the case were such that it was not in the public interest to grant the order. Although the parties had unequal financial resources, there was no evidence that without such an order the CPRE would be unable to continue the action, and the proposed order was not itself proportionate, since it would give substantially greater protection to the CPRE than to the other parties.[17]

The costs of preparing for and attending the CMC itself can be very significant, and in general are ordered to be costs in the case. However, where one party has adopted an uncooperative approach in relation to the preparation of the CMC materials or agreeing directions, it is open to the other party to seek an order for summary assessment of the costs incurred as a result.

- ## Who should attend the CMC?

It is essential to ensure that a legal representative with sufficient authority and knowledge of the case attends the CMC. The risks involved in using an agent, even if this reduces the cost of attendance, were clearly demonstrated in *Baron v Lovell*.[18] In that case the defendant failed to serve his medical

---

15 See Chapter 10 on costs for the considerations to take into account when preparing a costs estimate.
16 [1999] 21 LS Gaz R 39.
17 (20 January 2000, unreported).
18 (1999) Times, 14 September, CA.

expert's report within the time allowed under the automatic directions. The defendant's solicitors did not attend the pre-trial review, but sent an agent. The agent was not able to explain to the court why the evidence had not been served in time, and the first instance judge accordingly refused permission for the expert to be called at trial. On appeal, the Court of Appeal led by Lord Woolf upheld the decision, and re-stated the importance of ensuring that case management hearings were attended by someone with sufficient knowledge of the case to deal with any matters which might arise. This does not necessarily preclude agents from attending, provided that they are given full instructions and authority and are personally involved in the conduct of the case.

In the Commercial Court, it should be noted that the advocate dealing with the case must also attend case management hearings (although the court has been prepared to be flexible in this regard in at least one multi-party case where solicitors had only received instructions shortly before a preliminary CMC and had not at that point instructed counsel). There appears to have been a slight increase in the number of solicitor advocates dealing with case management hearings, although the extent to which this is directly due to the introduction of the CPR rather than simply the continuation of an existing trend is unclear.

Under CPR 3.1(2) the court may also require the parties to attend case management hearings. This provision gives the court an opportunity to put questions to the client directly about the scope for settlement or ADR, and to identify the commercial considerations which need to be taken into account when exercising its discretion. It also enables the court to ensure that the parties are fully aware of the legal costs they will incur if the case proceeds. This power has been exercised sparingly since the CPR were introduced and limited to cases where any costs estimates produced by the parties prior to the CMC appear to the courts to be disproportionate. In the Commercial Court the parties are not normally required to attend.[19]

- **Timetabling**

The CPR provide that certain milestone dates fixed by the court such as the CMC and pre-trial review may not be changed without the permission of the court, and there is an increased expectation that other deadlines will be met unless there is a very good reason for seeking an extension. Where an extension is sought, it is now frequently granted only on the basis that it will be a final order. So far as the fixing of timetables for trial preparation is concerned, these have, by and large, been realistic, although the parties are coming under greater pressure to justify requests for additional preparation time. Overall, this is good news for claimants, but as expected, is placing additional pressures (and increased costs) on defendants, particularly in terms of the amount of senior management time which has to be spent on the early stages of a case.

19 Commercial Court Guide, Section D7.8.

In the Commercial Court there have been several examples of speedy timetables being imposed in large cases since April 1999. Decisions in relation to fixing a trial date are generally being taken earlier, and the parties are being allocated the first available trial date, often irrespective of counsel's availability. The extent to which the court has been prepared to fix a date later than the first available slot has varied, and in some cases ambitious timetables have been set. Whilst the resources available to large corporate litigants (both in terms of large legal teams and financial resources) mean that they are able, with some difficulty, to meet these time limits, this can prove more expensive, and many commercial clients have yet to see the overall cost reductions forecast by Lord Woolf.

C   Interlocutory applications

One of Lord Woolf's aims was to reduce the number of opportunities for unproductive interlocutory skirmishes on peripheral matters. The overriding objective places a duty on the parties and their legal advisers to cooperate and to assist the court. The preliminary indications from the Queen's Bench Division and each of the specialist lists are that the parties are generally more co-operative in seeking to agree procedural matters, the number of interlocutory applications has reduced in accordance with CPR 1.4(2)(i) (which states that as part of active case management, the court will deal with as many aspects of the case as it can on the same occasion[20] and that such applications are being made if necessary at the CMC rather than by way of a separate hearing. For example, there has been a substantial reduction in the Commercial Court in the number of applications issued. From May–September 1998, 808 applications were issued, whereas between May and September 1999 the figure was 553 applications.[1] This reduction may be due in part to the lower number of cases issued during the same period, but the summary assessment of costs powers have undoubtedly also been an important factor in discouraging the parties from making 'borderline' applications which the court may consider to be tactical rather than central to the key issues in dispute.

This new willingness to reach agreement on procedural matters has reduced the costs incurred on interlocutory matters, although it is to some extent offset by the increase in the volume of correspondence on large commercial cases. Mindful of the requirements of the overriding objective and the costs sanctions available to the courts to penalise unreasonable or obstructive behaviour, there has been a tendency for the parties to record all their discussions in writing to guard against such accusations being made and demonstrate the 'proportionality' of their own approach.

---

20 See also CPR Pt 23, practice direction, para 2.8 and Pt 29, practice direction, paras 3.5 and 3.8.
1   Commercial Court Annual Report, September 1999.

D   Preliminary issues

The CPR place increased emphasis on managing litigation by splitting out and narrowing down the issues where appropriate, including through the determination of preliminary issues. Preliminary issues hearings have become more frequent in recent years, and this trend looks set to continue as a result of the further encouragement provided by the CPR. For example, the Commercial Court Guide[2] states that at the CMC and the pre-trial review 'consideration *will* be given to the possibility of preliminary issues in every case' (whether or not the parties have requested it). The parties should therefore always be prepared to make submissions on this point and to explain any reasons, which may not be readily apparent from the papers, why it may not be appropriate in the circumstances.

When deciding whether a preliminary issue hearing is appropriate for efficient case management the court will have to weigh up, as before, the advantages of a speedy determination of preliminary issues against the possibility that those findings may be appealed. In this situation there is a difficult balance to be struck when attempting to do justice between the parties—if the case is stayed pending the appeal it will delay the resolution of the case overall, rather than providing a speedy conclusion. However, if the case progresses pending the appeal, and the decision is ultimately upheld, costs will have been incurred unnecessarily. This problem is particularly acute given the current lengthy waiting times for hearings before the Court of Appeal, due to the limited resources available.[3] A significant increase in turnover of applications before the Court of Appeal is essential for the proper functioning of the case management principles underpinning the CPR. Where this problem arises, whether in relation to a preliminary issue or other interlocutory application, such as for an injunction, the court may prefer to order a speedy trial particularly where, as in the Chancery Division, an early date can currently be obtained.

E   Summary judgment

Part 24 of the CPR, which contains the provisions in relation to summary judgement, has two innovative features. It introduces the new summary judgment test of 'no real prospect of success' and provides that a defendant as well as a claimant may seek summary judgement, and that the court may also invoke it. Defendants have been taking advantage of this new provision, although with mixed success, but there have been no reported cases so far in which the court has instigated a summary judgment application. This may be due to concerns about the possibility of substantial delay in resolving the dispute if the summary judgment decision is appealed.

---

2   Section D 10.2.
3   See Court of Appeal Civil Division Review of the Year 1998/9.

There has been some initial confusion about the meaning of the 'no real prospect of success' test, particularly in the light of the practice direction to Pt 24 which appeared to apply a slightly different test. Paragraph 4.1 of the practice direction stated that where a claimant applied for judgment on his claim, the court would give judgment if:

(1) the claimant had shown a case which if unanswered would entitle him to judgment; and

(2) the defendant had not shown any reason why the claim should not be dealt with at trial.

Paragraph 4.2 stated that where a defendant applied for summary judgment, the court would allow judgment if either:

(1) the claimant had failed to show a case which if unanswered would entitle him to judgment; or

(2) the defendant had shown that the claim would be 'bound to be dismissed' at trial.

These paragraphs proved difficult to operate in practice and they were repealed with effect from 13 September 1999.

The courts have provided some further clarification as to what the 'no real prospect of success' test means. In *Swain v Hillman*,[4] a case before the Court of Appeal in which the defendant had applied for summary judgment in an action brought against him for personal injury, Lord Woolf stated that the words 'no real prospect of succeeding' did not need elaboration, as they spoke for themselves. The word 'real' directed the court to the need to see whether there was a realistic as opposed to fanciful prospect of success. However, in the circumstances of this case there were issues which were capable of being investigated at trial. Proper disposal of an issue under Part 24 should not involve the judge in conducting a 'mini-trial'. The objective of the provision was simply to enable cases which had no real prospect of success to be disposed of summarily.

F Pre-trial review/listing questionnaire[5]

The court will wish to ensure that the timetable set at the CMC is observed and that court resources are used effectively. If a party applies for an extension of time, while it may be granted this may well be with a potential sanction attached, such as an 'unless' order. Two cases heard before the Court of Appeal soon after the CPR were introduced illustrate the courts' likely approach to the prospect of a delay to the trial date. In *SJB Stephenson Ltd v Mandy*[6] the claimant obtained an injunction and the defendant appealed. The appeal was listed to be heard two weeks before trial, but was dismissed on the basis that it was a waste of costs and court resources when the point

4 (1999) Times, 4 November, CA.
5 Pre-trial review questionnaire in the Technology and Construction Court—49CPD, para 4.4.
6 (1999) Times, 21 July, CA.

could be dealt with at trial, and the defendant was protected by a cross undertaking in damages. In *Woods v Chalef*,[7] the Court of Appeal refused the claimant's application to amend particulars in a defamation case to add an allegation of malice, since the defendant would need time to deal with such an amendment in its own statement of case and the trial date was likely to be lost as a result.

There have also been a number of cases involving the late service of witness or expert evidence, where the court has had to decide whether to exclude this evidence.[8] On balance, the prevailing view appears to be that expressed in *Mealey Horgan plc v Horgan*[9] by Buckley J, namely that it would be unjust to exclude a party from adducing evidence at trial save in very extreme circumstances (although other penalties, including indemnity costs, may be imposed on the defaulting party). As part of proper case management, the defaulting party will certainly be expected to alert the court to the potential problem at the earliest opportunity.

In deciding whether to deprive a party of the opportunity of amending its case at a late stage, or to refuse to allow late evidence to be adduced, the court will exercise its discretion in order to achieve the overriding objective of dealing with the case justly. The courts will also have regard to the provisions of Article 6 of the European Convention on Human Rights, which provides that litigants are entitled to a fair trial.

G   Case management sanctions

The CPR provide a wide range of sanctions to ensure enforcement of the case management provisions. The courts are not hesitating to criticise poor case management but the emphasis is on setting a proportionate sanction rather than imposing an indiscriminate penalty. From October 2000, the courts will also have to take human rights considerations into account when exercising disciplinary powers on procedural matters.[10]

Under CPR 3.4 the court may strike out a statement of case if it appears to the court:

- that the statement of case discloses no reasonable grounds for bringing or defending the claim;
- that the statement of case is an abuse of the court's process or is otherwise likely to obstruct the just disposal of the proceedings; or
- that there has been a failure to comply with a rule, practice direction or court order.

This is the most extreme case management sanction available to the court. It has been implemented, but only in exceptional circumstances. An early warning was given by the Court of Appeal in *Shikari v Malik*.[11] In that case

---

7   (14 May 1999, unreported).
8   See Chapters 8 and 9 on witness evidence and expert evidence.
9   (1999) Times, 6 July, CA.
10 *Arrows Nominees Inc v Blackledge* (1999) Times, 8 December.
11 (1999) Times, 20 May.

the claimant's personal injury claim had been struck out by the Master for want of prosecution. On appeal, the judge found that there had been a wholesale disregard of the setting down obligations under the old rules, and upheld the decision (on abuse of process grounds rather than for want of prosecution). The case was then referred to the Court of Appeal which dismissed the claimant's appeal, holding that a case could be struck out on the abuse of process ground even if the abuse would not have been regarded as exceptional prior to the introduction of the case management requirements under the CPR. The court also warned that litigants could not rely on the court tolerating the sort of behaviour which has been tolerated under the old regime.

A contrasting approach was taken by the Court of Appeal in *Biguzzi v Rank Leisure plc.*[12] The case involved personal injuries sustained by Mr Biguzzi in 1993. The case became bogged down and on the defendant's application it was struck out by the district judge for 'wholesale disregard of the rules'. On appeal to the circuit judge the decision was reversed, on the basis that there were serious faults on both sides and that the case could still be tried fairly. The judge identified the central issue as 'Is there anything unfair in letting this case go to trial?' The Court of Appeal upheld this decision. Lord Woolf took the view that whilst the power to strike out was indeed available to the judge as part of his case management powers, it would not achieve justice in this particular case where other sanctions would be more proportionate. He pointed out that 'the advantage of the CPR over the previous rules is that the court's powers are much broader than they were. In many cases, there will be alternatives which enable a case to be dealt with justly without taking the draconian step of striking the case out'. Striking out the case in this instance would not bring an end to the litigation but would probably lead to lengthy satellite litigation between Mr Biguzzi and his legal advisers, which would simply transfer the problem to another part of the legal system and involve the deployment of further court resources.

Biguzzi only provides limited reassurance for defaulting parties. In the subsequent case of *UCB Corporate Services Ltd v Halifax (SW) Ltd*,[13] the claimant's case was struck out for abuse of process. Counsel for UCB argued that the judge at first instance should, following *Biguzzi*, have considered the alternative lesser sanctions available to him under the new rules. The Court of Appeal however distinguished *Biguzzi* and found that there was nothing to suggest that the judge had not been aware of these powers and that he was fully justified in asking himself whether on the facts there was a sufficient disregard of the rules to amount to an abuse of process and exercise his discretion accordingly. The court considered that it would be strange if they were required to take a more lenient approach under the CPR than under the old rules, and found that this could not have been the intention of Lord Woolf in *Biguzzi*. This decision was given further support by the Court of Appeal in *AXA Insurance Co Ltd v Swire Fraser Ltd*[14] which confirmed

12 [1999] 4 All ER 934, [1999] 1 WLR 1926, CA.
13 (1999) 144 Sol Jo LB 25, [2000] 01 LS Gaz R 24.
14 (2000) Times, 19 January.

that the CPR do not entitle the parties to expect a more lenient approach. The court observed that proof of prejudice to a party if the action were to proceed is not required (although the court will take this into account) and that CPR 3.4(2) enables the court to strike out a case for deliberate default or a failure to comply with a court order, without resorting to the court's inherent jurisdiction to strike out for abuse of the process.

It appears that *Biguzzi* is still the appropriate starting point, and that it will apply unless the facts are so extreme as obviously to warrant a strike out. Both *Biguzzi* and *UCB* were cases which were commenced under the old procedural regime and as a result were subject to its defects—under the principles of active case management the number of cases presenting themselves for consideration on strike out grounds should decrease rapidly once these old cases have worked their way through the system. Those cases which have not already been transferred to the new regime are at imminent risk of being stayed under CPR Pt 51, and parties to such cases (particularly claimants) are likely to find the courts reluctant to lift the stay without exceptional reasons. New cases commenced under the CPR will not be allowed to become dormant.

H   Appeals

The implementation in January 1999 of the almost universal requirement for permission to appeal was intended as a further step towards managing cases efficiently and ensuring that they do not take up a disproportionate share of the court's resources. This change has disappointed some litigants, although a refusal of permission to appeal is itself appealable. The Court of Appeal reports[15] that the introduction of this requirement has resulted in an initial reduction in the number of appeals, but that those cases where permission was granted are necessarily the more complex ones and therefore there has been a steep rise in the proportion of reserved judgments.

Waiting times for hearings before the Court of Appeal remain lengthy and a narrowing of the test for granting leave may ultimately be necessary as a practical matter if the objective of resolving cases promptly is to be met, and judges and Masters are to be able to make robust interlocutory decisions without the prospect that an appeal against the decision may delay the resolution of the case for many months.

15   The Court of Appeal Civil Division Review of the Year 1998/9.

7 DISCLOSURE

A Introduction

The process of discovery and disclosure of documents has been subject to widespread criticism for a number of years.[1] In Lord Woolf's Interim and Final Reports detailed consideration was given to addressing these criticisms.[2]

In his Interim Report Lord Woolf commented that:

'The scale of discovery, at the least in the larger cases, is completely out of control. The principle of full candid disclosure in the interests of justice has been devalued because discovery is pursued without sufficient regard to economy and efficiency in terms of the usefulness of the information which is likely to be obtained from the documents disclosed'.[3]

In his Final Report, Lord Woolf recommended that discovery (renamed 'disclosure of documents') should be retained, but subject to controls.[4] This approach has been adopted in the CPR.

Disclosure under the CPR, which applies to all claims except small claims,[5] is not automatic. Instead the court, exercising its powers of active case management,[6] usually determines by court order if and when and the extent to which parties to proceedings (and non parties) are required to give disclosure of documents having regard to the overriding objective of dealing with cases justly.[7] The concept of proportionality, which requires that the court deals with a case in ways which are proportionate:

(i)   to the amount of money involved;
(ii) to the importance of the case;
(iii) to the complexity of the issues; and
(iv) to the financial position of each party,[8]

is of particular importance in relation to disclosure.

---

1   See for example 'Civil Justice on Trial—The case for change'; report by Committee chaired by Hilary Heilbron QC (published in June 1993).
2   Final Report, Section III, Chapter 12, paras 37–52 and Interim Report, Section I, Chapter 3 and Section V, Chapter 21.
3   Interim Report, Section I, Chapter 3, para 10.
4   Final Report, page 311, para 134. See also Section III, Chapter 12, paras 37–46.
5   CPR 31.1.
6   Pursuant to CPR 1.4.
7   CPR 1.1(1).
8   CPR 1.1(2)(c).

The court will have regard to this principle when determining whether the parties should give standard disclosure or some more limited or wider form of disclosure or whether to restrict the inspection of disclosed documents. This is discussed further in this chapter. Also considered in this chapter is how the civil justice reforms having been working in practice in this area over the last twelve months.

B   Scoping the disclosure exercise

In line with the parties' duties to comply with any applicable pre-action protocol, or in its absence, paragraph 4 of the practice direction to protocols,[9] the process of identifying the issues in dispute and the documents relevant to those issues will have been carried out by the parties prior to the commencement of proceedings. The parties now play an integral role in the identification of documents and need to ensure that document management systems are in place to enable relevant documents to be easily identified and quickly retrieved. Inevitably this results in a greater time commitment from senior management and in-house lawyers at an earlier stage in the dispute. It is also necessary for one individual from within the party to continue to be closely involved in the document review process throughout the proceedings so that there is a company representative who is in a position to sign the disclosure statement when disclosure is given[10] and to deal with any questions raised by the court in relation to disclosure as part of case management.

Key documents will usually be exchanged between the parties prior to the commencement of proceedings or be attached to the parties' statements of case once proceedings are commenced. Much of the preliminary work of searching for and identifying the documents relevant to the issues in dispute will form the basis for disclosure given after proceedings are commenced. This exercise will inevitably involve the parties in significant front loading of time and costs.

Consistent with the parties' duty to help the court further the overriding objective[11] consideration should be given by the parties at the outset of proceedings as to the extent to which disclosure can be agreed. In particular the parties should consider whether it is possible to limit or even dispense with disclosure, give disclosure by sample or dispense with the preparation of disclosure lists. Any agreement reached in relation to disclosure will then take the form of proposed directions which will be subject to review by the court at the allocation stage or the case management conference.

However, in the event that it is not possible for the parties to agree the terms on which disclosure should take place, each party will need to prepare

---

9   See Chapter 1 on pre-action tactics.
10   It may be possible for a legal representative to sign the disclosure statement in Commercial Court cases. This is discussed further below.
11   CPR 1.3.

a disclosure strategy. This will usually be included within the party's case management plan and will consist of a range of proposals and fallbacks for management on disclosure. It will reflect factors such as whether one is acting for the claimant or defendant, the scope for ADR and at what stage, the case budget, what documents are readily available or can be easily obtained, and the court's likely attitude to disclosure bearing in mind the overriding objective.

C   What is disclosure?

A party is required to disclose documents which are or have been in his control. This includes documents held by a party's agent. Under the CPR, a party has or has had a document in his control if it is or was in his physical possession, he has or has had a right to possession of it; or he has or has had a right to inspect or take copies of it.[12] The duty to give disclosure continues until the proceedings are concluded.[13] However, a party is not obliged to give disclosure of documents or parts of documents that are irrelevant to the issues in dispute in the proceedings and a party may claim that he has a right to withhold a document or part of a document.[14]

Meaning of 'document'

A party discloses a document by stating that a document exists or has existed.[15] A 'document' is defined as 'anything in which information of any description is recorded'[16] and includes internal and external correspondence, agreements and other documents (including drafts), drawings, plans, manuscript notes, bank statements, computer records, word processing files, diary entries, company minutes, email messages, manuscript notes, notes of meetings, video and sound recordings and microfilms.

The term 'document' also includes a 'copy' which:
> 'in relation to a document means anything onto which information recorded in the document has been copied, by whatever means and whether directly or indirectly.'[17]

Where multiple identical copies of documents exist it is only necessary to disclose one copy of the document unless any additional copy documents contain modifications, obliterations or other markings which a party relies on to support his case or because it adversely affects his or another party's case or support's another party's case.[18]

---

12 CPR 31.8.
13 CPR 31.11. If a party becomes aware of further documents after disclosure has been given these documents should be disclosed by way of supplemental list. See CPR Pt 31, practice direction, para 3.3 and Commercial Court Guide, Section E2.5.
14 CPR 31.19(3).
15 CPR 31.2.
16 CPR 31.4.
17 CPR 31.4.
18 CPR 31.9.

D   The general principle of standard disclosure

Disclosure is usually restricted to standard disclosure unless the court orders, or the parties have agreed in writing, that it be dispensed with or otherwise limited.[19] Any agreement made between the parties must be lodged with the court.[20] For example, the court may order, or the parties may agree, that disclosure may be restricted to documents relating to a particular issue having regard to the number of documents involved and the nature and complexity of the proceedings. In the Chancery Division orders have been made limiting disclosure to less than standard disclosure in some cases on proportionality grounds. The Technology and Construction Court has also made orders requiring that disclosure be given in relation to particular issues only. However, when exercising their power to restrict or dispense with disclosure the courts need to be alive to the potential for claims being brought by disaffected parties who claim that they have been deprived of the right to a fair trial under Article 6(1) of the European Convention of Human Rights once the Human Rights Act 1998 is implemented.

There is some variation to the general principle discussed above depending upon whether or not a claim is brought in one of the specialist lists. For example, the Commercial Court Guide states that parties to Commercial Court cases can expect that disclosure beyond standard disclosure may be required either in a case as a whole or on particular issues although it will need to be justified.[1] Although the Patents Court Guide states that standard disclosure will usually be ordered it will not require the disclosure of documents in certain exempt classes.[2] To the extent that the practice and procedure in relation to disclosure has been varied by the specialist lists these differences are highlighted below.

Definition of 'standard disclosure'

Standard disclosure requires a party to disclose only:
- the documents on which he relies; and
- the documents which:
  — adversely affect his own case;
  — adversely affect another party's case; or
  — support another party's case; and
- the documents which he is required to disclose by a relevant practice direction.[3]

---

19   CPR 31.5. See also Chancery Guide, para 6.2.
20   CPR Pt 31, practice direction, para 1.4. This practice direction does not apply in the Commercial Court. See Commercial Court Guide, Section E1.4.
1   Commercial Court Guide, Section E1.2. This and the other provisions contained in the Commercial Court Guide may also apply to commercial cases dealt with in the Chancery Division of the High Court. Para 2.4 of the Chancery Guide states 'If a claim brought in the Chancery Division is a "commercial claim" within the meaning of paragraph 1.2 of the Practice Direction—Commercial Court…The court will in general, and to the extent that it is consistent with the CPR and relative Practice Directions adopt the same practice as the Commercial Court'.
2   See CPR Pt 49, practice direction E and the Patents Court Guide.
3   CPR 31.6.

E The parties' and their solicitors' obligations

1 The party's obligations

Under the CPR there is now clear emphasis on the client in terms of the obligation to the court to give disclosure and the client will need to be involved in the document selection process throughout the proceedings so that he is in a position to sign the disclosure statement. This is discussed further below.

When giving standard disclosure the party to the proceedings now has a duty to make a reasonable search for documents. Relevant factors in deciding the reasonableness of the search include the number of documents involved, the nature and complexity of the proceedings, the ease and expense of retrieval of particular documents and the significance of any document which is likely to be located during the search.[4] The overriding principle of proportionality must be borne in mind when conducting the search for documents and a party may decide not to search for a particular category or class of documents on the grounds that to do so would be unreasonable.[5] For example, a party may restrict his search to documents created after a certain date or located in a particular place or to email communications between key players. Where this approach is taken this must be reflected in the disclosure statement made by the party and included in his disclosure list. However, the judge may direct that a search takes place notwithstanding that the party considers that the search for a particular category of documents is unreasonable.[6]

The obligation to carry out a reasonable search does create difficulties for the client and until guidance is given by the courts as to how this concept is to be interpreted, clients (and their solicitors) will to some extent be carrying out this exercise in the dark. An assessment will have to be made at an early stage by the client (in conjunction with his solicitors) as to what documents are to be searched for and where, having regard to the factors set out above. The reasonableness of that search may be subject to attack at a later stage and the parties and their solicitors may well find that the exercise has to be carried out again, particularly where the client is later subject to an order for specific or special disclosure (discussed further below). In the light of this, it may be a good idea for the parties to obtain clarification from the court at the case management conference as to the scope and extent of the search for documents. Furthermore, if a party knows at the case management conference that he is likely to require a document or category of documents which is likely to fall outside standard disclosure, a request for that document or category of documents should if possible be made at that stage. If the

---

4 CPR 31.7.
5 CPR Pt 31, practice direction, para 2 and Commercial Court Guide, para E1.
6 See for example, Commercial Court Guide, Section E3.3.

request is made after the case management conference there is a danger that the party being asked to give additional disclosure raises arguments that he has already carried out his search and that it would be disproportionate to require him to carry out a further search.

Although in most cases there will therefore at least initially be a significant reduction in the amount of documents which will be disclosed by way of standard disclosure there is unlikely to be a corresponding reduction in the amount of documents identified for review.

2   The solicitor's obligations

The party's solicitor is under an obligation to ensure that his client understands his duty of disclosure.[7] The solicitor should make clear to his client at the outset of actual or potential litigation that documents must be disclosed even if they are damaging to his case, that all documents or other information which may be disclosed must be preserved and that documents should not be destroyed. In addition the solicitor should explain to his client that the obligation to give disclosure continues until proceedings are concluded. As an officer of the court, the solicitor should also review his client's documents to ensure that disclosure is properly given.

F   Timetable for disclosure

1   Fast track cases

In fast track cases disclosure will normally be ordered by the court at the allocation stage and is usually limited to standard disclosure.[8] The court may however order that more restricted disclosure be given in which case it will specify the documents or classes of documents which the parties must disclose or that no disclosure be given at all.[9] In addition, the parties can agree directions subject to court approval, which restrict disclosure to standard disclosure or less than that.[10]

In order to comply with the tight timetable for bringing a fast track case to trial (typically 30 weeks from the date of the notice of allocation), disclosure will usually be ordered to be given by the parties within four weeks of the date of notice of allocation.[11]

Although the timescale for providing disclosure in fast track cases will usually be tight the parties should be well placed to comply with it given that they

---

7   CPR Pt 31, practice direction, para 4.4. There is no equivalent provision in The Commercial Court Guide which does not apply the practice direction to Pt 31.
8   CPR 31.5, 28.3 and Part 28, practice direction, para 3.
9   CPR 28.3(2).
10 CPR Pt 28, practice direction, para 3.6.
11 CPR Pt 28, practice direction, para 3.12.

will already have front-loaded much of the work to identify documents relevant to the issues in dispute. This will have been done as part of the parties' compliance with any relevant pre-action protocol or paragraph 4 of the practice direction to protocols[12] and to enable them to state a positive case in their particulars of claim or defence.[13]

2 *Multi-track cases*

In multi-track cases an order for disclosure will usually be given by the court at the case management conference. If no case management conference is ordered, it will be dealt with by the court automatically as part of the directions given at the allocation stage. Directions for disclosure may be made at the court's own initiative or as a result of agreed directions having been proposed by the parties.[14] The usual order made by the court will initially be for standard disclosure although the court may order that standard disclosure is limited, for example that it is given in relation to particular issues only, or that it is dispensed with altogether. Any additional disclosure will be by court order.

For example, the Queen's Bench Division and the Technology and Construction Court have made orders limiting disclosure to particular issues in dispute, such as liability. The Technology and Construction Court has also made orders that disclosure be given on a sample basis.

In the Commercial Court a case management conference is mandatory,[15] and at this stage the court will consider whether to dispense with or limit standard disclosure, whether to order standard disclosure or whether to order specific disclosure, including whether to make a special disclosure order.[16] In practice, in the Commercial Court (where there is greater emphasis on documentation), disclosure will usually be ordered to be given on a standard basis although it will often be accompanied by an order for disclosure of additional specified categories of documents.

At the case management conference the court may also order that disclosure be given in stages. Alternatively, the parties may agree this in writing.[17]

G   Form of disclosure

Each party will normally give disclosure by making a list in the form of practice form N265[18] and serving it on the other parties to the proceedings.

---

12 See Chapter 1 on pre-action tactics.
13 See Chapter 4 on starting and defending a claim.
14 CPR 29.2 and Pt 29, practice direction, paras 3.3, 4.6, 4.7, 4.9, 4.10 and 5.3. See also Commercial Court Guide, Section E2 and Chancery Guide, paras 6.1–6.2.
15 Commercial Court Guide, para D1.4.
16 Commercial Court Guide, para E2.1.
17 CPR 31.13 and Commercial Court Guide, Section E.2.3.
18 Form CCN265 should be used in the Commercial Court.

Practice forms N265 and CCN 265 are reproduced at Appendices I and J. The parties can however agree to dispense with lists, including agreeing to dispense with each party making a disclosure statement.[19] The Commercial Court will also consider making an order that disclosure by list be dispensed with if an application is made at the case management conference. However each party may still be required to make a disclosure statement.[20]

The disclosure list must identify the documents in a convenient order and manner and as concisely as possible.[1] Each document will usually be listed in date order, numbered consecutively and described concisely although documents falling into one particular category, such as bank statements may be listed by category rather than individually.[2] The list must indicate those documents in respect of which the party claims a right or duty to withhold inspection and the grounds upon which the right or duty is claimed.[3] Those documents which are no longer in a party's control must also be indicated together with what has happened to those documents.[4]

H   Disclosure statements

One of the major changes introduced by the CPR is that a party's list of documents must now include a disclosure statement signed by the disclosing party or, his insurer, where the insurer has a financial interest in the result of the proceedings brought wholly or partly against the party.[5] Where the disclosing party or his insurer is a company, firm, association or other organisation, the statement must also identify the person making the statement and explain why he is considered an appropriate person to make it.

The disclosure statement must:
- set out the extent of the search made to locate documents which the party is required to disclose, including any limitations to the search adopted for proportionality reasons together with reasons why the limitations were adopted;[6]
- contain a statement that the disclosing party believes the extent of the search was reasonable and proportionate;[7]
- certify that the disclosing party understands the duty to disclose documents; and that to the best of his knowledge that he has carried out that duty;

---

19 CPR 31.10(8).
20 Commercial Court Guide, Section E2.2.
1   CPR 31.10(3).
2   CPR Pt 31, practice direction, para 3.2 and Commercial Court Guide, Section E3.4.
3   CPR Pt 31, practice direction, para 4.5.
4   CPR 31.10(4).
5   CPR 31.10(5) and practice direction, para 4.7.
6   CPR 31.10(6) and practice direction, para 4.2, which states that the disclosure statement should expressly state that the disclosing party believes the extent of the search to have been reasonable in all the circumstances.
7   CPR Pt 31, practice direction, para 4.2.

> - state where a party has not searched for a class of documents on the grounds of reasonableness and identify the class of documents;[8]
> - state if inspection of any of the documents disclosed is being withheld on the ground that it is disproportionate.[9]

The form of wording for the disclosure statement is set out in Annex A to the practice direction to CPR Pt 31.

In Commercial Court cases, unless the court directs otherwise, the disclosure statement must also:
- identify any respects in which the search has been limited;
- set out in detail the facts considered in arriving at the decision that it was reasonable to limit the search;
- specify by whom the search has been conducted.[10]

In Commercial Court cases 'an appropriate person' may also sign the disclosure statement. This person need not be an officer of the company which is party to the proceedings but 'someone in a position responsibly and authoritatively' to make the statements contained in the disclosure statement. For example, it may include a legal representative. An explanation why the person is considered an appropriate person must also be given in the disclosure statement.[11]

With effect from 2 May 2000, contempt of court proceedings may be initiated against a person who makes, or causes to be made a false disclosure statement without an honest belief in its truth.[12] The Commercial Court may also at any stage order that a disclosure statement be verified by affidavit or witness statement.[13] A false statement in an affidavit or witness statement is also a contempt of court punishable by fine and/or imprisonment.

The disclosure statement must be signed by someone with a detailed knowledge of the issues in the case, the disclosure process which has been undertaken and an understanding of what the duty of disclosure involves. This person is most likely to be an in-house lawyer or a member of senior management, although in the Commercial Court it can also be a legal representative.

The requirement to include information in the disclosure statement as to the scope of the search for documents, including the extent to which the search is limited and the reasons for or facts considered in arriving at the decision that it was reasonable to limit the search may involve the disclosure of privileged and certainly confidential information. To the extent that a party is required to disclose information which is subject to legal professional privilege in order to comply with the disclosure statement this may be subject

---

8 CPR 31.7(3).
9 CPR 31.3(2).
10 Commercial Court Guide, Section E3.6.
11 Commercial Court Guide, Section E3.10.
12 See Civil Procedure (Amendment) Rules 2000, SI 2000/221; CPR 31.23.
13 Commercial Court Guide, Section E3.9.

to challenge in the light of Toulson J's decision in *General Mediterranean Holdings SA v Patel & Patel*.[14]

I   Inspection of documents

Once a document has been disclosed to a party that party has a right to inspect the document and to take copies[15] unless the document is no longer in the control of the disclosing party[16] or the disclosing party has a right or duty to withhold inspection, for example because privilege is asserted.[17] The disclosing party must allow inspection to take place within seven days of receipt of written notice from the other party of his wish to inspect. Furthermore, if a disclosing party considers that it would be disproportionate to allow inspection of any class or category of documents disclosed within standard disclosure having regard to the issues in the case, the party will not be required to do so. As discussed above the party's disclosure statement will include a statement that inspection of those documents will not be permitted on grounds that it would be disproportionate to allow inspection.[18]

Although a party may apply for specific inspection of documents[19] where inspection is being withheld on proportionality grounds such an application will probably only succeed if the party is able to show that it would be more proportionate to grant inspection than not. This hurdle might in fact be fairly easy to overcome as there will be less work and cost involved in the inspection of documents than in their disclosure.

J   Specific and special disclosure

1   Specific disclosure

Pursuant to CPR 31.12[20] the court may make an order for specific disclosure requiring a party to:

---

14 [1999] 3 All ER 673, [2000] 1 WLR 272 in which Toulson J held that an application for disclosure of documents subject to legal professional privilege pursuant to CPR 48.7(3) in relation to a wasted costs order was ultra vires, and that even if it was intra vires it was in breach of the right to a fair trial and the right to confidentiality under Articles 6 and 8 of the European Convention on Human Rights.
15 CPR 31.15.
16 CPR 31.8.
17 CPR 31.19. The court does have a discretion under the CPR as to whether or not to order inspection. See *Morris v Banque Arabe et Internationale d'Investissement SA* [2000] 01 LS Gaz R 24. A party can also apply to withhold disclosure of a document on the ground that disclosure would damage the public interest. The application should be made without notice under Pt 23 and be supported by evidence.
18 CPR 31.3(2).
19 CPR 31.12(3).
20 See also the Commercial Court Guide, Section E4 and the Chancery Guide, paras 6.3–6.4.

- disclose specified documents or classes of documents;
- carry out a search to the extent stated in the order; and
- disclose any documents located as a result of that search.

An application for specific disclosure, which may be made where a party considers that the disclosure given by a party is inadequate, should be made under CPR Pt 23. The order which the applicant seeks should be specified in the application notice and should be supported by evidence setting out the grounds upon which the order is sought. In the Commercial Court, applications for specific disclosure may be made at the case management conference or by later application.[1] However, before an application for specific disclosure is made in the Chancery Division, the request for disclosure must first be communicated to the other party and an attempt made to reach agreement or narrow the issues before the matter is raised with the court.[2] An application for specific disclosure in the Chancery Division (outside of the case management conference) will not usually be heard without a prior written statement from the applicant that this step has been complied with.

In deciding whether to grant an order for specific disclosure the court will have regard to all the circumstances of the case and in particular, the overriding objective.[3] For example, in *Harrison v Bloom*[4] Neuberger J considered an application for specific disclosure part way through trial. He stated that the application was unusual but not unprecedented and since the overriding objective of the court was to do justice between the parties he was prepared to order specific disclosure of documents, notwithstanding the late application, albeit on a more restricted basis than that sought by the applicant.

Useful guidance has also been given generally in the Chancery Guide as to the circumstances in which the Chancery Division may be prepared to order specific disclosure. The Chancery Guide also suggests that where specific disclosure is sought the parties should give careful thought to ways in which disclosure might be limited such as by requiring disclosure of only sufficient documents to show a specified matter and whether the need for disclosure could be avoided by giving information under CPR Pt 18.[5]

Given the shift in emphasis to the concept of the reasonable search for documents under standard disclosure, applications for specific disclosure are likely to increase, especially where a party is concerned that his opponent has not disclosed documents adverse to his case. The threat of a specific disclosure application alone might be used as a tactical weapon to gain extra documents.

In both making and resisting an application for specific disclosure con-siderable emphasis will be placed by the parties upon whether the order

---

1 Commercial Court Guide, Section E4.2. The Commercial Court may also require specific disclosure to be verified by affidavit or witness statement. See Commercial Court Guide, Section E4.4.
2 Chancery Guide, para 5.6.
3 CPR Pt 31, practice direction, para 5.4.
4 [1999] 45 LS Gaz R 32.
5 Chancery Guide, paras 6.3–6.5.

sought furthers the overriding objective most. Where an application is made for disclosure of documents referred to in already disclosed documents it will probably be very difficult to resist the application unless the resisting party is able to show that a further search will be required to locate the specified documents and that the search will involve difficulty and expense.[6] Even then the court may still be prepared to order the search subject to proportionality arguments.

A successful party to an application for specific disclosure should generally be able to recover his costs of making the application. However the court does have a discretion in relation to costs and may decide to reserve costs pending the result of the specific disclosure order. For example if the documents obtained pursuant to the specific disclosure order prove to be irrelevant to the issues in the proceedings or the search ordered reveals nothing the court may take this into account when ordering costs.[7]

Indications appear to be that parties are applying for specific disclosure and, provided that such applications are properly framed, the courts are prepared to grant orders for specific disclosure, which may, where appropriate, include 'train of enquiry' documents.

2   Special disclosure

The Commercial Court may make an order for special disclosure substantially in the terms set out in Appendix 9 to the Commercial Court Guide[8] which is reproduced at Appendix K. An order made in the form of Appendix 9 requires:

> 'each party to carry out a thorough search for all documents relevant to [... the issues in the case], including (for the avoidance of doubt) all documents which may lead to a train of inquiry enabling a party to advance his own case or damage that of his opponent.'[9]

The Commercial Court effectively treats special disclosure as a form of specific disclosure under CPR 31.12(2) and suggests, without limiting the circumstances in which it may be appropriate, that such an order will be made where allegations of fraud, dishonesty or misrepresentation are alleged or where knowledge or lack of knowledge, or disclosure or non-disclosure are in issue.[10] In making the order the court will decide whether the special disclosure will enable the court to deal with the case justly and whether the likely costs of implementing the special disclosure order are proportionate to the amount of money involved and the importance of the case.[11]

---

6   It may be even harder to resist in the Commercial Court. See the comments in relation to resisting special disclosure orders discussed below.

7   CPR 44.5(3).

8   Commercial Court Guide, Section E5.1.

9   In the light of para 2.4 of the Chancery Guide the Chancery Division may also be prepared to make orders for special disclosure in relation to commercial cases. Appendix A(1) of the Mercantile Courts Guide which contains a case management information sheet for use in the Mercantile Courts and Business List also asks whether a full disclosure order is appropriate. This appears to be akin to the Commercial Court's special disclosure order.

10   Commercial Court Guide, Section E5.4.

11   Commercial Court Guide, Section E5.3.

An application for an order for special disclosure may be made at the case management conference or by later application and the Commercial Court may make a special disclosure order in relation to one or more issues in the case or the case as a whole[12] and against all or some of the parties.[13]

The Commercial Court may also order that special disclosure be verified by affidavit or witness statement.[14]

Arguments similar to those raised in relation to applications for specific disclosure orders are likely to made by the parties in the context of applications for special disclosure orders. However given the Commercial Court Guide's comment that:

> 'documents are of particular importance in commercial cases and of particular assistance in enabling the court to deal with cases justly'"[15]

parties resisting applications for special disclosure may face an uphill task.

Experiences suggest that the Commercial Court has been prepared to make special disclosure orders particularly where the parameters of standard disclosure have not been clear as between the parties.

K Sanctions for failure to comply with disclosure

If a party fails to disclose or allow inspection of a document he may not rely on the document unless the court gives permission.[16]

L Disclosure by a non-party

CPR 31.17 provides that a party may apply to court under any Act for an order for disclosure by a person who is not a party to the proceedings.[17] Previously such an application for disclosure of documents could only be made in respect of claims involving personal injury and death or by relying on the writ of subpoena *duces tecum* procedure. The latter only enabled a non party to be ordered to attend trial and produce documents and the party who made the application had no prior right of inspection as the documents were produced to the court.[18] Following *Khanna v Lovell White*

---

12 Commercial Court Guide, Section E5.2.
13 Commercial Court Guide, Section E5.3.
14 Commercial Court Guide, Section E5.5.
15 Commercial Court Guide, Section E1.2.
16 CPR 31.21.
17 Pursuant to the Supreme Court Act 1981, s 34(2) and the County Courts Act 1984, s 53 as amended by the Civil Procedure (Modification of Enactments) Order 1998, SI 1998/2940.
18 However, after *Khanna v Lovell White Durrant* [1994] 4 All ER 267, [1995] 1 WLR 121, the court did allow the trial date to be artificially advanced to enable documents to be produced.

Durrant[19] this practice is now embodied in CPR 34.2 which enables the court to issue a witness summons requiring a witness to attend court to produce documents on the date fixed for a hearing or on such other date as the court may direct. A party will need to obtain the court's permission where he wishes to have a summons issued for a witness to attend court to produce documents on any date except the date fixed for the trial or at any hearing except the trial.[20] All parties should be given notice of the hearing at which the witness is required to produce the documents. If the applicant and the witness are able to agree the documents to be produced, the hearing at which the documents are to be produced may be vacated and the summons discharged or, if there is some doubt, it may be adjourned to a later date. In some circumstances this procedure may be quicker and more economic than an application for disclosure against a non party under CPR 31.17, however, the procedure is unlikely to be appropriate if there are many categories of documents to be produced or if there is any possibility of contention surrounding the production of documents sought such as questions of privilege.

An application for disclosure under CPR 31.17 must be made in accordance with CPR Pt 23 and must be supported by evidence.[1] As a general rule the application notice should be served on the non party (the respondent).[2] If this is not done the respondent may apply to set aside or vary the court's order.[3] The applicant will usually bear the costs of the application and the costs incurred by the non party in complying with any order made by the court although the court does have a discretion to vary this general rule.[4]

An order for disclosure against a non party will only be made by the court where the disclosure of documents sought are likely to support the applicant's case or adversely affect the case of another party to the proceedings and disclosure is necessary in order to dispose fairly of the claim or to save costs.[5]

The order made by the court must specify the documents or classes of documents which the non party must disclose and require the non party when making disclosure to specify which documents are no longer in his control or in relation to which documents he claims a right or duty to withhold inspection. He may also be ordered to indicate what has happened to any documents which are no longer in his control and to specify the time and place for disclosure and inspection.[6] These requirements do however go beyond the witness summons procedure contained in CPR 34.2 which

---

19   [1994] 4 All ER 267, [1995] 1 WLR 121.
20   CPR 34.3(2)(b) and (c).
1   CPR 31.17(2). The evidence may be contained in an application notice verified by a statement of truth or witness statement.
2   CPR 23.4.
3   CPR 23.10.
4   CPR 48.1. The court will consider all the circumstances, including the extent to which it was reasonable for the person against whom the order was sought to oppose the application and whether the parties complied with any relevant pre-action protocols. For example, para 3.13 of the protocol for the resolution of clinical disputes requires third party healthcare providers to cooperate in providing health records.
5   CPR 31.17(3).
6   CPR 31.17(4) and (5).

simply requires the recipient of the witness summons to produce documents to the court on the date fixed for trial or earlier if directed by the court.

Rule 31.17 does not limit any other power which the court may have to order disclosure before proceedings start or against a non-party. For example, pursuant to CPR 31.18 disclosure may still be obtained against a non-party under the *Norwich Pharmacal*[7] principle which allows an action to be commenced against a third party solely for discovery in order to identify the wrong-doer or pursuant to the Bankers' Book Evidence Act 1879.[8]

The procedure contained in CPR 31. 17 certainly simplifies the basis upon which a party to proceedings may obtain disclosure from a non party and may in certain circumstances result in the witness summons procedure contained in CPR 34.2 being less widely used.

Both claimants and defendants should give consideration to whether additional disclosure from a third party might help to dispose of the claim or to save costs as soon as proceedings are commenced.[9] If it appears likely that it will do so, an application for non party disclosure should be made to the court.

Although there is a risk that non party disclosure applications may increase litigation by enabling parties to embark on fishing expeditions, as long as the courts apply strictly the criteria set out in CPR 31.17 this risk should be fairly small. At present there is no case law to provide any guidance as to how strictly the courts are likely to interpret this.

7   *Norwich Pharmacal Co v Customs and Excise Comrs* [1974] AC 133, [1973] 2 All ER 943, HL.
8   See *Civil Procedure* (2nd edn) paragraph 31.18.3.
9   It is not at present possible to obtain disclosure of documents from a non party before proceedings are commenced. This is discussed in detail in Chapter 1 on pre-action tactics.

8 WITNESS EVIDENCE

A Introduction

The process of gathering witness evidence has assumed greater importance under the CPR and at an earlier stage in proceedings. Parties must now thoroughly research their case prior to commencing proceedings. This includes identifying at an early stage the issues in dispute and the key factual witness evidence in support of each party's case in order to comply with any relevant pre-action protocols and, in their absence, paragraph 4 of the practice direction to pre-action protocols.[1] Preliminary witness statements are likely to have been taken either prior to or at the outset of proceedings and certainly prior to serving one's statement of case to enable a positive case to be pleaded. Preliminary witness statements may even be served with each party's statement of case, although it appears that this practice is not at present being widely adopted.

CPR Pt 32 has now addressed the concerns raised by Lord Woolf in relation to witness evidence and witness statements in particular. In Lord Woolf's Interim and Final Reports the use of witness statements in litigation came under attack.[2] Although in favour of the 'cards on the table' approach, which allows each party to know in advance of trial the evidence to be put forward by the other side, Lord Woolf expressed concern that witness statements 'have ceased to be the authentic account of the lay witness; instead they have become an elaborate, costly branch of legal drafting'.[3] Moreover, there is

> '…the fear that a witness will not be permitted to depart from or amplify his statement at the trial itself. Whether or not this fear is well-founded, it has led to…elaborate over-drafting…with a view to ensuring that the witness statement is complete in every detail'.[4]

Lord Woolf's recommendations that:
- a court should be able to allow evidence to be given at trial which was not contained in a witness statement where admitting it will not cause any injustice to another party;

---

1 See Chapter 1 on pre-action tactics.
2 See Lord Woolf's Interim Report, Section V, Chapter 22 and Final Report, Section III, Chapter 12, paras 53–60.
3 Final Report, Section III, Chapter 12, para 54.
4 Final Report, Section III, Chapter 12, para 55.

- witness statements should:
  — as far as possible, be in the witness's own words;
  — not discuss legal propositions;
  — not comment on documents; and
  — conclude with a statement, signed by the witness, that the evidence is a true statement and that it is in his own words,[5]

are now reflected in the CPR.

In addition, Lord Woolf's recommendation that the courts should actively manage cases[6] is now deeply enshrined within CPR Pt 32 and in the courts' approach to witness evidence since the implementation of the CPR. This chapter considers developments in this area over the last twelve months.

B   The court's power to control evidence

Pursuant to CPR 32.1 the court may control evidence by giving directions as to the issues on which it requires evidence, the nature of the evidence which it requires to decide those issues and the way in which the evidence is to be placed before the court. Furthermore the court has the power to exclude evidence which would otherwise not be admissible and to limit cross-examination. These powers will be exercised in accordance with the overriding objective contained in CPR 1.1 of dealing with cases justly. As a general rule any fact which needs to be proved by witness evidence at trial will be by way of oral evidence given in public. A witness statement or witness summary of the evidence to be given at trial must be served in advance of the trial. For all other hearings any facts which need to be proved will be done so by the witness's evidence in writing.[7]

In fast track cases, parties can expect the courts to make use of their power to control evidence to restrict the time allotted to oral evidence within the trial timetable. In multi-track cases at the case management conference parties should be prepared for the courts controlling the amount of factual evidence to be given on a particular issue and limiting the number of witnesses who may give evidence, or ordering that factual evidence is only to be given in relation to certain issues.[8]

The courts have already demonstrated their willingness to exclude evidence which is otherwise admissible in *Grobbelaar v Sun Newspapers Ltd*.[9] In that case the Court of Appeal (Henry, Potter and Mummery LJJ), on an appeal from an interlocutory application in a defamation action, confirmed that the trial judge now has the power to exclude evidence under Pt 32 and that there were no express limitations as to the manner and extent of the exercise

---

5   Final Report, Section III, Chapter 12, para 59.
6   See Chapter 6 on case management.
7   CPR 32.2.
8   For example, the Technology and Construction Court has made orders that witness evidence should only be given in relation to certain issues.
9   (1999) Times, 12 August, CA. See also *GKR Karate UK Ltd v Yorkshire Post Newspapers Ltd* [2000] 04 LS Gaz R 32, CA.

of that power, although it had to be exercised in accordance with the overriding objective. The Court of Appeal in reaching its decision referred to the judgment of Lord Woolf in an earlier defamation action before the Court of Appeal, *McPhilemy v Times Newspapers Ltd*[10] in which Lord Woolf stated:

> 'while under the CPR a party cannot be prevented from putting forward an allegation which is central to his or her defence, the court can control the manner in which this is done and thus limit the costs involved'.

Furthermore, with a view to saving court time and expense, the court was willing in *Mullan v Birmingham City Council*[11] (a case involving a claim for damages for personal injuries), after hearing and testing the claimant's evidence, to find that grounds arose for contending that the claimant had no reasonable prospect of success and that it could hear a submission of no case to answer without putting the defendant to his election as to not to call evidence.

In contrast there may be circumstances where the court considers it appropriate to admit further evidence even at an apparently late stage in proceedings. For example, in *Charlesworth v Relay Roads Ltd (in liquidation)*[12] Neuberger J was prepared to allow further evidence (and statements of case to be amended) even though judgment had been given, providing that the order recording his decision had not been drawn up.

Cases over the last twelve months generally suggest that the courts are willing to use their new power to control evidence to assist in complying with the overriding objective. However, when controlling evidence, the courts need to be mindful of the impact of the Human Rights Act 1998 (currently due to be implemented in October 2000). In particular the courts may face claims from aggrieved parties who consider that their right to a fair trial under Art 6(1) of the European Convention on Human Rights has been infringed as a result of decisions by the courts to exclude or limit evidence which would otherwise be admissible.

C Timetable for preparing witness evidence

1 Fast track cases

In fast track cases parties might typically be expected to exchange witness statements within ten weeks of the date of the notice of allocation with trial taking placing within thirty weeks.[13] Although the parties will have already

---

10 [1999] 3 All ER 775, [1999] EMLR 751, CA.
11 (1999) Times, 29 July, Birmingham District Registry, David Foskett QC See also *Al Malik Carpets Ltd v London Buildings (Highgate) Ltd* (17 September 1999, unreported), Ch D, Neuberger J.
12 [1999] 4 All ER 397, [2000] 1 WLR 230, Ch D.
13 CPR Pt 28, practice direction, para 3.12.

identified key factual witnesses and probably taken preliminary witness statements prior to the allocation stage, it is only when the court gives directions at the allocation stage that the parties can be sure of the areas on which the court will require evidence at trial and the extent of the evidence required. Parties need to ensure that witnesses are available for witness statement preparation immediately after the allocation stage if they are to be in a position to comply with the court's timetable through to trial. Given the court's powers to control evidence, preparation of witness statements in advance of directions being given by the court may result in a party incurring costs which may not subsequently be recovered even if successful at trial. Costs are discussed in detail in Chapter 10.

2   *Multi-track cases*

A party will be expected to be in a position to identify the number and nature of its witnesses at the case management conference. At the case management conference directions will be given by the court as to what factual evidence should be given and by what date. The court may also give directions as to the order in which witness statements should be exchanged and whether or not witness statements are to be filed.[14] If no case management conference is ordered, directions for the disclosure of witness statements will be made either on the court's own initiative or as a result of agreed directions having been proposed by the parties.[15] An order will usually be made for witness statements to be exchanged simultaneously and filed at court, however in the Commercial Court witness statements will not usually be ordered to be filed.[16]

It is probably unwise to spend considerable time on the detailed preparation and drafting of witness statements for multi-track cases for use at trial prior to the case management conference, given the court's powers of active case management contained in CPR Pt 3 (in particular the court's power to order the trial of certain issues before others), and the court's power to control evidence. However, the parties will need to have carried out a careful analysis of the issues raised in the case and the evidence required to prove those issues in order to discuss the timetable for the case through to trial with the court.

D   Form and content of witness statements

The practice direction to CPR Pt 32 sets out in detail the form and content of witness statements.[17] Witness statements must comply with the practice

---

14   CPR 32.4(3).
15   CPR 29.2 and Pt 29, practice direction, paras 4.7, 4.8, 4.9, 4.10 and 5.3.
16   Commercial Court Guide, Appendix 8.
17   CPR Pt 32, practice direction, paras 17–20.

direction.[18] Failure to do so may lead to evidence not being admitted or the costs of its preparation not being allowed. In line with Lord Woolf's recommendations, witness statements must as far as possible be in the witness's own words,[19] should not argue the law[1] and should specify which statements are within the witness's own knowledge and which are matters of information and belief.[2] Appendix L contains a pro forma witness statement which complies with the requirements of the practice direction to Pt 32.

Additional guidance on the form and content of witness statements for use in the Chancery Division of the High Court and the Commercial Court has also been given.

In summary, the Chancery Guide adds the following:
- witness statements should be as concise as the circumstances of the case allow;
- inadmissible material should not be included nor should irrelevant material;
- solicitors and counsel should not allow the costs of preparation of witness statements to become increased by over-elaboration of the statements. Unnecessary elaboration may be subject to special costs orders;[3]
- witness statements should contain the truth, the whole truth and nothing but the truth. No pressure should be exerted on a witness to give anything other than a true and complete account of his evidence. A professional adviser may be under an obligation to check the truth of a witness statement where practical. If a party discovers that there is something incorrect or inaccurate in the statement the other parties should be informed immediately;
- a witness statement should not be used to provide a commentary on the documents in the bundle and should be used to give evidence in chief.[4]

The Commercial Court Guide contains similar guidance but in addition states that a witness statement should not be longer than necessary and should not contain lengthy renditions of correspondence.[5]

Over the last twelve months witness statements do not appear to have changed significantly and witness statements are still regarded by many members of the judiciary as being too long. Unless witness statements do

18 CPR 32.8.
19 CPR Pt 32, practice direction, para 18.1.
1 *Alex Lawrie Factors Ltd v Morgan* (1999) Times, 18 August, in which the Court of Appeal (Brooke and Walker LJJ) held in an action seeking payment under a deed of indemnity that 'the purpose of an affidavit, or a statement of truth was for a witness to say, in her own words, what the relevant evidence was. It was not to be used by the lawyer who settled it as a vehicle for complex legal argument to which the witness herself would not be readily able to speak if cross-examined on it...Those considerations applied just as much to statements of truth under the CPR as they did to affidavits'.
2 CPR Pt 32, practice direction, para 18.2.
3 See Chapter 10 on costs.
4 Chancery Guide, Appendix 4.
5 Commercial Court Guide, Section H, paras1.2–1.4.

change to take into account Lord Woolf's criticisms, parties may well find themselves unable to recover the full costs of their preparation.

E   Statements of truth

A witness statement should also include a statement of truth made by the witness confirming that the contents of the witness statement are true.[6] If a witness makes a statement without an honest belief in its truth, contempt of court proceedings may be initiated against the witness.[7] The court has already considered an application to commence committal proceedings in *Malgar Ltd v RE Leach (Engineering) Ltd.*[8] In this case the claimant applied to commence committal proceedings against the defendants on the basis that they had made false statements of truth in their witness statements. Sir Richard Scott V-C held that the nature of the claimant's committal proceedings were tenuous since the defendants had not persisted in their alleged false statements of truth. As the defendants would be leading witnesses at trial Sir Richard Scott V-C held that:

> 'it would be undesirable to have an application or prosecution for contempt at the same time. However, if the sanctity of the administration of justice needed protecting it could be otherwise.'

This case emphasises the importance which the court attributes to statements of truth and that in appropriate circumstances it will be prepared to use its powers to allow contempt of court proceedings to be commenced pre-trial against a witness who makes a false statement. To date, no guidance has been given in the CPR, the accompanying practice directions or guides produced by the specialist lists as to how the court should exercise this power.

Where a case involves a dispute as to fact there is a danger that one party may make an application to commence committal proceedings for tactical reasons in an attempt to exclude the other party from giving evidence at trial. Such applications are, in our view, likely to be discouraged by the courts save in exceptional circumstances, however clarification is needed from the courts on this point.

Guidance is also needed as to the circumstances in which contempt of court proceedings may be commenced where a trial judge has determined a question of fact in dispute between the parties to the proceedings by favouring the evidence of one witness in preference to another. On the face of it, the successful party could apply to the court to bring contempt of court proceedings against the maker of the statement which the trial judge chose not to believe. However issues have been raised as to whether or not it is appropriate for such an application to be made in these circumstances and, if an application can be made, whether the trial judge should hear it.[9]

---

6   CPR 22.1 and accompanying practice direction and Pt 32, practice direction, para 20.
7   CPR 32.14.
8   (2000) Times, 17 February.
9   See the commentary to CPR 32.14 in *Commercial Court Procedure* (2nd edn).

F Hearsay evidence

Pursuant to the Civil Evidence Act 1995 a more relaxed approach is now taken towards hearsay evidence at trial. Hearsay evidence, including multiple hearsay, can be relied upon at trial provided notice has been given and the evidence would not be inadmissible for reasons other than hearsay, for example because it consists of opinion evidence or relates to any matter which is scandalous, irrelevant or otherwise oppressive. The Act applies to all proceedings commenced on or after 31 January 1997 and to proceedings commenced before that date unless, prior to 26 April 1999, directions were given or orders made as to the evidence to be given at trial or the trial had begun.[10]

CPR 33.2 simplifies the notice requirements for hearsay evidence. It provides that where a party intends to rely on hearsay evidence at trial and the evidence is to be given by a witness giving oral evidence or the evidence is contained in a witness statement of a person not being called to give evidence, a party will comply with the notice provisions contained in the Civil Evidence Act 1995, s 2(1)(a) simply by serving a witness statement on the other parties to the proceedings in accordance with the court's order.[11]

Where the hearsay evidence is contained in a witness statement, at the same time as the witness statement is served, the party intending to rely on the hearsay evidence must inform the other parties to the proceedings that the witness will not be giving oral evidence at trial and state reasons why the witness is not being called.[12] CPR 33.2 (3) states that in order to rely on hearsay evidence in all other cases a party must serve a notice on the other parties which identifies the hearsay evidence, states that the party intends to rely on that evidence and give the reasons why the witness will not be called. Pursuant to CPR 33.2(4) the notice must be served no later than the latest date for serving the witness statement.

Under the Civil Evidence Act 1995 it is possible for a notice to be served after the witness statement has been served and for the hearsay evidence still to be admissible. However, given the court's power to control or exclude otherwise admissible evidence under CPR 32.1 it would be unwise to delay service of a notice for tactical reasons. At best the court may decide to adjourn the proceedings or impose cost penalties. At worst the evidence may be excluded completely.

As a matter of good practice as soon as a party is aware that a witness will not or may not be able to give evidence at trial, that party should serve notice on the other party to the proceedings and apply to the court for directions at the next case management conference or pre-trial review as appropriate.

The court may, upon the application of the other party to the proceedings, permit the maker of a statement containing hearsay evidence to be cross-

---

10 CPR Pt 33, and practice direction thereto.
11 CPR 33.2 sets out the circumstances in which a notice of intention to rely on hearsay evidence is not required.
12 CPR 33.2.

examined on the contents of his statement. This application must be made within 14 days after the day on which the notice of intention to rely on hearsay evidence is served on the party. Provision also exists within the CPR to attack the credibility of the maker of the hearsay statement.[13] Notice of intention to do so must again be given within 14 days of the date on which the party was served with the hearsay notice.

G   Witness summaries

Where a party is unable to obtain a signed witness statement from a witness for use at trial a party may apply for permission to serve a witness summary. The summary should consist of the evidence, if known, or the matters about which the witness will be questioned at trial. A witness summary must be served at the same time as a witness statement, unless the court orders otherwise, and is subject to the same requirements as to form and amplification of evidence as witness statements. A witness summary is most likely to be used where a witness is unwilling to sign a statement but the party still anticipates calling the witness to give evidence at trial.[14]

H   Service of witness statements and summaries

Pursuant to CPR 32.4 the court will order a party to serve on the other parties to the proceedings the witness statements or summaries of the oral evidence upon which it intends to rely at trial.[15] Failure to serve a witness statement or summary within the time specified by the court (or as agreed by minor variation between the parties) will result in the witness not being called to give oral evidence unless the court gives permission.[16] However, the court has a general discretion to extend the time for complying with any court order for service of witness statements or summaries.[17]

There have been a number of cases to date involving the late service of witness evidence.

For example, in *Rose Stroh v London Borough of Haringey*[18] the Court of Appeal (Brooke and Walker LJJ) upheld the order of Judge Knight QC in a personal injury action at the Central London County Court and prevented a defendant

---

13   CPR 33.5.
14   CPR 32.9.
15   The parties can agree minor variations to the date for exchange of witness statements or witness summaries as long as this does not affect the pre-trial timetable.
16   CPR 32.10. It is still possible to rely on the witness statement as hearsay evidence under the Civil Evidence Act 1995. Although notice of intention to rely on hearsay evidence should be given no later than the date by which witness statements must be served, failure to do so does not render the statement inadmissible. See the Civil Evidence Act 1995, s 2(4).
17   CPR 3.1(2)(a).
18   (13 July 1999, unreported).

from adducing the evidence of four witnesses served on the claimant only two weeks before trial on the ground that the prejudice to the claimant outweighed the prejudice to the defendant.

In contrast, in *Mealey Horgan plc v Horgan*[19] Buckley J held that it would be unjust to exclude a party from adducing evidence at trial save in very extreme circumstances. Examples cited by Buckley J included deliberate flouting of court orders or inexcusable delay. In the instant case a defendant who had served witness statements two weeks late, but still six weeks before trial, was given permission under CPR 32.10 for the witnesses to give oral evidence.

In *Cowland and Kendrick v District Judges of The West London County Court*[20] the Court of Appeal (Lord Woolf MR, Brooke and Walker LJJ) allowed an appeal from the decision of Mr Assistant Recorder Sycamore in the Manchester County Court in which he had refused the claimants' application for leave to adduce evidence on the morning of the trial. The Court of Appeal held that the defendants had not been prejudiced by the application but that the claimants had been prevented from adducing evidence which was crucial to their case, which prevented justice from being done. Furthermore, in *Dean v Dean*[1] Jacob J held on appeal from an order of Master Bowles that the strike out sanction for breach of procedural rules where there was late compliance (in this case the failure to serve a witness statement) had to be exercised with care.

Although on balance these cases suggest that the court will be extremely unwilling to deprive a party from relying on oral evidence at trial because the party failed to serve its witness statements on time, parties should still do everything in their power to comply with the court prescribed deadline for serving witness statements. As soon as it appears that it will be impossible for a party to do so, an application should be made to the court for a case management conference to determine with the court the time period in which witness statements might be served.

I Use of witness statements and affidavits to support interlocutory applications

As a general rule it is no longer necessary to file affidavits as evidence in support of interlocutory applications unless required by the court, a provision contained in a rule or a practice direction or any other enactment. Instead witness statements, application notices or statements of case verified by statements of truth are to be used.[2]

When preparing evidence in support of an interlocutory application consideration should be given as to whether it is necessary to prepare a

---

19 (1999) Times, 6 July, QBD.
20 (20 July 1999, unreported).
1   (19 November 1999, unreported), Ch D.
2   CPR 32.6.

witness statement in support and not simply deal with the application by way of an application notice or statement of case. For example, if a witness statement is produced consisting of legal argument in support of an application to strike out there may be a risk that the court regards the production of the witness statement as unnecessary with the result that the costs of its preparation may not be recovered even if the party is successful in its application.

The Commercial Court has adopted something of a halfway house in relation to interlocutory applications and still allows evidence to be given by affidavit as well as by witness statement, application notice or statement of case verified by statement of truth except where the practice direction supplementing CPR Pt 32 requires evidence to be by affidavit only (for example in relation to applications for freezing orders).[3] The form and content of affidavits is governed by CPR Pt 32 and the accompanying practice direction.

J   Use of witness summons

In advance of trial a party may issue a witness summons requiring a party to attend court to give evidence. The summons is usually binding on the witness if it is served at least seven days before the witness is required to attend although the court does have the power to vary or set aside a witness summons under CPR 34.3(4).[4] The procedure is not suitable however where a witness is resident out of the jurisdiction. Instead the letter of request procedure contained in CPR 34.13 should be used.

K   Giving evidence at trial

A party who has served a witness statement and intends to rely on the evidence of that witness at trial must call the witness to give oral evidence or state that the evidence is being put in as hearsay unless the court orders otherwise.[5] Where a witness is called to give oral evidence his witness statement will usually stand as his evidence in chief.[6] If a party who has served a witness statement does not call the witness to give evidence at trial or does not serve a hearsay notice in relation to it, any other party may put the witness statement in as hearsay evidence.[7] Under the CPR once a witness statement has been served, the party serving it no longer has the option not to rely on

---

3   Commercial Court Guide, Section F6.1.
4   See also *Harrison v Bloom* [1999] 45 LS Gaz R 32.
5   CPR 32.5(1).
6   Unless the court orders otherwise under CPR 32.5(2). The Commercial Court Guide states at Section H1.7 that in an appropriate case the trial judge *may require* the whole or any part of a witness's evidence to be given orally.
7   CPR 32.5(5). In the Commercial Court prompt notice of the decision not to call a witness whose witness statement has been served including whether or not it is intended to put the statement as hearsay evidence should be given to all other parties. See Commercial Court Guide, Section H1.9.

that evidence at trial and at the same time prevent other parties from using the evidence.

As part of the court's powers of case management, parties to proceedings will usually be subject to a pre-set timetable for trial and in fast track cases each party will be given a limited period in which to present its evidence.[8] Cross-examination of a witness's evidence is also likely to be restricted.[9] In multi-track cases however, much will depend on the size and complexity of the case as to whether or not the court considers it appropriate to restrict the evidence which the parties will give, including limiting the cross-examination of witnesses. In the Chancery Guide specific provision is made for the court to fix limits for oral submissions, speeches and the examination and cross-examination of witnesses at any time,[10] however the Commercial Court Guide is silent on this point. As discussed above, when exercising powers to restrict evidence at trial, the courts need to be aware of potential human rights arguments which may be raised by parties who consider that they have been deprived of their right to a fair trial under Art 6(1) of the European Convention on Human Rights.

1 Amplification of evidence

In order to avoid the problems of over-drafting of witness statements Lord Woolf recommended that a witness should be allowed to give evidence at trial which was not contained in a witness statement provided that admitting it would not cause injustice to any other party. This recommendation has now been implemented by CPR 32.5 which provides that a witness may amplify upon his statement or raise new matters since his statement was served, but only where the courts consider that there is good reason to do so. As a matter of caution however a witness should not expect to be able to amplify or add to his evidence at trial.

This practice is discouraged in any event in the Commercial Court, which requires that a witness serve a supplemental statement where the witness intends to materially add to or alter his earlier served statement[11] and in the Chancery Division of the High Court which recommends that a supplementary witness statement should be prepared where practicable.[12]

As a matter of best practice in either of these specialist lists, a party should consider serving a supplemental statement where a witness wishes to add to, alter, correct or retract the contents of an earlier statement. It may also be appropriate to serve a supplemental statement to deal with a peripheral issue which has assumed greater importance as the proceedings have progressed or to deal with significant amendments to statements of case after witness statements have been exchanged. The court's permission will be required to

8   CPR Pt 28, practice direction, Appendix.
9   CPR 32.1(3).
10 Chancery Guide, para 9.3. See also Mercantile Courts Guide, para 8.
11 Commercial Court Guide, Section H1.8.
12 Chancery Guide, para 9.12.

serve the supplemental statement and this should be sought at the earliest opportunity.

2   *Giving evidence by video link or other means*

CPR 32.3 provides that witness evidence may now be given by video link or other means. An application will usually be made at the case management conference or, if later, as soon as it becomes known that a witness will not be able to attend the trial. There has been no real guidance as to what is meant by giving evidence by other means although it could conceivably include giving evidence by telephone or email. The courts have already shown a willingness to allow evidence to be given by video link where witnesses are located abroad or are otherwise unable to attend the court room to give oral evidence. Such orders have been made notwithstanding concerns that it is not possible to cross-examine as effectively or that the court can not observe the demeanour of witnesses as easily where credibility issues are raised. For example, in *Yamaichi International Europe Ltd v Anthony*,[13] a case concerning allegations of dishonesty and forgery, Douglas Brown J held, dismissing an appeal, that it was possible for a judge to decide issues of credibility using a live video link and although there were some difficulties with cross examination when using the link it should be used when in the interests of justice.

The Commercial Court is keen to allow oral evidence to be given by video link in appropriate cases and guidance is given in the Commercial Court Guide on its use.[14]

---

13 (22 April 1999, unreported), QBD. In this case however the judge considered that the witnesses who had sought to give evidence by video link had only given evidence of their temporary incapacity to attend at trial and that as a result the listing judge should be provided with the availability of the witnesses for an adjourned trial date.
14 Commercial Court Guide, Section H3 and Appendix 15.

9 EXPERT EVIDENCE

A Introduction

One of the major planks of the civil justice reforms has been the changes introduced in relation to expert evidence. In his Interim and Final Reports Lord Woolf criticised heavily the use of expert evidence in civil litigation.[1] In particular, Lord Woolf commented that 'two of the major generators of unnecessary cost in civil litigation were uncontrolled discovery and expert evidence'[2] and that 'experts sometimes take on the role of partisan advocates instead of neutral fact finders or opinion givers.'[3]

In the light of these criticisms, Lord Woolf considered that the court should have complete control over the calling of expert evidence and that there:

'should be no expert evidence at all unless it will help the court, and no more than one expert in any one speciality unless this is necessary for some real purpose'.[4]

Moreover, the function of the expert should be to assist the court; he should be impartial and independent and this should override any duty which he owes to his client.[5]

Lord Woolf also suggested that there should be greater use of single experts to determine matters of expert evidence in dispute between parties. Whilst he accepted that

'there are in all areas some large, complex and strongly-contested cases where the full adversarial system, including oral cross-examination of opposing experts on particular issues, is the best way of producing a just result. That will apply particularly to issues on which there are several tenable schools of thought, or where the boundaries of knowledge are being extended. It does not, however, apply to all cases.'[6]

Lord Woolf considered that:

'as a general principle, single experts should be used wherever the case (or the issue) is concerned with a substantially established area of knowledge and where it is not necessary for the court directly to sample a range of opinions.'[7]

1 See Final Report, Section III, Chapter 13 and Interim Report, Section V, Chapter 23.
2 Final Report, Section III, Chapter 13, para 1.
3 Final Report, Section III, Chapter 13, para 5.
4 Final Report, Section III, Chapter 13, para 11.
5 Final Report, Section III, Chapter 13, para 29.
6 Final Report, Section III, Chapter 13, para 19.
7 Final Report, Section III, Chapter 13, para 19.

Lord Woolf's recommendations have largely been implemented by the CPR and these are discussed further in this chapter. In addition this chapter considers how the civil justice reforms are working in practice in this area.

B   The role of the expert

'Expert' for the purpose of the CPR refers to an expert who has been instructed to give or prepare evidence for the purpose of court proceedings.[8] Accordingly, an expert whose instructions never include giving or preparing evidence for court proceedings, and whose role is confined to advising a party on the strengths or weaknesses of a particular issue in dispute, will not be subject to CPR Pt 35. This distinction is recognised in the revised draft code of guidance for experts prepared by a working party chaired by Sir Louis Blom-Cooper of the Expert Witness Institute.[9] It is understood that the revised draft code of guidance for experts is currently with the Vice Chancellor, Sir Richard Scott, for consideration. It may be subject to further revision and possibly another consultation process. The current form of the revised draft code of guidance seeks to apply to all disputes, both prior to and after the commencement of litigation. It even seeks to regulate the private relationship between a client and his expert adviser outside the litigation process.[10] There have been suggestions that the code of guidance for experts, when in its final form, will be given the same status as a practice direction. If this is the case, there will be sanctions, such as costs penalties for failure to comply with the code.

In the light of the distinction referred to above there may be an increase in the number of experts instructed in relation to a dispute, particularly for high value disputes. For example, each party may instruct an expert adviser to give initial advice on the merits of a case at the pre-action stage and/or to assist in the preparation of statements of case as part of early case analysis or to assist in early ADR. This will be important to enable the party to comply with its pre-action obligations and to meet the tight deadlines imposed by the CPR and the court once proceedings are commenced. If the parties subsequently agree or the court orders that it is appropriate to use a single joint expert, neither of the experts initially retained by the parties on an advisory basis is likely to be a suitable candidate for the single joint expert.[11] Instead a new expert who is seen to be independent from both parties is likely to be appointed as the single joint expert. Each party is likely to continue to instruct his initial expert to shadow the single joint expert, perhaps assisting in drafting instructions or written questions, identifying points for cross-examination or providing advice in the event of settlement discussions or ADR. However, this will inevitably increase costs and the costs of the expert adviser are unlikely to be recovered.[12]

8   CPR 35.2.
9   Revised draft code of guidance for experts, dated 11 January 2000, para 1.
10 For example, the revised draft code of guidance appears to attempt to apply some CPR Pt 35 duties to those who are never more than advisers.
11 Revised draft code of guidance for experts, para 30d.
12 Again this is reflected in the revised draft code of guidance for experts, para 30c.

The number of experts retained in a dispute may increase further if each party is allowed separate experts to give evidence in court. In this situation, if a party wishes to retain his expert in an advisory capacity to advise on the merits, in addition to acting as an expert witness to the court, the current version of the revised draft code of guidance for experts states that the expert witness's overriding duty to the court renders any relevant 'advice' given by the expert, including that given pre-litigation, disclosable.[13] To avoid the risk of having to disclose their expert's advice on the merits of their case, each party may instruct yet another expert, this time as an expert witness, to give evidence to the court. Again, if this approach is adopted, it will increase costs substantially, with the expert adviser's costs being unlikely to be recovered. Any suggestion that a client might appoint a team of experts from within the same organisation with different people within the team being appointed to act solely as expert adviser or solely as expert witness may not be well-received by the courts given the recent concerns which have been expressed as to the ability to effectively preserve Chinese walls within, for example the litigation support services department of an accountancy firm.[14] These issues will be discussed further below.

C The court's duty to restrict expert evidence

Pursuant to CPR 35.1 expert evidence should be restricted to that which is reasonably required to resolve the proceedings. This forms part of the court's general power to control evidence contained in CPR 32.1.[15] When exercising its power to restrict expert evidence the court must act in accordance with the overriding objective contained in CPR 1.1 of dealing with cases justly.

Pursuant to CPR 35.4 no party may call an expert or use an expert's report in evidence unless the court's permission has been obtained and where the court gives such permission it will only be in relation to the expert named or the field of expert evidence identified by the party.[16]

When exercising its powers of case management[17] the court will usually limit the number of experts who may be called to give evidence at trial, or direct that evidence be given by a single joint expert. In both fast track and

---

13 Revised draft code of guidance for experts, para 3. If this provision is implemented in its current form there is an argument that an order to disclose 'advice' might be subject to challenge under Art 8 of the European Convention on Human Rights in light of Toulson J's comments in *General Mediterranean Holdings SA v Patel & Patel* [1999] 3 All ER 673, [2000] 1 WLR 272. This is discussed in more detail later in this chapter. 'Advice' is defined in para 2 of the revised draft code of guidance for experts as 'things said and done (including any draft report) by the expert outwith the litigation process' ie before Pt 35 comes into play, on the grounds that the 'advice' attracts legal professional privilege/ litigation privilege; the 'advice' would not be disclosable.

14 *Prince Jefri Bolkiah v KPMG (a firm)* [1999] 2 AC 222, [1999] 1 All ER 517, HL.

15 Pursuant to CPR 32.1 the court may control the issues on which it requires evidence, the nature of the evidence and the way in which it is to be placed before the court. This includes expert evidence. See Chapter 8 on witness evidence.

16 CPR 35.4(2) and (3).

17 See also Chapter 6 on case management.

multi-track cases (save for in the Commercial Court) there is a stated presumption in favour of using single joint experts.[18] The court's power to order that evidence be given by a single joint expert is a vital tool in enabling the court to restrict expert evidence to that which is reasonably necessary. This is discussed further below.

The court may also direct that expert evidence be given in relation to a particular issue which, if determined in advance of other issues, may be dispositive of the case. For example, the Technology and Construction Court has made such orders.

In exercising its duty to restrict expert evidence the court will also require the parties to cooperate with each other. For example, the court may order a party which has access to information which is not reasonably available to another party to prepare and file a document recording that information, including sufficient details of all facts, tests and assumptions which underlie the information and serve a copy of that document on the other party.[19]

Parties can expect the courts to scrutinise carefully applications for permission to use expert evidence and there have already been a number of cases which demonstrate the court's willingness to restrict its use. For example, in *Skandia Property (UK) Ltd v Thames Water Utilities Ltd*,[20] a case involving damage by escape of water, the court considered that the advice of an expert was 'a highly significant factor' in testing the reasonableness of an assumption of damage which was 'accessible and inspectable' but 'simple reliance...on an expert could not be the test'.

In *Gumpo v Church of Scientology Religious Education College Inc*[1] the claimant requested expert evidence from a psychiatrist in the context of a claim for the tort of intimidation and breach of contract of employment arising out of the same circumstances. Smedley J overturned a decision by a Master to allow evidence not in relation to psychiatric injury but on whether the employment regime alleged by the claimant would intimidate the reasonable man. On appeal it was held that the issue was a question of fact and in determining it:

> 'the judge would obtain little, if any, advantage from having the views of a psychiatrist expressed on that issue. If that be right then clearly the cost of calling psychiatric evidence would also be out of all proportion to the advantage which the judge would gain from hearing it'.

Orders have been made restricting the use of expert evidence in the Chancery and Queen's Bench Divisions and in the Technology and Construction Court (although in the latter such orders were also being made before the

---

18 See CRP 35.7, Pt 28, practice direction, para 3.9 and Pt 29, practice direction, paras 4.10 and 4.11. However see also Commercial Court Guide, Section H2.4.

19 CPR 35.9 and practice direction, para 2. However the courts need to be alive to the fact that a party may seek to challenge such an order under the Human Rights Act 1998 (when implemented in October 2000) on the basis that disclosure of the document is an infringement of the right to privacy under Art 8 of the European Convention on Human Rights.

20 [1999] BLR 338, CA.

1   (26 July 1999, unreported).

implementation of the civil justice reforms). In the Commercial Court too, expert evidence is now frequently limited in terms of the areas on which expert evidence will be admitted and orders for more than one expert per party per area have become rare. The Patents Court has also already warned that care should be taken before allowing expert evidence in registered design cases.[2]

However, when exercising its duty to restrict expert evidence the courts will soon need to consider potential human rights arguments which may be brought by disgruntled parties once the Human Rights Act 1998 is implemented in October 2000. In particular, parties may seek to argue that they have been deprived of their right to a fair trial under Art 6(1) of the European Convention on Human Rights as a result of the court's decision to restrict or exclude expert evidence.

D The expert's duty to the court

An expert has an overriding duty to the court to help on matters within his expertise. This duty overrides any obligation to the person who has instructed him or by whom he is paid.[3]

The rule contained in CPR 35.3 embodies the principles set out by Cresswell J in *The 'Ikarian Reefer'*.[4] These principles now form part of the Commercial Court Guide[5] and the Mercantile Court Guide[6] and have general application to Commercial Court cases (and Mercantile Court cases). The duties and responsibilities of expert witnesses in the Commercial and Mercantile Courts, are as follows:

'2. Expert evidence presented to the court should be, and should be seen to be, the independent product of the expert uninfluenced by the exigencies of litigation.

3. An expert witness should provide independent assistance to the court by way of objective unbiased opinion in relation to matters within his expertise. An expert witness should never assume the role of an advocate.

4. An expert witness should not omit to consider material facts which could detract from his concluded opinion.

5. An expert witness should make it clear when a particular question or issue falls outside his expertise.

6. If an expert's opinion is not properly researched because he considers that insufficient data is available, then this must be stated with an indication that the opinion is no more than a provisional one.

---

2 *Thermus v Aladdin Sales* (26 October 1999, unreported).
3 CPR 35.3.
4 [1993] Lloyd's Rep 58 at 81–82; see also the Court of Appeal decision at [1995] 1 Lloyd's Rep 455.
5 Commercial Court Guide, Appendix 12. See also Chancery Guide, paras 6.8 and 6.9 which emphasis the expert's duties to the court.
6 Mercantile Court Guide, Appendix B.

7. In a case where an expert witness who has prepared a report could not assert that the report contained the truth, the whole truth and nothing but the truth without some qualification, that qualification should be stated in the report.

8. If, after exchange of reports, an expert witness changes his view on a material matter having read the other side's expert's report or for any other reason, such change of view should be communicated (through legal representatives) to the other side without delay and when appropriate to the court.'

The revised draft code of guidance for experts also emphasises the expert's duty to the court, and in particular to maintain professional objectivity at all times.[7] However, it is submitted that all experts should adhere to the principles set out above, and that an expert should be made aware of these points at the outset of his retainer.[8]

The courts have already taken a strong line in ensuring that experts fully understand the duty which they owe to the court when giving or preparing evidence for court proceedings. For example, in *Stevens v Gullis (Pile, third party)*[9] the Court of Appeal upheld the decision of Judge Hywel Moseley QC made in the Cardiff County Court debarring the defendant's expert from giving evidence on the basis that the expert had demonstrated by his own conduct that he had no conception of the requirements placed on an expert under the CPR. In that case, although the expert had been ordered to produce a report which complied with the requirements set out in CPR Pt 35,[10] he had failed to do so.

In addition, in *Matthews v Tarmac Bricks & Tiles Ltd*[11] the Court of Appeal, (Lord Woolf MR) commented in the context of a personal injury case that experts holding themselves out as practising in the medico-legal field:

'...must be prepared to arrange their affairs to meet the commitments of the courts where this is practical.'

In that case the Court of Appeal upheld the decision of Judge Overend in the Plymouth County Court to fix a trial date notwithstanding that neither of the defendant's two experts were available. The Court of Appeal also criticised the defendant for failing to recognise the spirit behind CPR Pt 1 and for failing to provide the court with reasons for the expert's unavailability.

---

7   Revised draft code of guidance for experts, para 13. However, the Court of Appeal (Lord Woolf MR, Waller and May LJJ) held in *Field v Leeds City Council* (2000) Times, 18 January, that if an expert was properly qualified to give evidence, the fact that he was employed by one of the parties would not disqualify him from giving evidence.

8   Pursuant to the Commercial Court Guide, Section H2.9 these principles apply to all aspects of expert evidence, including experts reports, meetings of experts and oral expert evidence.

9   (1999) Times, 6 October.

10   CPR Pt 35, practice direction, para 1.2.

11   (1999) Times, 1 July.

E   Timetable for preparing expert evidence

1   *Fast track cases*

For fast track cases the criteria for allocation to that track is that the trial is likely to last for no more than one day and that oral expert evidence at trial will be restricted to one expert per party in relation to any expert field and expert evidence in two expert fields.[12] As a result, it is anticipated that expert evidence in fast track cases is likely to be limited.

Where the parties have agreed directions which are acceptable to the court, provision will usually be made for the use of a single joint expert or where this has not been agreed between the parties, the exchange and agreement of expert evidence. Experts' reports may be exchanged simultaneously or sequentially and there will usually be provision for without prejudice discussions between the experts.[13] If the court makes directions on its own initiative it will usually give directions for a single joint expert unless there is good reason not to do so.[14] However, where this is inappropriate, the court will direct disclosure of experts' reports by simultaneous exchange, for discussions to take place between the experts if the experts' reports are not agreed, and for the subsequent preparation of a report.[15] Where each party is to retain his own expert, a direction will usually be given requiring exchange of experts' reports within fourteen weeks of the date of the notice of allocation with trial taking place within thirty weeks.[16]

As discussed in Chapter 1 on pre-action tactics, a party is likely to have obtained preliminary expert advice prior to commencing proceedings. A preliminary expert report may even have been prepared and disclosed to the other party prior to commencement of proceedings or when serving statements of case. However the parties can not be certain whether or not they will be able to rely on expert evidence until the allocation stage when any directions agreed between the parties are approved by the court or the court makes directions of its own initiative. In view of the court's duty to restrict expert evidence coupled with the emphasis given to the use of single experts in fast track cases, the parties would be unwise to spend significant time and money instructing their own experts and obtaining reports prior to the allocation stage as any costs incurred may not be recovered, even if successful at trial.

However the tight timetable for fast track cases does present problems for the parties where the court directs that expert evidence, whether or not by a single expert, is to be given. Prior to the allocation stage the parties should therefore make every effort to agree the areas where they believe expert evidence will be required, to identify a single joint expert agreeable to both parties, or failing this, their own expert, and to ascertain that expert's availability for preparation of the report and attendance at trial.

12   CPR 26.6(4) and (5).
13   CPR Pt 28, practice direction, para 3.7.
14   CPR Pt 28, practice direction, para 3.9(4).
15   CPR Pt 28, practice direction, para 3.9(5).
16   CPR Pt 28, practice direction, para 3.12.

2   *Multi-track cases*

In multi-track cases the issue of expert evidence will usually be considered at the case management conference stage. As in fast track cases, the parties may agree directions for the use of a single joint expert or where this is not agreed, the exchange of expert evidence either simultaneously or sequentially, and for without prejudice discussions to take place between the experts.[17]

If those directions are not agreed by the court and the court decides to give directions of its own initiative without holding a case management conference the practice direction to CPR Pt 29 states that it will usually direct that a single joint expert give evidence on any appropriate issue unless there is good reason not to do so.[18] In practice however there are indications in the Technology and Construction Court and the Chancery and Queen's Bench Divisions that, a single joint expert is unlikely to be imposed on parties without their consent, unless for example, the court considers that the parties are behaving wholly unreasonably or the issues on which expert evidence is required are considered by the court to be on the periphery of the case and are not seen as controversial. However, as a halfway house, the Chancery Division has made orders requiring each party's expert to undertake a joint investigation and produce a joint report.

Where the court directs that each party may retain his own expert, a direction will usually be given that experts' reports be exchanged simultaneously[19] and that if experts' reports are not agreed, direct a discussion between the experts and the preparation of a statement. This is discussed further below. If expert evidence is required on both liability and quantum issues, the court may also direct that experts' reports on liability issues be exchanged simultaneously and those in relation to quantum, exchanged sequentially.[20]

Alternatively, a case management conference may be held. The court will consider what expert evidence is reasonably required and how and when that evidence is to be obtained and disclosed.[1] The parties will be required to identify at the case management conference the field or fields in which they wish to rely on expert evidence and where practicable, the expert in that field on whose evidence each party wishes to rely.[2] In addition, the party wishing to rely on expert evidence will need to state whether the expert's evidence is to be given orally or by report.

---

17   CPR Pt 29, practice direction, para 4.8. Part 29 and the practice direction thereto do not apply in the Commercial Court. The position in the Commercial Court is discussed further below.
18   CPR Pt 29, practice direction, para 4.10.
19   In an appropriate case the Chancery Division will direct that experts' reports are delivered sequentially. See Chancery Guide, para 6.15.
20   CPR Pt 29, practice direction, para 4.11.
1   CPR Pt 29, practice direction, para 5.3.
2   CPR 35.4(2) and Pt 29, practice direction, para 5.5. The court will not make an order permitting expert evidence to be used unless this can be stated in its order. The Chancery Division has also made orders on close of pleadings requiring the parties to prepare a document setting out the propositions of fact which each party wishes to establish by expert evidence thus ensuring the early identification of issues which are to be the subject of expert evidence.

In Commercial Court cases, applications for permission to call an expert witness or serve an expert's report should be made at the case management conference.[3] If permission is granted, at this stage the Commercial Court will also consider whether experts' reports should be exchanged sequentially rather than simultaneously.[4] In the Commercial Court there is no presumption in favour of the use of single joint experts.

Given the court's duty to restrict expert evidence to that which is reasonably required and the general presumption stated in the practice direction to CPR Pt 29, (save in the Commercial Court), that a single joint expert should be used unless it is unjust to do so, as a matter of caution, parties should think carefully before incurring significant costs instructing experts to prepare reports prior to obtaining the court's permission to use expert evidence. The CPR specifically warn that a party who obtains expert evidence before obtaining a direction that it may do so, is at risk as to costs, except where that evidence was obtained in compliance with a pre-action protocol.[5] However, where there is no applicable pre-action protocol but the parties act in accordance with paragraph 4 of the practice direction to protocols by exchanging information and documentation relating to the claim (including potentially the exchange of preliminary experts' reports) it is not clear at present whether the costs incurred in preparing such reports will be recoverable. Clarification is needed on this point.[6]

F   The single joint expert

As discussed above one of the key aspects of Lord Woolf's recommendations in relation to expert evidence was that the use of single joint experts should be encouraged where possible. Although the court had the power to appoint a single expert upon the application of one of the parties to proceedings under the old system this power was rarely used.[7] The position has now changed dramatically under the CPR with the court having the power to appoint a single joint expert on its own initiative.

Pursuant to CPR 35.7 where two or more parties wish to submit expert evidence on a particular issue, the court may direct that evidence on that issue be given by one expert only. If the parties cannot agree who should be the expert the court may select the expert from a list prepared or identified by the instructing parties or in such other manner as the court may direct. Where the court gives directions as to expert evidence on its own initiative, as discussed above, there is a stated presumption in favour of single joint experts in all fast track and multi-track cases,[8] except in relation to

3   Commercial Court Guide, Section H2.1.
4   Commercial Court Guide, Section H2.18 and Appendix 8.
5   CPR Pt 29, practice direction, para 5.5(2).
6   The recoverability of pre-action costs generally is currently being considered by the Civil Procedure Rule Committee.
7   RSC Ord 40.
8   See CPR Pt 28, practice direction, para 3.7 and Pt 29, practice direction, para 4.10.

Commercial Court cases.[9] Although the Commercial Court recognises that a direction for a single joint expert may be made in an appropriate case it suggests that such a direction may be made infrequently where both parties wish to instruct separate experts. Alternatively, the Commercial Court suggests that a single joint expert may be used to chair and facilitate meetings of separate experts.[10]

Where the court directs that evidence will be given by a single joint expert in relation to an issue but there are a number of disciplines relating to the issue, the court may direct that a leading expert in the dominant discipline be identified as the single expert. He will then prepare the general part of the report and be responsible for annexing or incorporating the contents of any reports from experts in other disciplines.[11] However use of this procedure will be infrequent in the Commercial Court and it will need to be persuaded before allowing evidence to be given other than directly by each expert in the relevant field or discipline.[12]

Experiences suggest that in many disputes the parties now actively consider either before the commencement of, or at an early stage in the proceedings, whether or not it is appropriate to appoint a single joint expert. Indeed the parties may soon be required to do so in some types of disputes if some of the draft pre-action protocols[13] come into force.[14]

To date there have been relatively few cases where the courts have made directions for single joint experts without the parties' consent. For example, in *Knight v Sage Group plc*[15] the Court of Appeal (Evans and Sedley LJJ) considered whether to direct that a joint expert be appointed to report on the claimant's medical condition in a personal injury case but decided not to do so as the defendant was unwilling.[16]

The lack of cases on this point is probably due, at least in part, to the parties' increased willingness to propose the use of single joint experts to the courts. As a general rule it appears that the courts will be sympathetic to the single joint expert approach where expert evidence is required on issues which are on the periphery of the case and which are not seen as being controversial. It has been suggested that a single joint expert might be appointed in the Technology and Construction Court where valuation issues are raised or where the Technology and Construction Court requires uncontroversial technical expert evidence for educational purposes. In the Queen's Bench Division a single joint expert might typically be appointed to assess the quantum of damages (for example, using accountancy expert evidence) provided that the amount of damages is not itself a central issue in the case.

---

9   Commercial Court Guide, Section H2.4.
10 Commercial Court Guide, Section H2.6.
11 CPR Pt 35, practice direction, para 5.
12 Commercial Court Guide, Section H2.7.
13 See Chapter 1 on pre-action tactics.
14 See for example, the draft pre-action protocol on debt claims.
15 (28 April 1999, unreported).
16 See also *S (A Minor) v Birmingham Health Authority* (23 November 1999, unreported), in which Curtis J held that the order of District Judge Marsh that the parties jointly instruct a medical expert was premature having regard to the stage reached in the case.

The Chancery Guide suggests that the fact the parties have already instructed their own experts will not necessarily be a sufficient objection to the court making an order for a single joint expert. In particular it recognises that where a single expert is appointed the parties may also wish to instruct their own experts to advise the party although the party may be unable to recover the costs of employing their own expert if successful at trial.[17]

Although the Commercial Court has stated that orders for single joint experts will be infrequently made in the Commercial Court, parties can expect such orders to be made by the court where expert evidence is required on issues such as quantum, foreign law and share valuations. This approach has already been confirmed by the Court of Appeal in *North Holdings Ltd v Southern Tropics Ltd*,[18] a case involving the valuation of shares. In addition, a single joint expert might also be appointed where it is agreed by the court and the parties that there is one individual with outstanding expertise.

Lord Woolf's recommendation that single joint experts be used where possible was intended, at least in part, to save costs. In practice this may not happen as parties are likely to appoint their own experts to shadow the single joint expert. Indeed this practice has already been recognised in the Chancery Guide and the revised draft code of guidance for experts. The costs of the shadow expert or expert adviser are unlikely to be recovered from the other party even if successful at trial.

However, if a party or the court proposes that a single joint expert be used, the party or parties resisting the appointment of the single joint expert may face an uphill task. For this reason the party proposing a single joint expert may gain a tactical advantage by doing so, particularly if he succeeds in getting his nominated expert appointed as single joint expert.[19] Following the comments made by Lord Woolf in his Final Report[20] a party is unlikely to be successful in resisting such a proposal unless it can be argued that the case is large and complex, that there are several tenable schools of thought on the issue which is to be the subject of expert evidence or that the boundaries of knowledge are being extended.

At present there is very little guidance as to how the parties and the court should manage a single joint expert once he has been appointed and the revised draft code of guidance provides little assistance on this point. For example, at present the revised draft code of guidance for experts deals with issues such as the payment of the single joint expert's fees, ensuring that advice given by a single joint expert to a party is copied to all parties and that if a single joint expert is invited to attend a conference with counsel, an opportunity is given to solicitors for the other parties to attend also.[1] Guidance is needed however on a whole range of issues such as dealing with conflicting instructions given to the single joint expert, requests by the single

---

17 Chancery Guide, para 6.13. See also the revised draft code of guidance, para 30b and c.
18 [1999] 2 BCLC 625, [1999] BCC 746, CA.
19 However, any expert proposed by a party should not ordinarily have given advice in the case. See revised draft code of guidance for experts at para 30d.
20 Final Report, Section III, Chapter 13, para 19.
1   Revised draft code of guidance, para 30 e and f.

joint expert for disclosure of additional documentation or to interview the claimant or defendant for additional information.

Finally in the context of single joint experts, human rights arguments may well be raised by parties under the Human Rights Act 1998 (when implemented in October 2000) who claim that their right to a fair trial under Art 6(1) of the European Convention on Human Rights has been infringed if the court decides to appoint a single joint expert without the consent of the parties.

G   Instructing experts

1   *Instructing the expert adviser*

As discussed above, a party may retain an expert to act solely in an advisory capacity, in which case the expert adviser owes a duty to his client. The terms of his appointment should be agreed at the outset and the revised draft code of guidance for experts sets out proposals as to what this should include.[2] A pro forma letter of instruction is at Appendix M.

If it is envisaged that an expert adviser may subsequently be appointed to act as an expert witness in court proceedings the instructing party should draw this possibility to the expert's attention at the outset of his appointment as an adviser. He should also be reminded that in the event that he is appointed as expert witness he will have an overriding duty to the court. The revised draft code of guidance for experts specifically contemplates the possibility that an expert adviser may subsequently be appointed as an expert witness.[3] At that stage the recommended approach is that the expert be given a fresh letter of appointment setting out his new terms of reference and his instructions. (See for example the pro forma letter of appointment of an expert witness at Appendix N.) However the expert witness is unlikely to continue to act also in an advisory capacity, particularly in high value or evidentially contentious cases, given the fact that if he does so the revised draft code of guidance for experts recommends that his overriding duty to the court as an expert witness renders any relevant 'advice' given by him, including that given pre-litigation disclosable.[4]

Whilst instructions given to an expert retained to advise on the merits of the case are privileged this does not apply to instructions given to an expert retained to give evidence to the court.[5] This is discussed further below. Concerns have been raised as to whether privileged or confidential documents or information disclosed to an expert in his capacity as expert adviser retain their privilege if that expert adviser is subsequently retained as an expert witness to give or prepare expert evidence for the court. The

---

2   Revised draft code of guidance for experts, paras 5–9.
3   Revised draft code of guidance for experts, para 3.
4   Revised draft code of guidance for experts, para 3. See also comments on p 125 at fn 14. There is also an argument that an expert witness's overriding duty to the court is inconsistent with him continuing to act at the same time for a party as an expert adviser.
5   CPR 35.10(4), practice direction, para 3.

answer may differ from case to case and may depend on the basis on which the expert was first instructed as adviser and then later as expert witness.[6] At present the revised draft code of guidance for experts does not deal with this point, however clarification is certainly needed on this.

2 Instructing the expert witness

When instructing an expert to give or prepare evidence for court proceedings, it is extremely important to check that the witness will be available to attend trial. If he is not able to attend the court may be reluctant to vacate trial dates which have already been set as a result of the expert's unavailability.[7] However a party will need to be armed with this information at the case management conference before the court has given the party permission to rely on expert evidence. It is suggested therefore that the party retains the expert prior to the case management conference in order to obtain this information and to obtain preliminary soundings from him. However if he obtains expert evidence prior to a direction being given from the court he does so at his own risk as to costs.[8] Once the court has given permission for the expert to give evidence this can be followed up with a formal letter of appointment. Again the revised draft code of guidance sets out proposals as to what this should include.[9] A pro forma letter of appointment is at Appendix N.

Instructions to an expert witness must be clear and the revised draft code of guidance suggests that if clear instructions are not received the expert witness should indicate that he is not prepared to act unless and until clear instructions are received.[10] An alternative course of action might be for the expert witness to make a written request to the court for directions under CPR 35.14. Save in the Commercial Court, this can be made without giving notice to the instructing party.[11] Where the court gives directions it may also direct that a party be served with the copy of the directions together with a copy of the request. These will then form part of the expert's instructions.

Pursuant to CPR 35.10(4) instructions to experts (whether oral or in writing) are no longer protected by privilege and the substance of an expert's instructions must be summarised in his report. The court will not however allow an expert to be cross-examined on the contents of his instructions unless the court permits it or the party who has given instructions to the expert consents to it. Permission will not normally be given for cross-

6   See for example the pro forma letter of appointment at Appendix N.
7   *Linda Rollinson v Kimberley Clark Ltd* (1999) Times, 22 June, CA. See also *Matthews v Tarmac Brick & Tiles* (1999) Times, 1 July, CA, discussed above.
8   CPR Pt 29, practice direction, para 5.5(2).
9   Revised draft code of guidance, paras 5–9.
10 Revised draft code of guidance for experts, para 10.
11 CPR 35.14. See also Chancery Guide, para 6.20. However if notice is not given to the instructing party and the court does not give the instructing party an opportunity to make representations in relation to the expert's request for directions, objections might be raised under the Human Rights Act 1998 on the basis that there has been an infringement of the right to a fair trial under Art 6(1) of the European Convention on Human Rights. In the Commercial Court notice must be given to the party who has instructed him to avoid the risk of an expert accidentally disclosing privileged or confidential information. See Commercial Court Guide, Section H2.16. and 2.17.

examination unless the court is satisfied that there are reasonable grounds to consider that the statement in the expert's report as to the substance of the instructions is inaccurate or incomplete and it is in the interests of justice to allow cross-examination.[12] This provision may be subject to challenge in the light of the decision of Toulson J in *General Mediterranean Holdings SA v Patel & Patel*.[13] In that case Toulson J held in the Commercial Court that an application to disclose privileged documents for the purpose of determining whether a wasted costs order should be made was ultra vires. Toulson J also held that even if it was intra vires the defendant had a right to confidentiality under Art 8 of the European Convention on Human Rights and that the right to a fair trial under Art 6(1) did not give a right to interfere with another person's right to legal confidentiality. Although Toulson J expressed the view that CPR 35.10 did not seem to infringe a person's substantive right to legal confidentiality, but was a matter of procedure, the point did not arise for decision in the case and Toulson J's views remain obiter. Until this point is clarified the parties need to be aware that privileged or confidential documentation or information given to an expert witness as part of his instructions may be potentially disclosable.

3   *Instructing the single joint expert*

When instructing a single joint expert the expert must be informed at the outset if the court has given a direction that his fees or expenses are to be limited[14] so that the expert can decide whether to accept the appointment on the terms which are proposed. Given that all instructing parties are jointly and severally liable for payment of the expert's fees[15] a single joint expert should try to agree identical terms with all parties.

Pursuant to CPR 35.8 where the court directs the use of a single joint expert, each party may give instructions to the expert. At the same time as sending instructions to the expert the instructing party must send a copy of the instructions to the other instructing parties.[16]

The parties will be expected to cooperate in developing and agreeing terms of reference for a single joint expert as far as possible. The terms of reference should state what the expert is being asked to do, identify any documentary material the expert is being asked to consider and specify any assumptions the expert is being asked to make.[17] Care should be taken to ensure that no privileged or confidential information is disclosed to the single joint expert as part of his instructions.

Very little guidance has been given to the parties, or the single joint expert, as to how to deal with the more difficult issues which may arise when instructing a single joint expert such as how to deal with conflicting instructions or no instructions or with amended or supplementary instructions. At present

---

12 CPR Pt 35, practice direction, para 3.
13 [1999] 3 All ER 673, [2000] 1 WLR 272.
14 CPR 35.8(4).
15 CPR 35.8(5).
16 CPR 35.8(2).
17 Commercial Court Guide, Section H2.8 and Chancery Guide, para 6.14. See also the revised draft code of guidance for experts, paras 9, 10 and 29.

the single joint expert may make a written request to the court for directions or the parties may apply to the court for directions perhaps by requesting a case management conference. However if the single joint expert (or the parties) resort to either of these procedures whenever a difficulty of the type described above arises this may lead to a disproportionate amount of time being spent by the courts on cases involving single joint experts. Guidance is needed as to how the parties and the single joint expert should deal with these issues without always having to apply to the court. This could be included within the code of guidance for experts.

H Form and content of the expert's report

Where the court permits expert evidence to be used under CPR 35.4 the court will require that evidence be given in a written report unless it directs otherwise.[18]

Rule 35.10 and the accompanying practice direction[19] set out what an expert's report, including a report prepared by a single joint expert, must contain.

The report must contain the following:
- it must be addressed to the court;
- details of the expert's qualifications and details of any materials upon which the expert has relied when making the report;
- where tests or experiments have been carried out state who performed them, giving the qualifications of that person and state whether or not they were carried out under the expert's supervision;
- where there is a range of opinion on matters dealt with in the report summarise the range of opinion and give reasons for the expert's own opinion;
- a summary of the conclusions reached;
- a statement setting out the substance of all material instructions (whether written or oral) on the basis of which the report was written;[20]
- summarise the facts and instructions given to the expert which are material to the opinions expressed in his report or upon which his opinions are based;[1] in the Commercial Court where any of the facts stated are within the expert's direct knowledge this should be made clear and where any stated assumptions are also in the opinion of the expert unreasonable or unlikely, this should also be stated;[2]
- be verified by a statement of truth signed by the expert in which he confirms that he understands his duty to the court and that he has complied with that duty.[3]

---

18 In the Commercial Court an order will usually be made for an expert to give oral evidence. See Commercial Court Guide, Appendix 8.
19 CPR Pt 35, practice direction, paras 1.1–1.6. See also revised draft code of guidance for experts, paras 15–18.
20 CPR 35.10(3).
1 CPR 35.10(3) and practice direction, para 1.2(8).
2 Commercial Court Guide, Section H2.12.
3 CPR 35.10(2) and Pt 35, practice direction, para 1.4.

A different form of statement of truth to that contained in CPR Pt 35, practice direction, para 1.4 must be signed by the expert in Commercial Court cases.[4] Both forms of wording are at Appendix O. It is submitted that the Commercial Court statement of truth wording is to be preferred, as it reflects the fact that the expert's opinion may be based on assumptions whose accuracy he may not be able to verify.

Proceedings for contempt of court may be brought against an expert who makes a false statement in a report verified by a statement of truth without an honest belief in its truth.[5]

One of the major concerns arising from the civil justice reforms is the loss of privilege over instructions to experts as a result of the requirement contained in CPR 35.10(3) that an expert disclose in his report the substance of all material instructions on the basis of which his report is written. As discussed earlier this may be subject to challenge in the light of *General Mediterranean Holdings SA v Patel & Patel*. However, in any event, an expert will not be required to give inspection of his instructions (nor will the court permit questioning on those instructions) unless the court is satisfied that there are reasonable grounds to consider that the statement of instructions given in the report is inaccurate or incomplete.[6]

Failure by a party to disclose an expert's report will result in the party being unable to use the report at trial or to call the expert to give evidence orally unless the court otherwise gives permission.[7] The courts have already taken a tough line in relation to compliance with the provisions as to form and content of an expert's report in *Stevens v Gullis* discussed above. A similar approach has been taken by the Court of Appeal in *Baron v Lovell* in relation to a defendant's failure to properly disclose his expert's report in a personal injury case.[8] In that case, Brooke LJ upheld the decision of Judge Hamilton in the Luton County Court which had the effect of preventing the defendant from calling his expert evidence. However, where a party is late in serving his expert's report but applies for an extension of time this may be granted if the court considers that it is proportionate to do so.[9]

I   Written questions to experts

Once an expert has served his report a party may put to the expert (including to a single joint expert) written questions about his report. The questions may be put once only within 28 days of service of the expert's report and must be for clarification purposes only unless the court gives permission or

---

4   Commercial Court Guide, Section H2.14–2.15. A similar form of wording also appears in the Mercantile Courts Guide.
5   CPR 32.14.
6   An expert will however be required to give inspection of any documents referred to in his report other than his instructions. See CPR 31.14(e) and Commercial Court Guide, Section H2.29.
7   CPR 35.13.
8   (1999) Times, 14 September.
9   *Kevin Newton v Dorset Travel Service Ltd* (5 May 1999, unreported), CA.

the other party agrees. An expert's answers in response will be treated as part of the expert's report and must be verified by a statement of truth. The sanctions for failure to answer any written question put to him are severe as the court may order that the party may not be able to rely on that expert's evidence or that the party may not recover the expert's fees and expenses from the other party to proceedings, or both.[10] The expert's costs in answering the questions will be borne by his instructing party.

Although this procedure is likely to be a useful tool for the parties (especially where an expert is being asked to deal with a matter not contained within his report but within his field of expertise), both the Commercial Court and the Chancery Division warn that they will pay close attention to its use. If it is considered that the written questions put are oppressive in number or content or are not for clarification purposes the questions will be disallowed and an order for costs will be made against the party putting the questions.[11]

J Expert discussions or meetings

At any stage the court may order that one or more discussions take place between experts to enable the experts (without lawyers) to meet or discuss on a without prejudice basis and decide those areas on which they agree and those areas on which they disagree. They may also be required to give a summary of their reasons for disagreeing.[12]

In the Commercial Court meetings, rather than discussions, usually take place between the experts. These will normally take place before trial although they may also be held during the trial itself.[13] A similar procedure exists in the Chancery Division however unless the court orders otherwise, the procedure to be adopted is a matter for the experts, who may, for example, hold discussions by telephone.[14]

The court may direct that a statement be produced for the court reporting on the outcome of the experts' meeting. In Commercial Court cases a joint memorandum must be produced either at or following the meeting.[15] The parties will not be bound by any agreement reached by the experts at their meetings unless they expressly agree to do so.[16] In Commercial Court cases each expert may also prepare a short supplemental report highlighting why the expert adheres to his views where there is a difference of expert opinion.[17]

Under the revised draft code of guidance, the parties and their lawyers are also encouraged to seek to reach agreement or clarify the issues by conferences

---

10 CPR 35.6 and practice direction, paras 4.1–4.2.
11 Commercial Court Guide, Section H2.28 and Chancery Guide, para 6.19.
12 CPR 35.12. See also Commercial Court Guide, Section H2.19–2.26 and Chancery Guide, paras 6.16–6.18.
13 Commercial Court Guide, Section H2.19.
14 Chancery Guide, para 6.16.
15 CPR 35.12(3) and Commercial Court Guide, Section H2.24.
16 CPR 35.12(5). See also Commercial Court Guide, Section H2.25.
17 Commercial Court Guide, Section H2.26.

or discussions with experts and/ or discussions between experts for opposing parties. The revised draft code also proposes that concise agendas be produced for discussions between experts which should be circulated 28 days before the date fixed for discussion and that these should be agreed seven days in advance of the date fixed for discussion. The agreed agenda should consist of a series of questions, some of which may be closed, which enable the experts to state their agreement on issues or their reasons for disagreement. Whilst this proposal is generally welcome it should be recognised that in some cases the costs incurred in preparing an agenda may be disproportionate to the case.

The revised draft code of guidance also proposes that a statement of the areas of agreement and disagreement be prepared and agreed promptly between the experts, usually before the discussion is concluded. This may have to be produced to the court.[18] In practice however it may prove quite difficult for experts to produce a statement which includes a summary of their reasons for disagreeing before the discussion is concluded, particularly if production of the statement might involve the disclosure of potentially privileged or confidential information. Given that lawyers will not usually be present at experts' meetings or discussions an expert witness may wish to check with his client's lawyers what he can properly include in the joint statement without disclosing privileged or confidential information. This may require detailed consideration before an expert is in a position to produce a joint statement.

Although the courts had the power to order experts to meet under the old system, and such orders were routinely made in the Commercial Court and the Technology and Construction Court, it is likely that the power to order discussions or meetings will be used extensively by the courts as part of active case management. Indeed such orders are now made in the Queen's Bench Division and the Chancery Division as a matter of course. The court's ability to order discussions, rather than meetings, is designed to save time and costs, enabling experts to make use of telephone conferencing or video conferencing.

In addition, discussions between experts may now be ordered to take place at any time, including prior to the preparation of reports. This will enable experts to narrow the issues in dispute between them before positions become entrenched in reports, thereby saving time and costs. Parties may wish to consider applying for such an order at the case management conference although in the Commercial Court it is still contemplated, at least at present, that meetings between experts will take place after exchange of reports.[19]

K   Giving expert evidence at trial

Expert evidence will be given in a written report unless the court directs otherwise. Consideration will usually be given by the court at the case

---

18 Revised draft code of guidance for experts, paras 21–25.
19 Commercial Court Guide, Appendix 8.

management stage as to whether an expert should give evidence orally and in fast track cases the court will not direct an expert to attend a hearing unless it is necessary to do so in the interests of justice.[20]

Where separate experts have been instructed to give oral evidence at trial, the same procedure as under the old system will apply with each expert giving evidence in chief and amplifying particular points contained within his report. This will be followed by cross-examination by the other party's advocate and re-examination by one's own advocate.

As a general rule, where a single joint expert has been instructed to give evidence at trial, both parties will be able to cross-examine the expert, although probably not as to credit or competence. However, where the single joint expert's report is so supportive of one party's case it may be unfair to allow that party to cross-examine the expert and ask leading questions. In this situation the party may only be permitted to re-examine the expert. Neither party will be able to prepare the single joint expert for trial.

L   Experts' costs

Where a single joint expert is ordered by the court it may at the same time make directions about the payment of the expert's fees and expenses and direct that the instructing parties pay that amount into court. Unless otherwise directed the instructing parties will be jointly and severally liable for the payment of the expert's fees and expenses.[1]

The court has a general power to limit the amount of expert's fees and expenses which may be paid to a single joint expert or which a party may recover from the other party when permitting a party to rely on expert evidence.[2] For example, orders have been made to limit the expert fees which a party may recover from his opponent in the Queen's Bench Division.

Costs in general are discussed in detail in Chapter 10, however a party's use of expert evidence will be one of the factors which the court will consider when exercising its discretion as to costs after trial. For example, if a party unreasonably raises or pursues a point which requires expert evidence, the court may take this in to account when awarding costs and may decide that all or part of the expert's costs may not be recoverable. Similarly, any failure to agree on the appointment of a single joint expert pre-action in circumstances where the court subsequently considers that such an appointment would have been reasonable or to refuse to exchange expert evidence pursuant to a relevant pre-action protocol may also result in the party in default being penalised as to costs.[3]

---

20   CPR 35.5.
1   CPR 35.8.
2   CPR 35.4(4) and CPR 35.8(4).
3   CPR 44.3. Fast track trial costs will be limited. See CPR Pt 46.

Conditional fee agreements for experts

Given that solicitors may now be remunerated on a conditional fee basis, there has been some debate recently as to whether experts should also be remunerated on this basis. The revised draft code of guidance for experts proposes that payments contingent upon the nature of expert evidence given in court proceedings be expressly prohibited. To do otherwise might contravene the expert witness's overriding duty to the court (and the *Law Society's Guide to the Professional Conduct of Solicitors*).[4] If an expert witness does enter into CFA he may also face judicial scrutiny.[5] However there may be pressure for an expert (whether providing advice work or acting as an expert witness) to accept deferred payment terms or to agree to a fixed fee.[6] Conditional fees are discussed in detail in Chapter 3 on funding.

M   Use of assessors

Provision also exists for the court to appoint an assessor to assist the court in dealing with a matter within his skill and expertise and for the assessor to prepare a report for the court.[7] Where the court intends to make such an appointment the court will notify each party in writing at least 21 days in advance of the name of the proposed assessor, the matter on which the assessor will give assistance and his qualifications. Any party may object to the identity of the assessor or to his qualification within seven days of the receipt of the notification and the court will take this into account when deciding whether or not to make the appointment. Where an appointment is made the fees of the assessor will be determined by the court and will form part of the costs of the proceedings. Parties may also be asked to deposit a sum at court in respect of the assessor's fees. Although copies of any report prepared by the assessor will be sent to the parties the assessor will not give oral evidence or be open to cross-examination.[8]

The revised draft code of guidance for experts also proposes that a party should be able to apply to the court at the outset of proceedings for the appointment of an assessor, either in place of or in addition to experts.[9] A party may also request the court to appoint an assessor to preside over discussions between parties pursuant to CPR 35.12.[10]

---

4   Revised draft code of guidance for experts, para 6.
5   *Vista Maritime Inc v Sesa Goa* [1997] CLC 1600, in which Coleman J stated 'The weight given to an expert's evidence may in some cases be affected by the fact that he is giving evidence under, or subject to an arrangement which involves contingent fees. I therefore propose to adopt the practice...that if an expert witness is called and counsel does not ask the witness whether he is being remunerated on a contingent basis, the court will do so'.
6   The revised draft code of guidance for experts, para 7 provides that agreement may be reached to delay payment of an expert's fees until after the conclusion of the case as long as the amount of the fee does not depend on the outcome of the case.
7   CPR 35.15. See also Chancery Guide, para 6.21.
8   CPR Pt 35, practice direction, paras 6.1–6.4.
9   Revised draft code of guidance, para 32.
10   See also revised draft code of guidance, para 33.

The Admiralty Court has already confirmed its intention to continue the use of assessors in *Owners of the ship 'Pelopidas' v Owners of the ship 'TRSL Concord'*,[11] however it is not currently clear to what extent the other courts will use them. If the court does order the use of assessors without the agreement of the parties there is a risk that the court will fall foul of the Human Rights Act 1998 on the basis that the parties have been deprived of their right to a fair trial under Art 6(1) of the European Convention on Human Rights in view of the fact that, as the CPR are currently drafted, the parties have no right of cross-examination of an assessor.

11 [1999] 2 All ER (Comm) 737, [1999] 2 Lloyd's Rep 675.

10 COSTS

A Introduction

Lord Woolf observed in his Final Report that:

> 'the problem of costs is the most serious problem besetting our litigation system…Costs are central to the changes I wish to bring about. Virtually all my recommendations are designed at least in part to tackle the problem of costs'.[1]

He identified three particular problems:

- litigation is so expensive that the majority of the public cannot afford it unless they receive financial assistance;
- the costs incurred in the course of litigation are out of all proportion to the issues involved; and
- the costs are uncertain in amount so that the parties have difficulty in predicting what their ultimate liability might be if the action is lost.

Lord Woolf also noted that these problems did not just affect individual litigants. During his inquiry, concerns about the relative cost of litigating in England as compared with other jurisdictions were expressed by many corporate litigants, including investment banks and other financial institutions.

Lord Woolf recommended a variety of measures to control costs, and in particular advocated the imposition of more stringent costs sanctions by the courts as part of their new 'active case management' role, in order to ensure that the parties observed their procedural obligations. These objectives were widely welcomed by court users, and are reflected in the new costs provisions in the CPR Pts 43–48. However, commercial practitioners also expressed some concerns about the new regime before it came into operation, particularly in relation to the extent to which the courts would take advantage of the costs sanctions to penalise uncooperative or dilatory litigants and whether these sanctions would be effective.

This chapter looks at the principal costs reforms and how they have been applied by the courts during the last 12 months. It also considers the impact which the new provisions have had on the management of commercial litigation, and whether they have delivered more proportionate costs to litigants in practice.

---

1 'Access to Justice', July 1996, Chapter 7.

B   The costs reforms in context

The new costs rules form part of a wider government programme of funding and costs reform,[2] including the extension of CFAs to all civil cases and the restructuring of the legal aid system under the Access to Justice Act 1999 which are intended to promote access to justice for those who would not otherwise be able to afford legal costs. The new costs rules in the CPR are intended to ensure that once litigants have secured adequate funding arrangements and proceedings have been commenced, the costs of those proceedings will be more predictable, and proportionate to the amount in dispute. The rationale is that if overall costs reductions can be achieved and budgeting for litigation made simpler, this should result in the civil justice system becoming more accessible to prospective litigants.

The costs changes introduced by the CPR focus on improving transparency in relation to costs between the parties. A number of other initiatives are also underway to increase transparency in relation to costs between solicitors and their clients. With effect from 3 September 1999 Rule 15 of the Solicitors' Practice Rules 1990 was revised to provide that solicitors should:

- give the client the best information possible about the likely overall costs, including a breakdown between fees, VAT and disbursements;
- discuss with the client whether the likely outcome in a matter would justify the expense or risk involved including, if relevant, the risk of having to bear an opponent's costs; and
- keep the client properly informed about costs as the matter progresses.[3]

The Lord Chancellor's Department also issued a consultation paper[4] proposing a number of further changes to keep clients informed of their potential costs liability, including:

- solicitors will be required to provide evidence to the court at the allocation stage that they have informed the client of the basis on which they propose to charge and, where relevant, their hourly rate;
- solicitors will be required to provide an inclusive charging basis, abolishing the uplift for 'care and conduct' previously claimed in a bill of costs;
- in fast track cases, solicitors will be required to file a final estimate of costs at the listing stage, which will set the maximum recoverable costs both between the parties and between the solicitor and his client.

It therefore seems likely that the CPR will be supplemented in due course by further provisions regulating the costs information to be provided to the client from the outset.

2   See Chapter 3 on funding litigation.
3   Solicitors' Practice Costs Information and Client Care Amendment Rule 1999.
4   'Controlling Costs' May 1999.

C Costs under the CPR

The costs provisions in Pts 43–48, examined in more detail below, do not exist in isolation, and should be read in the light of the overriding objective of 'dealing with cases justly' set out in CPR 1.1. The concept of dealing with cases justly is elaborated under CPR 1.1(2), which places a great emphasis on wider financial considerations, including:

(a) 'ensuring that the parties are on an equal footing' (this may include taking into account their respective financial resources);

(b) 'saving expense';

(c) 'dealing with the case in ways which are proportionate–
   (i) to the amount of money involved...
   (iv) to the financial position of each party...'

(e) 'allotting to it an appropriate share of the court's resources, while taking into account the need to allot resources to other cases'.

The court therefore has a very wide ranging discretion in relation to costs in order to achieve the overriding objective. Once a costs decision has been made by the judge or Master responsible for managing the case, there is very limited scope for appealing it. In *Customs and Excise Comrs v Anchor Foods Ltd (No 2)*[5] the court made it clear that only in the most exceptional circumstances such as those involving fraud or the slip rule, could the court re-visit a costs order and act as an appellate court. There has been no change to the common law rule that an interlocutory order for costs cannot be varied except in exceptional circumstances.

The reference to proper allocation of the court's resources is significant, the implication being that whatever the financial resources of the parties themselves and their willingness to meet high costs, they cannot necessarily insist on a 'Rolls Royce' service for all aspects of the case, if the effect could be to deprive other litigants of the opportunity for their dispute to be dealt with justly (eg within a reasonable period of time). This was illustrated by the case of *Adoko v Jemal*[6] in which the Court of Appeal stressed, when dismissing an appeal, that the use of court resources should be considered. Modern litigation culture required that litigation was conducted justly and economically and the parties had a duty to assist the court in achieving this. It remains to be seen whether litigants who disagree with the court's interpretation of what amounts to 'an appropriate share of the court's resources' may seek to challenge this approach as incompatible with Art 6 of the European Convention on Human Rights, which entitles the parties to a 'fair hearing'.

The costs rules in Pts 43–48 (and accompanying practice directions) deal with the following areas:
- Part 43 provides a general introduction and definitions. The practice direction deals with estimates of costs;
- Part 44 sets out the key principles on which orders for costs are

---

5 (1999) Times, 28 September.
6 (1999) Times, 8 July, CA.

> based and how costs should be quantified;
> - Part 45 sets out the rules in relation to fixed costs (ie costs recoverable on certain types of application, such as summary judgment);
> - Part 46 deals with fast track fixed trial costs;[7]
> - Part 47 sets out the procedure for detailed cost assessments;
> - Part 48 provides for particular types of costs including those between solicitors and clients.

D   Costs estimates

Lord Woolf placed great emphasis in his reports on the importance of introducing transparency in relation to costs, in order to bring home to litigants at an early stage the financial consequences of litigating, and to focus their minds on the real issues in dispute. Whilst commercial litigants have long been used to receiving costs estimates and reports on progress against budget, the CPR now regulate the way in which costs estimates have to be exchanged between the parties and provided to the court to facilitate case management.

Section 4 of the practice direction to Pt 43 deals with the provision of costs estimates. Under Section 4, estimates have to be provided to the court and to the other parties when filing the allocation questionnaire and later when filing the listing questionnaire. A copy of the estimate must also be provided to the client. In addition, the court can require a party to file an estimate of costs and serve copies on the other parties at any stage.[8] Such a direction is likely where one of the parties is proposing a potentially expensive course of action (such as the trial of a preliminary issue, or disclosure beyond standard disclosure).

The allocation questionnaire[9] requires the parties to state their estimate of costs incurred to date, and the overall costs of the action, in the form of a statement of costs.[10] It appears that the current practice in large multi-track cases is for such cost estimates to be very general in nature, although in lower value, more easily predictable cases it may be possible to provide a more accurate estimate. Unless there is a very wide discrepancy between the parties' estimates, they are not generally being challenged or queried at the allocation stage.

There is no provision in the CPR for the filing of a costs estimate specifically for consideration at the case management conference.[11] It is clearly good practice in any event to prepare a case budget (which is likely to be more comprehensive than a cost estimate) for internal case management purposes

---

7   This chapter focuses on costs on the multi-track. Separate provisions apply in relation to fast track and small claims track costs.
8   CPR Pt 43, practice direction, para 4.3.
9   Form N150.
10   Form 1, Schedule of Costs Forms.
11   Other than in the Technology and Construction Court where this information is required in the CMC Questionnaire.

and for the client. Moreover, the nature of the issues which the court will address at the case management conference (such as the scope of disclosure and witness and expert evidence) mean that a costs estimate may be needed. The court will need to satisfy itself that the proposed directions are proportionate to the parties' financial positions and that the likely benefit of taking a particular step justifies the cost of taking it. An outline costs estimate may assist with this exercise, particularly where there is a wide disparity between the financial resources of the parties and their willingness to undertake expensive procedures.

A party who can demonstrate at the case management conference that it has budgeted for the various ways in which the litigation may progress and is able if necessary to argue for its preferred course of action on the basis of estimates provided to the court is likely to have the advantage in any argument as to the proportionality of its approach. It will also protect that party against the situation which arose in *Mars UK Ltd v Teknowledge Ltd (No 2)*,[12] where Jacob J held that for one side to run up unforeseeably large bills without warning the other side was a matter to be taken into account on detailed assessment (and the result may be that such costs, though properly incurred, are not recoverable).

At the listing stage, the procedure is straightforward. The parties are required to draw up a statement of costs in the same format as for the allocation questionnaire, to file it with the listing questionnaire and to serve a copy on all parties and the client.[13] By this stage the parties should be in a position to provide accurate estimates of solicitors' and counsel's fees.

The practice direction does not give any additional guidance as to how a costs estimate should be calculated, and whether for example it should be on the basis of solicitor and own client costs, or estimated recoverable costs (ie applying the principles of proportionality and reasonableness which will apply on detailed costs assessment on the standard basis).[14] It is difficult to predict how the court will allocate costs, given the number of factors it will have to take into account, and there is a risk that if the estimate is drawn up on the basis of anticipated recoverable costs, the court may nevertheless reduce it further. On balance, it is advisable to submit a costs estimate based on the actual hourly rate to be charged, and leave the court to decide whether or not it is proportionate in all the circumstances.

Lord Woolf indicated in his Final Report that costs estimates were not intended to be binding, but were primarily to assist the court in exercising its costs discretion. He stated that 'estimates need not go into detail and would not therefore disclose confidential information which might be of tactical value to an opponent...The estimates would be indications to help the procedural judge decide the best course of action rather than budgets which limited what the parties could recover'.[15] The estimate will normally only need to be in outline form (together with an estimate of counsel's fees

---

12 (1999) Times, 8 July.
13 CPR Pt 43, practice direction, section 4.
14 See CPR 44.5.
15 Final Report, Section II, Chapter 7.

and any other significant disbursements, such as experts' fees) to enable the court to decide how to proceed, rather than a detailed budget setting out amounts by stage or activity, which might be seen as a limit on what the parties are allowed to do or could recover in costs. The CPR are silent as to the position if the costs estimate is exceeded or is likely to be exceeded and there are as yet no reported decisions on this point. This is however likely to be the subject of comment at subsequent case management conferences or the pre-trial review and may be used by the court as a lever to promote ADR or settlement. The paying party is also likely to object if the estimate originally submitted is exceeded, and a larger sum is sought on detailed assessment.

E   Assessment of costs: core principles

Under CPR 44.3(2), the general rule is that an unsuccessful party will be ordered to pay the costs of the successful party. However the 'winner takes all' approach, which was the usual result under the old rules no longer applies. Under the CPR there is a move away from the presumption that the successful party should be awarded costs irrespective of the way in which the litigation was conducted, and there are more opportunities for a losing party to challenge this assumption, and for the courts to make more flexible costs orders. Overbearing and aggressive claimants or applicants who win on the main issue, may nonetheless find themselves penalised on costs.

In the past, a party who raised a number of issues, succeeding on some and failing on others, tended to be awarded the entire cost of the proceedings. Under the new regime he may be at risk, even if he has not acted improperly or unreasonably, since the court must give consideration to apportioning the cost where a party does not win on all issues. The court has considerable leeway in deciding what costs order to make—in addition to refusing the claimant recovery of all his costs, it is open to the court to allow the defendant to recover some costs to reflect his partial success.[16] CPR 44.3(6)(f) provides that the court may make an order for costs relating to a distinct part of the proceedings only. However, given the difficulty of identifying accurately the costs incurred in relation to a particular step or part of the proceedings, a more practicable order is that a specified proportion of the costs should be paid, or that the costs payable should span a particular period.[17] There have been a number of recent examples of such creative costs orders. In *Liverpool City Council v Rosemary Chavasse Ltd*[18] the Council was the overall winner, but the second defendant was successful on at least two issues. The judge took this into account, and also noted that the Council had left matters until the last minute which resulted in greater expense to the parties and led to the defendants having less time to consider settling or conceding certain issues. The Council's conduct cost them approximately a third of their costs.

16   See *Liverpool City Council v Rosemary Chavasse Ltd* [1999] 36 LS Gaz R 29, CA.
17   See CPR 44.3(7).
18   [1999] 36 LS Gaz R 29, CA.
19   (4 November 1999, unreported).

In *BCCI v Munawar Ali*[19] both sides had incurred costs in excess of £1m. Although the defendants had technically won, in that they successfully established a breach of contract, they failed to establish loss and so made no recovery. Mr Justice Lightman decided that the approach to costs established before the CPR was of no consequence, and that the proper course was to make no order as to costs, which also reflected what justice required in the circumstances.

> **The considerations which the court will take into account**
> **when assessing costs under CPR 44.3(5) are:**
> * conduct before, as well as during, the proceedings and in particular the extent to which the parties followed any relevant pre-action protocol;
> * whether it was reasonable for a party to raise, pursue or contest an allegation or issue;
> * the manner in which a party has pursued or defended his case or a particular allegation or issue;
> * whether a claimant who has succeeded in his claim in whole or in part exaggerated his claim;
> * whether any payment into court or admissible offer to settle has been made, whether or not in accordance with Pt 36.[20]

Pre-action conduct is now a relevant factor when costs are assessed. The parties are obliged to cooperate in the exchange of information and documents in relation to a potential claim before proceedings are commenced, and a failure to follow a pre-action protocol may lead to an adverse costs order, or an order for a payment into court of a sum of money.[1] The courts have proved willing to penalise successful litigants for pre-action conduct which does not accord with the spirit of the overriding objective. In *Mars UK Ltd v Teknowledge Ltd (No 2)*[2] the court took into account the claimant's pre-action behaviour (including its failure to consider settlement discussions and the aggressive tone of its letter before action) and significantly reduced the amount of costs recoverable. The claimant was also criticised for including an allegation which was bound to fail if its main allegation failed.

F The basis of assessment

Under CPR 44.4(1) costs are assessed either on the standard basis or the indemnity basis.

Under CPR 44.4(2), where the amount of costs is to be assessed on the standard basis, the court will only allow costs which are proportionate to the matters in issue, and will resolve any doubt which it may have as to

---

20 For considerations to take into account in relation to offers to settle/Pt 36 offers, and subsequent assessment of costs, see Chapter 5 on Part 36 offers.
1 CPR 3.1(5).
2 (1999) Times, 8 July.

whether the costs were reasonably incurred, or reasonable and proportionate in amount in favour of the paying party.

Indemnity basis costs are likely to be limited, as previously, to cases where a party has demonstrated abuse of court procedure, lack of bona fides, tenuous claims, or time wasting practices. However, it may also include situations where one party fails to comply with the spirit of the overriding objective, for example by repeatedly failing to meet court deadlines. Under CPR 44.4(3), where costs are awarded on the indemnity basis the court will resolve any doubt it may have as to whether costs were reasonably incurred or were reasonable in amount in favour of the receiving party. There is no additional requirement for proportionality.[3] As a result, if the receiving party has been put to significant expense beyond what he could have achieved as a result of the standard basis costs order, he may well be able to recover in full. A protest by the paying party that the particular costs are not proportionate is likely to carry very little weight, and any doubt is likely to be resolved in favour of the receiving party.

The additional hurdle of proportionality imposed by the indemnity basis test has given rise to some debate as to whether there is a material difference between 'reasonableness' and 'proportionality'. The concept is causing concern amongst practitioners because it places a wide discretion in the hands of the court and during the transitional period since April 1999, it has been difficult to predict how it will be applied in practice.

This concern led the Civil Procedure Rule Committee to provide additional guidance as follows:[4]

- In applying the test of proportionality, the court will have regard to CPR 1.1(2)(c) which requires the court to take account of the amount of money involved, the importance of the case, the complexity of the issues and the financial position of the parties. The relationship between the total of the costs incurred and the financial value of the claim may not be a reliable guide. A fixed percentage cannot be applied in all cases to the value of the claim in order to ascertain whether or not the costs are proportionate.
- There will be costs which will inevitably be incurred in any proceedings and which are necessary for the successful conduct of the case. Solicitors are not required to conduct litigation at rates which are uneconomic. In a relatively small claim, the proportion of cost is likely to be higher than in a large claim, and may even in some circumstances exceed the amount in dispute.
- Furthermore, when a trial takes place, the time taken by the court in dealing with a particular issue may not be an accurate guide to the amount of time properly spent by the legal representatives in preparing for the trial of that issue.

---

3   But note *Sun Valley Foods Ltd v Vincent* (1 December 1999, unreported), Ch D—although indemnity costs were not subject to test of being proportionate, they would still be disallowed if they were unnecessarily incurred or unreasonable in amount.
4   CPR Pt 44, practice direction, paras 3.1–3.3.

The factors to take into account when assessing the amount of costs to be awarded on the standard or indemnity basis are set out in CPR 44.5. In addition to determining whether the costs were proportionately and reasonably incurred and are proportionate and reasonable in amount (for standard basis costs) or were unreasonably incurred or are unreasonable in amount (for indemnity costs) the court must consider the conduct of all the parties, both before and during the proceedings; the efforts made (if any) before and during proceedings to decide to resolve the dispute; the amount or value of any money or property involved; the importance of the matter to all the parties; the particular complexity of the matter or the difficulty or novelty of the questions raised; the skill, effort, specialised knowledge and responsibility involved; the time spent on the case; and the place where and the circumstances in which work or any part of it was done.

G   The 'pay as you go' approach

As part of the new regime of transparency on costs, the CPR introduced the concept of summary assessment of costs[5] whereby the costs of applications lasting one day or less are assessed immediately after the hearing, by the same judge or Master who heard the application. Summary assessment enables a successful party to be compensated at an appropriate stage in the proceedings and imposes an immediate penalty (usually payable within 14 days) on the paying party.

When requesting a summary assessment, the applicant should give the details specified in the costs practice direction. Where a party is asking for costs which may appear to the judge to be substantial, having regard to the nature of the application, the party should be prepared to give further details to support the request for costs.[6] It may be appropriate in certain circumstances for a costs draftsman to be involved in the production of a bill of costs. If so, the costs draftsman's costs of preparing the bill can be included in the assessment, even if charged as a percentage of the bill.

The courts are readily carrying out summary assessments in relation to hearings of one day or less (other than where the appropriate order is for costs in the case). The court may also be prepared to carry out summary assessment of costs in relation to applications lasting for more than one day if the parties request it and there is no substantial dispute as to costs. However where there is a substantial dispute it is more likely that the court will refer the costs for detailed assessment and order an interim payment of costs on account.

There have been some initial reports of an inconsistent judicial approach in relation to summary assessment, which was perhaps inevitable given that judges and Masters have not previously had to deal with quantification issues on costs applications (other than in relation to security for costs) and often have had little practical experience on which to base costs assessments. In

---

5   CPR 44.7.
6   This applies even where the costs have been agreed between the parties—see CPR 1998, Pt 44, practice direction, para 4(10).

some cases, the courts have taken a fairly rough and ready approach, limiting their consideration to a few minutes only, whereas others have been prepared to consider detailed submissions. The amounts allowed have also varied widely, as the general guidance set out in the guide to the summary assessment of costs is not appropriate in every situation.

Summary assessment will normally be granted in the Commercial Court where one party requests it, even though the parties' respective estimates may be some way apart. Summary assessments are being made as a matter of course on Friday summonses, on most applications of less than one day, and in some cases on longer applications where an interlocutory decision has brought the matter to an end (eg following summary judgment or the determination of a jurisdiction issue). The usual practice is to allow between 10 and 25 minutes, providing a fairly rough and ready calculation. Some judges are allowing the parties time to try to agree a figure, but the more usual option is to indicate the likely award and give the receiving party the option to accept it or to proceed instead to detailed assessment, with the attendant delay and costs that involves. The procedure appears to work well for shorter, more modest applications but can be more problematic for longer applications lasting several days, where although there was no obligation to use the procedure, the parties have been tempted to volunteer for summary assessment. It has been pointed out by Mr Justice Rix during the Commercial Court's regular 'CPR surgeries' that in these circumstances the court has other, and probably more appropriate options, such as ordering an interim payment on account of costs.

Preliminary indications from the courts (including the specialist lists) are that the summary assessment provisions have discouraged litigants and their lawyers from making obstructive or time-wasting applications, and that this is one of the most productive areas of the reforms in terms of its immediate effect on litigants' behaviour. It is also popular with many litigants, who are opting for summary assessment in order to recover some proportion of their costs immediately even though in some cases they might obtain a greater sum if they proceeded to detailed assessment.

It has been suggested by some practitioners that recoverable costs are rising as a result of this procedure. Judges appear to be accepting that the solicitor/client rates charged by City and other firms can be recovered from the other side, whereas under the old regime costs judges tended not to allow the full amount. This acceptance is pragmatic—judges do not have time to deal with issues about whether or not an hourly rate is reasonable, or the purpose of the summary procedure would be defeated.

The summary assessment provisions compensate to some extent for the frustrations which successful litigants feel at the fact that whilst successful in court, they have to wait many months to recover any of the costs which they have been awarded. There are two further provisions under the CPR which have been introduced to improve their position. CPR 44.3(8) provides for interim payment of costs 'on account' to the winner, pending detailed assessment. This provision was considered by Mr Justice Jacob in the Chancery Division in *Mars UK Ltd v Teknowledge Ltd (No 2)*.[7] In that case

---

7   (1999) Times, 8 July.

the claimant had succeeded in its copyright claim but failed in its secondary claim for breach of confidence. The judge took the view that the court should make an immediate award of costs, for less than the amount of costs the claimant would eventually recover. In calculating the amount to award he took into account the pre-action conduct of the parties, penalising the claimant for its heavy handed approach. The interim award made was for £80,000, on the basis that the claimant's costs would be approximately £200,000 of which it would recover no less than 40%. CPR 47.15 enables an application for an interim costs certificate to be made immediately upon filing a request for a detailed assessment hearing. An interim costs hearing is likely to take place within weeks rather than months, and the Supreme Court Costs Office reports a steady rise in the number of CPR 47.15 applications.

H   Costs sanctions

Under the CPR a wide range of sanctions is available, including adverse costs orders. Some rules make provision for an automatic sanction in the event of default although in many cases the burden remains on the non defaulting party to apply to the court for relief (accompanied if appropriate by an application for summary of assessment of the associated costs), not least because the courts do not currently have the IT facilities necessary to enable them to monitor the progress of cases between hearings. It has not been the courts' general practice to impose a sanction (such as an unless order or a costs penalty) when giving directions, unless there is reason to believe that the party is likely to default (based for example on previous conduct).

Where a party or his legal representative has failed to act in accordance with the spirit of the rules during detailed assessment proceedings (or before or during the action that gave rise to those proceedings) they may be penalised under CPR 44.14 if it appears to the court that the conduct of a party or his representative was unreasonable or improper.

The court also has the power to make wasted costs orders against a legal representative under CPR 48.7. There have been a number of cases involving the wasted costs provisions. The most notable is *General Mediterranean Holdings SA v Patel & Patel*.[8] The wasted costs provisions originally envisaged that the court could order disclosure of solicitor/client correspondence in order to investigate allegations of misconduct. This was intended to overcome difficulties caused by privilege where advisers could not rely on documents which might exonerate them. However, in *General Mediterranean* Toulson J held that a court order that privileged documents should be disclosed to the court for the purposes of determining whether a wasted costs order should be made was ultra vires, and that even if it had not been, it would have been in breach of Arts 6 and 8 of the European Convention on Human Rights.

8   [1999] 3 All ER 673, [2000] 1 WLR 272.

In the past, applications for wasted costs orders have often led to costly and expensive satellite litigation. In *Drums & Packaging Ltd v Martin Freeman*[9] the court confirmed that the wasted costs provisions are not to be invoked lightly or as a tactical ploy. It was held that the jurisdiction to order a wasted costs order should be exercised cautiously since the existence of the jurisdiction could operate to put pressure on clients to waive privilege.

A further discipline has been imposed on solicitors by the introduction of the obligation to notify the client[10] of adverse costs orders within seven days of the order being made.[11] The introduction of the summary assessment procedure for costs increases the likelihood of such orders being made and combined with the notification requirement appears to have led to a reduction in minor interlocutory disputes.

I   The practical impact of the costs rules

Inevitably, the parties will look to extract what tactical advantage they can from the costs rules. However, the scope for tactical manoeuvring is very limited given the continuing obligation on the parties and their legal advisers to observe the overriding objective. The courts are likely to favour litigants who make early Pt 36 offers; abandon weak issues; are proactive in seeking to agree costs; apply for interim payments promptly; are realistic about when summary assessment is appropriate; apply for abridged assessment at the end of the case if appropriate; and know the sanctions and when it is appropriate to invoke them. Tactics to avoid include wrangling over the effectiveness of Pt 36 offers; resorting too early to wasted costs orders; failing to agree costs unless there is a point of principle in issue; and appearing uncooperative in correspondence about costs.

At this relatively early stage it is difficult to make a reliable assessment of the impact which the new costs regime is having on commercial litigants in terms of the overall cost of litigation, although there appears to be a general recognition that the costs of the early stages of a case have increased significantly. The costs of preparing the documentation needed for the case management conference in particular can be high, and the time spent on case budgets and costs estimates has not always delivered tangible short term benefits for the client (although it is likely to prove beneficial in the longer term). Reaction to the implementation of the summary assessment provisions has been mixed, but they do appear to be discouraging peripheral applications and thereby contributing to more proportionate costs overall.

---

9   (27 August 1999, unreported).
10 CPR Pt 44, practice direction, para 1.1 states that for these purposes 'client' includes the party for whom a solicitor is acting and any other person (for example an insurer or trade union) who has instructed the solicitor to act or who is liable to pay his fees.
11 CPR 44.14(3).

APPENDIX A

List of pre-action protocols in draft or development

There are a number of protocols in draft form which relate to the following areas:

- road traffic accidents
- contentious probate
- defamation
- debt claims
- professional negligence
- solicitor's negligence
- uninsured motorists (MIB protocol)
- Y2K
- Technology and Construction Court

There are currently also a number of protocols in development (but with no draft) in relation to:

- holidays
- housing disrepair
- racial discrimination and equal opportunities (may also encompass disability discrimination)
- intellectual property
- police malpractice
- model protocol
- mortgage possession
- rent arrears
- wrongful dismissal
- disease (occupational health claims)

APPENDIX B

Draft pre-action protocol for professional negligence

For further details please contact either CAP's direct line (020 7367 3944) or a member of the Steering Committee:

Mark Swinbank, R J Wallace & Others 020 7488 2233
Bill Pearce, Norwich Union 020 7558 0000
Stuart Clarke, Hiscox 020 7448 6231
David Siddle, Independent 020 7623 8877
John Kopczynski, D J Marshall & Others 020 7369 3000
Ian Bryant, Solicitors Indemnity Fund 020 7566 6000
Stephen Tester, CMS Cameron McKenna 020 7367 3000
Peter Mansfield, CMS Cameron McKenna 0117 930 0200

A   Introduction

A1 This protocol is designed to apply when a claimant wishes to claim against a professional (other than solicitors and healthcare providers) as a result of that professional's alleged negligence or equivalent breach of contract. Although negligence claims will be the usual situation in which the protocol will be used, there may be other claims for which the protocol could be appropriate. For a more detailed explanation of the scope of the protocol see **Guidance Note C**2.

A2 The aim of this protocol is to establish a framework in which there is an early exchange of information so that the claim can be fully investigated and, if possible, resolved without the need for litigation. This includes:
(a)   ensuring that the parties are on an equal footing
(b)   saving expense
(c)   dealing with the dispute in ways which are proportionate:
    (i)   to the amount of money involved
    (ii)   to the importance of the case
    (iii) to the complexity of the issues
    (iv)   to the financial position of each party
(d)   ensuring that it is dealt with expeditiously and fairly.

A3 This protocol is not intended to replace other forms of pre-action dispute resolution (such as internal complaints procedures, the Surveyors and Valuers Arbitration Scheme, etc). Where such procedures are available, parties are encouraged to consider whether they should be used. If, however, these other procedures are used and fail to resolve the dispute, the protocol should be used before litigation is started, adapting it where appropriate. See also **Guidance Note C**3.

A4 The Courts will be able to treat the standards set in this protocol as the normal reasonable approach to pre-action conduct. If litigation is started, it will be for the court to decide whether sanctions should be imposed as a result of non-compliance with a protocol. Guidance on the courts' likely approach will be given from time to time in Practice Directions. As between the parties it is intended that minor infringements should not entitle the innocent party to abandon the protocol.

A5 Both in operating the timetable and in requesting and providing information during the protocol period, the parties are expected to act reasonably, in line with the court's expectations of them. See also **Guidance Note C1**.2.

B   *The Protocol*

B1. Preliminary notice (See also Guidance Note C3.1)

B1.1 If a claimant has a grievance against a professional and is considering whether to bring a claim, the claimant should inform the professional in writing as soon as possible.

B1.2 This letter should contain the following information:
(a)   the identity of the claimant and any other parties
(b)   a brief outline of the claimant's grievance against the professional
(c)   if possible, a general indication of the financial value of the potential claim

B1.3 This letter should be addressed to the professional and should ask the professional to inform his professional indemnity insurers, if any, immediately.

B1.4 The professional should acknowledge receipt of the claimant's letter within 21 days. Other than this acknowledgement, the protocol places no obligation upon either party to take any further action.

B2. Letter of claim

B2.1 As soon as the claimant decides there are grounds for a claim against the professional, the claimant should write a detailed Letter of Claim to the professional.

B2.2 The Letter of Claim will normally be an open letter (as opposed to being 'without prejudice') and should include the following:
(a)   The identity of any other parties involved in the dispute or a related dispute.
(b)   A clear chronological summary (including key dates) of the facts on which the claim is based. Key documents should be identified, copied and enclosed.

(c)   The allegations against the professional. What has he done wrong? What has he failed to do?

(d)   An explanation of how the alleged error has caused the loss claimed.

(e)   An estimate of the financial loss suffered by the claimant and how it is calculated. Supporting documents should be identified, copied and enclosed. If details of the financial loss cannot be supplied, the claimant should explain why and should state when he will be in a position to provide the details. This information should be sent to the professional as soon as reasonably possible. If the claimant is seeking some form of non-financial redress, this should be made clear.

(f)   Confirmation whether or not an expert has been appointed. If so, providing the identity and discipline of the expert, together with the date upon which the expert was appointed.

(g)   A request that a copy of the Letter of Claim be forwarded immediately to the professional's insurers, if any.

B2.3 The Letter of Claim is not intended to have the same formal status as a Statement of Case. If the Letter of Claim differs materially from the Statement of Case in subsequent proceedings, however, the court may decide, in its discretion, to impose sanctions.

B2.4 If the claimant has sent other Letters of Claim (or equivalent) to any other party in relation to this dispute or related dispute, those letters should be copied to the professional. (If the claimant is claiming against someone else to whom this protocol does not apply, please see **Guidance Note C**4.)

B3. The letter of acknowledgment

B3.1 The professional should acknowledge receipt of the Letter of Claim within 21 days.

B4. Investigations

B4.1 The professional will have three months from the date of the Letter of Acknowledgment to investigate.

B4.2 If the professional is in difficulty in complying with the three month time period, the problem should be explained to the claimant as soon as possible. The professional should explain what is being done to resolve the problem and when the professional expects to complete the investigations. The claimant should agree to any reasonable request for an extension of the three month period.

B4.3 The parties should supply promptly, at this stage and throughout the pre-action period, whatever relevant information or documentation is reasonably requested. (Please see **Guidance Note C**5).

(If the professional intends to claim against someone who is not currently a party to the dispute, please see **Guidance Note C**4.)

B5. Letter of response and letter of settlement

B5.1 As soon as the professional has completed his investigations, the professional should send to the claimant:

(a) a Letter of Response, or
(b) a Letter of Settlement; or
(c) both.

The letters of response and settlement can be contained within a single letter.

The Letter of Response

B5.2 The Letter of Response will normally be an open letter (as opposed to being 'without prejudice') and should be a reasoned answer to the claimant's allegations:
(a) if the claim is admitted the professional should say so in clear terms
(b) if only part of the claim is admitted the professional should make clear which parts of the claim are admitted and which are denied.
(c) if the claim is denied in whole or in part, the Letter of Response should include specific comments on the allegations against the professional and, if the claimant's version of events is disputed, the professional should provide his version of events.
(d) if the professional is unable to admit or deny the claim, the professional should identify any further information which is required.
(e) if the professional disputes the estimate of the claimant's financial loss, the Letter of Response should set out the professional's estimate. If an estimate cannot be provided, the professional should explain why and should state when he will be in a position to provide an estimate. This information should be sent to the claimant as soon as reasonably possible.
(f) where additional documents are relied upon, copies should be provided

B5.3 The Letter of Response is not intended to have the same formal status as a defence. If the Letter of Response differs materially from the defence in subsequent proceedings, however, the court may decide, in its discretion, to impose sanctions.

The Letter of Settlement

B5.4 The Letter of Settlement will normally be a without prejudice letter and should be sent if the professional intends to make proposals for settlement. It should:
(a) set out the professional's views to date on the claim identifying those issues which the professional believes are likely to remain in dispute and those which are not. (The Letter of Settlement does not need to include this information if the professional has sent a Letter of Response).
(b) make a settlement proposal or identify any further information which is required before the professional can formulate its proposals.
(c) where additional documents are relied upon, copies should be provided.

Effect of Letter of Response and/or Letter of Settlement

B5.5 If the Letter of Response denies the claim in its entirety and there is no Letter of Settlement, it is open to the claimant to commence proceedings.

B5.6 In any other circumstance, the professional and the claimant should commence negotiations with the aim of concluding those negotiations within

6 months of the date of the Letter of Acknowledgment (NOT from the date of the Letter of Response).

B5.7 If the claim cannot be resolved within this period:
(a)   the parties should agree within 14 days of the end of the period whether the period should be extended and, if so, by how long.
(b)   the parties should seek to identify those issues which are still in dispute and those which can be agreed.
(c)   If an extension of time is not agreed it will then be open to the claimant to commence proceedings.

B6. Alternative Dispute Resolution

B6.1 The parties can agree at any stage to take the dispute (or any part of the dispute) to mediation or some other form of alternative dispute resolution (ADR).

B6.2 In addition, any party at any stage can refer the dispute (or any part of the dispute) to an ADR agency for mediation or some other form of ADR.

B6.3 When approached by a party or an ADR agency with a proposal that ADR be used, the other party or parties should respond within 14 days stating that:
(a)   they agree to the proposal; or
(b)   they agree that ADR will be or may be appropriate, but they believe it has been suggested prematurely. They should state when they anticipate it would or may become appropriate; or
(c)   they agree that ADR is appropriate, but not the form of ADR proposed (if any). They should state the form of ADR which they believe to be appropriate; or
(d)   they do not accept that any form of ADR is appropriate. They should state their reasons.

This letter should be copied to the other party or parties and can be disclosed to the court on the issue of costs.

B6.4 It is expressly recognised that no party can or should be forced to mediate or enter into any other form of ADR.

B7. Experts

B7.1 If the claimant has obtained expert evidence prior to sending the Letter of Claim, the professional will have equal right to obtain expert evidence prior to sending the Letter of Response/Letter of Settlement.

B7.2 If the claimant has not obtained expert evidence prior to sending the Letter of Claim, the parties should consider whether to appoint a joint expert. If so, they should seek to agree the identity of the expert and the terms of the expert's appointment.

B7.3 If agreement about a joint expert cannot be reached, all parties are free to appoint their own experts. (For further details on experts see **Guidance Note C**6)

B8. Proceedings

B8.1 Unless it is necessary (for example, to obtain protection against the expiry of a relevant limitation period) the claimant should not start court proceedings until:
(a) the Letter of Response denies the claim in its entirety and there is no Letter of Settlement (see paragraph B5.5 above); or
(b) the end of the negotiation period (see paragraphs B5.6 and B5.7 above); or
(c) there has been an infringement (which should be more than minor) by the professional of the time limits in this protocol (see paragraph A4).

(For further discussion of statutory time limits for the commencement of litigation, please see **Guidance Note C**7)

B8.2 Where possible 14 days written notice should be given to the professional before proceedings are started, indicating the court within which the claimant is intending to commence litigation.

B8.3 Proceedings should be served on the professional, unless the claimant is advised to the contrary.

C. *Guidance notes*

C1. Introduction

C1.1 The protocol has been kept simple to promote ease of use and general acceptability. The guidance notes which follow relate particularly to issues on which further guidance may be required.

C1.2 The Woolf reforms envisage that parties will act reasonably in the pre-action period. Accordingly, in the event that the protocol and the guidelines do not specifically address a problem, the parties should comply with the spirit of the protocol by acting reasonably.

C2. Scope of protocol

C2.1 The protocol is specifically designed for claims of negligence against professionals. This will include claims in which the allegation against a professional is that they have breached a contractual term to take reasonable skill and care.

C2.2 The protocol is not intended to apply to claims against:
(a) Solicitors—for which there is a separate, but similar, draft protocol. A copy can be obtained from the Solicitors Indemnity Fund, 100 St John Street, London, EC1M 4EH.
(b) Healthcare providers—for which there is an approved protocol.

C2.3 'Professional' is deliberately left undefined in the protocol. If it becomes an issue as to whether a defendant is or is not a professional, parties are reminded of the overriding need to act reasonably in the pre-action period (see paragraphs A4 and C1.2 above). Rather than argue about the definition of 'professional', therefore, the parties are invited to use this protocol (which sets out a reasonable approach to pre-action conduct), adapting it where appropriate.

C2.4 The protocol may not be suitable for disputes with professionals concerning intellectual property claims, defamation etc. Until specific protocols are created for those claims, however, parties are invited to use this protocol, adapting it where necessary.

C2.5 Allegations of professional negligence are sometimes made in response to an attempt by the professional to recover outstanding fees. Where possible these allegations should be raised before litigation has commenced, in which case the parties should comply with the protocol before either party commences litigation. If litigation has already commenced it will be a matter for the court whether sanctions should be imposed against either party. In any event, the parties are encouraged to consider applying to the court for a stay to allow the protocol to be followed.

C3. Inter-action with other pre-action methods of dispute resolution

C3.1 There are a growing number of methods by which disputes can be resolved without the need for litigation, eg internal complaints procedures, the Surveyors and Valuers Arbitration Scheme, and so on. The Preliminary Notice procedure of the protocol (see paragraph B1) is designed to enable both parties to take stock at an early stage and to decide before work starts on preparing a Letter of Claim whether the grievance should be referred to one of these other dispute resolution procedures. (For the avoidance of doubt, however, there is no obligation on either party under the protocol to take any action at this stage other than giving the acknowledgment provided for in paragraph B1.4.)

C3.2 Accordingly, parties are free to use (and are encouraged to use) any of the available pre-action procedures in an attempt to resolve their dispute. If appropriate, the parties can agree to suspend the protocol timetable whilst the other method of dispute resolution is used.

C3.3 If these methods fail to resolve the dispute, however, the protocol should be used before litigation is commenced. Because there has already been an attempt to resolve the dispute, it may be appropriate to adjust the protocol's requirements. In particular, unless the parties agree otherwise, there is unlikely to be any benefit in duplicating a stage which has in effect already been undertaken. However, if the protocol adds anything to the earlier method of dispute resolution, it should be used, adapting it where appropriate. Once again, the parties are expected to act reasonably.

C4. Multi-party disputes

C4.1 Paragraph B2.2 (a) of the protocol requires a claimant to identify any other parties involved in the dispute or a related dispute. This is intended to ensure that all relevant parties are identified as soon as possible.

C4.2 If the dispute involves more than two parties, there are a number of potential problems. It is possible that different protocols will apply to different defendants. It is possible that defendants will claim against each other. It is possible that other parties will be drawn into the dispute. It is possible that the protocol timetable against one party will not be synchronised with the protocol timetable against a different party. How will these problems be resolved?

C4.3 As stated in paragraph C1.2 above, the parties are expected to act reasonably. What is 'reasonable' will, of course, depend upon the specific facts of each case. Accordingly, it would be inappropriate for the protocol to set down generalised rules. Whenever a problem arises, the parties are encouraged to discuss how it can be overcome. In doing so, parties are reminded of the protocol's aims which include the aim to resolve the dispute without the need for litigation (paragraph A2 above).

C5. Investigations

C5.1 Paragraph B4.3 is intended to encourage the early exchange of relevant information, so that issues in the dispute can be clarified or resolved. It should not be used as a 'fishing expedition' by either party. No party is obliged under paragraph B4.3 to disclose any document which a court could not order them to disclose in the pre-action period.

C5.2 This protocol does not alter the parties' duties to disclose documents under any professional regulation or under general law.

C6. Experts

C6.1 The use and role of experts in professional negligence claims is usually crucial. However, the way in which expert evidence is used in, say, an engineers' negligence case, is not necessarily the same as in, say, an accountants' case. Similarly, the approach to be adopted in a £10,000 case does not necessarily compare with the approach in a £10 million case. The protocol therefore is designed to be flexible and does not dictate a standard approach. On the contrary it envisages that the parties will bear the responsibility for agreeing how best to use experts in the pre-action period.

C6.2 If a joint expert is used, therefore, the parties are left to decide issues such as: the payment of the expert, whether joint or separate instructions are used, how and to whom the expert is to report, how questions may be addressed to the expert and how the expert should respond, whether an agreed statement of facts is required, and so on.

C6.3 If separate experts are used, the parties are left to decide issues such as: whether the expert's reports should be exchanged, whether there should be an expert's meeting, and so on.

C6.4 Even if a joint expert is appointed, it is possible that parties will still want to instruct their own experts. The protocol does not prohibit this.

C7. Proceedings

C7.1 This protocol does not alter the statutory time limits for starting court proceedings. Unless there is prior agreement between the parties, a claimant must start proceedings within those time limits.

C7.2 If proceedings have already been started, the parties are encouraged to consider applying to the court for a stay whilst the protocol is followed.

THIS PROTOCOL IS A DRAFT. IT HAS NOT YET BEEN APPROVED BY THE LORD CHANCELLOR'S DEPARTMENT.

APPENDIX C

Pre-action protocol for the resolution of clinical disputes (Clinical Disputes Forum, December 1998)

Executive summary

1. The Clinical Disputes Forum is a multi-disciplinary body which was formed in 1997, as a result of Lord Woolf's 'Access to Justice' inquiry. One of the aims of the Forum is to find less adversarial and more cost-effective ways of resolving disputes about healthcare and medical treatment. The names and addresses of the Chairman and Secretary of the Forum can be found at Annex E.

2. This protocol is the Forum's first major initiative. It has been drawn up care-fully, including extensive consultations with most of the key stakeholders in the medico-legal system.

3. The protocol—
- encourages a climate of openness when something has 'gone wrong' with a patient's treatment or the patient is dissatisfied with that treatment and/or the outcome. This reflects the new and developing requirements for clinical governance within healthcare;
- provides general guidance on how this more open culture might be achieved when disputes arise;
- recommends a timed sequence of steps for patients and healthcare providers, and their advisers, to follow when a dispute arises. This should facilitate and speed up exchanging relevant information and increase the prospects that disputes can be resolved without resort to legal action.

4. This protocol has been prepared by a working party of the Clinical Disputes Forum. It has the support of the Lord Chancellor's Department, the Department of Health and NHS Executive, the Law Society, the Legal Aid Board and many other key organisations.

1 Why this Protocol?

Mistrust in healthcare disputes

1.1 The number of complaints and claims against hospitals, GPs, dentists and private healthcare providers is growing as patients become more prepared to question the treatment they are given, to seek explanations of what happened, and to seek appropriate redress. Patients may require further treatment, an apology, assurances about future action, or compensation. These trends are unlikely to change. The Patients' Charter encourages patients to have high expectations, and a revised NHS Complaints Procedure was implemented in 1996. The civil justice reforms and new Rules of Court should make litigation quicker, more user friendly and less expensive.

1.2 It is clearly in the interests of patients, healthcare professionals and providers that patients' concerns, complaints and claims arising from their treatment are resolved as quickly, efficiently and professionally as possible. A climate of mistrust and lack of openness can seriously damage the patient/clinician relationship, unnecessarily prolong disputes (especially litigation), and reduce the resources available for treating patients. It may also cause additional work for, and lower the morale of, healthcare professionals.

1.3 At present there is often mistrust by both sides. This can mean that patients fail to raise their concerns with the healthcare provider as early as possible. Sometimes patients may pursue a complaint or claim which has little merit, due to a lack of sufficient information and understanding. It can also mean that patients become reluctant, once advice has been taken on a potential claim, to disclose sufficient information to enable the provider to investigate that claim efficiently and, where appropriate, resolve it.

1.4 On the side of the healthcare provider this mistrust can be shown in a reluctance to be honest with patients, a failure to provide prompt clear explanations, especially of adverse outcomes (whether or not there may have been negligence) and a tendency to 'close ranks' once a claim is made.

What needs to change

1.5 If that mistrust is to be removed, and a more co-operative culture is to develop—
- healthcare professionals and providers need to adopt a constructive approach to complaints and claims. They should accept that concerned patients are entitled to an explanation and an apology, if warranted, and to appropriate redress in the event of negligence. An overly defensive approach is not in the long-term interest of their main goal: patient care;
- patients should recognise that unintended and/or unfortunate consequences of medical treatment can only be rectified if they are brought to the attention of the healthcare provider as soon as possible.

1.6 A protocol which sets out 'ground rules' for the handling of disputes at their early stages should, if it is to be subscribed to, and followed—
- encourage greater openness between the parties;
- encourage parties to find the most appropriate way of resolving the particular dispute;
- reduce delay and costs;
- reduce the need for litigation.

Why this Protocol now?

1.7 Lord Woolf in his Access to Justice Report in July 1996, concluded that major causes of costs and delay in medical negligence litigation occur at the pre-action stage. He recommended that patients and their advisers, and healthcare providers, should work more closely together to try to resolve disputes co-operatively, rather than proceed to litigation. He specifically recommended a pre-action protocol for medical negligence cases.

1.8 A fuller summary of Lord Woolf's recommendations is at Annex D.

Where the Protocol fits in

1.9 Protocols serve the needs of litigation and pre-litigation practice, especially—
- predictability in the time needed for steps pre-proceedings;
- standardisation of relevant information, including records and documents to be disclosed.

1.10 Building upon Lord Woolf's recommendations, the Lord Chancellor's Department is now promoting the adoption of protocols in specific areas, including medical negligence.

1.11 It is recognised that contexts differ significantly. For example: patients tend to have an ongoing relationship with a GP, more so than with a hospital; clinical staff in the National Health Service are often employees, while those in the private sector may be contractors; providing records quickly may be relatively easy for GPs and dentists, but can be a complicated procedure in a large multi-department hospital. The protocol which follows is intended to be sufficiently broadly based, and flexible, to apply to all aspects of the health service: primary and secondary; public and private sectors.

Enforcement of the Protocol and sanctions

1.12 The civil justice reforms will be implemented in April 1999. One new set of Court Rules and procedures is replacing the existing rules for both the High Court and county courts. This and the personal injury protocol are being published with the Rules, practice directions and key court forms. The courts will be able to treat the standards set in protocols as the normal reasonable approach to pre-action conduct.

1.13 If proceedings are issued it will be for the court to decide whether non-compliance with a protocol should merit sanctions. Guidance on the court's likely approach will be given from time to time in practice directions.

1.14 If the court has to consider the question of compliance after proceedings have begun it will not be concerned with minor infringements, eg failure by a short period to provide relevant information. One minor breach will not entitle the 'innocent' party to abandon following the protocol. The court will look at the effect of non-compliance on the other party when deciding whether to impose sanctions.

2 The aims of the Protocol

2.1 The **general** aims of the protocol are—
- to maintain/restore the patient/healthcare provider relationship;
- to resolve as many disputes as possible without litigation.

2.2 The **specific** objectives are—

Openness
- to encourage early communication of the perceived problem between patients and healthcare providers;
- to encourage patients to voice any concerns or dissatisfaction with their treatment as soon as practicable;
- to encourage healthcare providers to develop systems of early reporting and investigation for serious adverse treatment outcomes and to provide full and prompt explanations to dissatisfied patients;
- to ensure that sufficient information is disclosed by both parties to enable each to understand the other's perspective and case, and to encourage early resolution;

Timeliness
- to provide an early opportunity for healthcare providers to identify cases where an investigation is required and to carry out that investigation promptly;
- to encourage primary and private healthcare providers to involve their defence organisations or insurers at an early stage;
- to ensure that all relevant medical records are provided to patients or their appointed representatives on request, to a realistic timetable by any healthcare provider;
- to ensure that relevant records which are not in healthcare providers' possession are made available to them by patients and their advisers at an appropriate stage;
- where a resolution is not achievable to lay the ground to enable litigation to proceed on a reasonable timetable, at a reasonable and proportionate cost and to limit the matters in contention;
- to discourage the prolonged pursuit of unmeritorious claims and the prolonged defence of meritorious claims.

Awareness of options
- to ensure that patients and healthcare providers are made aware of the available options to pursue and resolve disputes and what each might involve.

2.3   This protocol does not attempt to be prescriptive about a number of related clinical governance issues which will have a bearing on healthcare providers' ability to meet the standards within the protocol. Good clinical governance requires the following to be considered—

(a) **Clinical risk management:** the protocol does not provide any detailed guidance to healthcare providers on clinical risk management or the adoption of risk management systems and procedures. This must be a matter for the NHS Executive, the National Health Service Litigation

Authority, individual trusts and providers, including GPs, dentists and the private sector. However, effective co-ordinated, focused clinical risk management strategies and procedures can help in managing risk and in the early identification and investigation of adverse outcomes.

(b) **Adverse outcome reporting:** the protocol does not provide any detailed guidance on which adverse outcomes should trigger an investigation. However, healthcare providers should have in place procedures for such investigations, including recording of statements of key witnesses. These procedures should also cover when and how to inform patients that an adverse outcome has occurred.

(c) **The professional's duty to report:** the protocol does not recommend changes to the codes of conduct of professionals in healthcare, or attempt to impose a specific duty on those professionals to report known adverse outcomes or untoward incidents. Lord Woolf in his final report suggested that the professional bodies might consider this. The General Medical Council is preparing guidance to doctors about their duty to report adverse incidents and to co-operate with inquiries.

3   The Protocol

3.1 This protocol is not a comprehensive code governing all the steps in clinical disputes. Rather it attempts to set out **a code of good practice** which parties should follow when litigation might be a possibility.

3.2 The **commitments** section of the protocol summarises the guiding principles which healthcare providers and patients and their advisers are invited to endorse when dealing with patient dissatisfaction with treatment and its outcome, and with potential complaints and claims.

3.3 The **steps** section sets out in a more prescriptive form, a recommended sequence of actions to be followed if litigation is a prospect.

Good practice commitments

3.4 **Healthcare providers** should—
(i)   ensure that **key staff**, including claims and litigation managers, are appropriately trained and have some knowledge of healthcare law, and of complaints procedures and civil litigation practice and procedure;
(ii) develop an approach to **clinical governance** that ensures that clinical practice is delivered to commonly accepted standards and that this is routinely monitored through a system of clinical audit and clinical risk management (particularly adverse outcome investigation);
(iii) set up **adverse outcome reporting systems** in all specialties to record and investigate unexpected serious adverse outcomes as soon as possible. Such systems can enable evidence to be gathered quickly, which makes it easier to provide an accurate explanation of what happened and to defend or settle any subsequent claims;
(iv) use the results of **adverse incidents and complaints positively** as a guide to how to improve services to patients in the future;
(v)   ensure **that patients receive clear and comprehensible information** in an accessible form about how to raise their concerns or complaints;

(vi) establish **efficient and effective systems of recording and storing patient records**, notes, diagnostic reports and X-rays, and to retain these in accordance with Department of Health guidance (currently for a minimum of eight years in the case of adults, and all obstetric and paediatric notes for children until they reach the age of 25);

(vii) **advise patients** of a serious adverse outcome and provide on request to the patient or the patient's representative an oral or written explanation of what happened, information on further steps open to the patient, including where appropriate an offer of future treatment to rectify the problem, an apology, changes in procedure which will benefit patients and/or compensation.

3.5 **Patients and their advisers** should—

(i) **report any concerns and dissatisfaction** to the healthcare provider as soon as is reasonable to enable that provider to offer clinical advice where possible, to advise the patient if anything has gone wrong and take appropriate action;

(ii) consider the **full range of options** available following an adverse outcome with which a patient is dissatisfied, including a request for an explanation, a meeting, a complaint, and other appropriate dispute resolution methods (including mediation) and negotiation, not only litigation;

(iii) **inform the healthcare provider when the patient is satisfied** that the matter has been concluded: legal advisers should notify the provider when they are no longer acting for the patient, particularly if proceedings have not started.

Protocol steps

3.6 The steps of this protocol which follow have been kept deliberately simple. An illustration of the likely sequence of events in a number of healthcare situations is at Annex A.

Obtaining the health records

3.7 Any request for records by the **patient** or their adviser should—

* **provide sufficient information** to alert the healthcare provider where an adverse outcome has been serious or had serious consequences;
* be as **specific as possible** about the records which are required.

3.8 Requests for copies of the patient's clinical records should be made using the Law Society and Department of Health approved **standard forms** (enclosed at Annex B), adapted as necessary.

3.9 The copy records should be provided **within 40 days** of the request and for a cost not exceeding the charges permissible under the Access to Health Records Act 1990 (currently a maximum of £10 plus photocopying and postage).

3.10 In the rare circumstances that the healthcare provider is in difficulty in complying with the request within 40 days, the **problem should be explained** quickly and details given of what is being done to resolve it.

3.11 It will not be practicable for healthcare providers to investigate in detail each case when records are requested. But healthcare providers should **adopt**

a policy on which cases will be investigated (see paragraph 3.5 on clinical governance and adverse outcome reporting).

3.12 If the healthcare provider fails to provide the health records within 40 days, the patient or their adviser can then apply to the court for an **order for pre-action disclosure**. The new Civil Procedure Rules should make pre-action applications to the court easier. The court will also have the power to impose costs sanctions for unreasonable delay in providing records.

3.13 If either the patient or the healthcare provider considers **additional health records are required from a third party**, in the first instance these should be requested by or through the patient. Third party healthcare providers are expected to co-operate. The Civil Procedure Rules will enable patients and healthcare providers to apply to the court for pre-action disclosure by third parties.

Letter of claim

3.14 Annex C1 to this protocol provides **a template for the recommended contents of a letter of claim**: the level of detail will need to be varied to suit the particular circumstances.

3.15 If, following the receipt and analysis of the records, and the receipt of any further advice (including from experts if necessary—see Section 4), the patient/adviser decides that there are grounds for a claim, they should then send, as soon as practicable, to the healthcare provider/potential defendant, a **letter of claim.**

3.16 This letter should contain a **clear summary of the facts** on which the claim is based, including the alleged adverse outcome, and the **main allegations of negligence**. It should also describe the **patient's injuries**, and present condition and prognosis. The **financial loss** incurred by the plaintiff should be outlined with an indication of the heads of damage to be claimed and the scale of the loss, unless this is impracticable.

3.17 In more complex cases a **chronology** of the relevant events should be provided, particularly if the patient has been treated by a number of different healthcare providers.

3.18 The letter of claim **should refer to any relevant documents**, including health records, and if possible enclose copies of any of those which will not already be in the potential defendant's possession, eg any relevant general practitioner records if the plaintiff's claim is against a hospital.

3.19 **Sufficient information** must be given to enable the healthcare provider defendant to **commence investigations** and to put an initial valuation on the claim.

3.20 Letters of claim are **not** intended to have the same formal status as a **pleading**, nor should any sanctions necessarily apply if the letter of claim and any subsequent statement of claim in the proceedings differ.

3.21 **Proceedings should not be issued until after three months from the letter of claim**, unless there is a limitation problem and/or the patient's position needs to be protected by early issue.

3.22 The patient or their adviser may want to make an **offer to settle** the claim at this early stage by putting forward an amount of compensation which would be satisfactory (possibly including any costs incurred to date). If an offer to settle is made, generally this should be supported by a medical report which deals with the injuries, condition and prognosis, and by a schedule of loss and supporting documentation. The level of detail necessary will depend on the value of the claim. Medical reports may not be necessary where there is no significant continuing injury, and a detailed schedule may not be necessary in a low value case. The Civil Procedure Rules are expected to set out the legal and procedural requirements for making offers to settle.

The response

3.23 Attached at Annex C2 is a template for the suggested contents of the **letter of response.**

3.24 The healthcare provider should **acknowledge** the letter of claim **within 14 days of receipt** and should identify who will be dealing with the matter.

3.25 The healthcare provider should, **within three months** of the letter of claim, provide a **reasoned answer**—
*   if the **claim is admitted** the healthcare provider should say so in clear terms;
*   if only **part of the claim is admitted** the healthcare provider should make clear which issues of breach of duty and/or causation are admitted and which are denied and why;
*   if it is intended that any **admissions will be binding**;
*   if the claim is denied, this should include specific comments on the allegations of negligence, and if a synopsis or chronology of relevant events has been provided and is disputed, the healthcare provider's version of those events;
*   where additional documents are relied upon, eg an internal protocol, copies should be provided.

3.26 If the patient has made an offer to settle, the healthcare provider should **respond to that offer** in the response letter, preferably with reasons. The provider may make its own offer to settle at this stage, either as a counter-offer to the patient's, or of its own accord, but should accompany any offer by any supporting medical evidence, and/or by any other evidence in relation to the value of the claim which is in the healthcare provider's possession.

3.27 If the parties reach agreement on liability, but time is needed to resolve the value of the claim, they should aim to agree a reasonable period.

4   Experts

4.1 In clinical negligence disputes expert opinions may be needed—
*   on breach of duty and causation;
*   on the patient's condition and prognosis;
*   to assist in valuing aspects of the claim.

4.2 The civil justice reforms and the new Civil Procedure Rules will encourage economy in the use of experts and a less adversarial expert culture. It is recognised that in clinical negligence disputes, the parties and their advisers will require flexibility in their approach to expert evidence. Decisions on whether experts might be instructed jointly, and on whether reports might be disclosed sequentially or by exchange, should rest with the parties and their advisers. Sharing expert evidence may be appropriate on issues relating to the value of the claim. However, this protocol does not attempt to be prescriptive on issues in relation to expert evidence.

4.3 Obtaining expert evidence will often be an expensive step and may take time, especially in specialised areas of medicine where there are limited numbers of suitable experts. Patients and healthcare providers, and their advisers, will therefore need to consider carefully how best to obtain any necessary expert help quickly and cost-effectively. Assistance with locating a suitable expert is available from a number of sources.

5 *Alternative approaches to settling disputes*

5.1 It would not be practicable for this protocol to address in any detail how a patient or their adviser, or healthcare provider, might decide which method to adopt to resolve the particular problem. But, the courts increasingly expect parties to try to settle their differences by agreement before issuing proceedings.

5.2 Most disputes are resolved by **discussion and negotiation**. Parties should bear in mind that carefully planned face-to-face meetings may be particularly helpful in exploring further treatment for the patient, in reaching understandings about what happened, and on both parties' positions, in narrowing the issues in dispute and, if the timing is right, in helping to settle the whole matter.

5.3 Summarised below are some other alternatives for resolving disputes—
- The revised **NHS Complaints Procedur**e, which was implemented in April 1996, is designed to provide patients with an explanation of what happened and an apology if appropriate. It is not designed to provide compensation for cases of negligence. However, patients might choose to use the procedure if their only, or main, goal is to obtain an explanation, or to obtain more information to help them decide what other action might be appropriate.
- **Mediation** may be appropriate in some cases: this is a form of facilitated negotiation assisted by an independent neutral party. It is expected that the new Civil Procedure Rules will give the court the power to stay proceedings for one month for settlement discussions or mediation.
- Other methods of resolving disputes include **arbitration, determination by an expert, and early neutral evaluation** by a medical or legal expert. The Lord Chancellor's Department has produced a booklet on '**Resolving Disputes Without Going to Court**', LCD 1995, which lists a number of organisations that provide alternative dispute resolution services.

Annex A   Illustrative Flowchart

Patient (P)   *Healthcare Provider* (HCP)

INITIAL STAGES

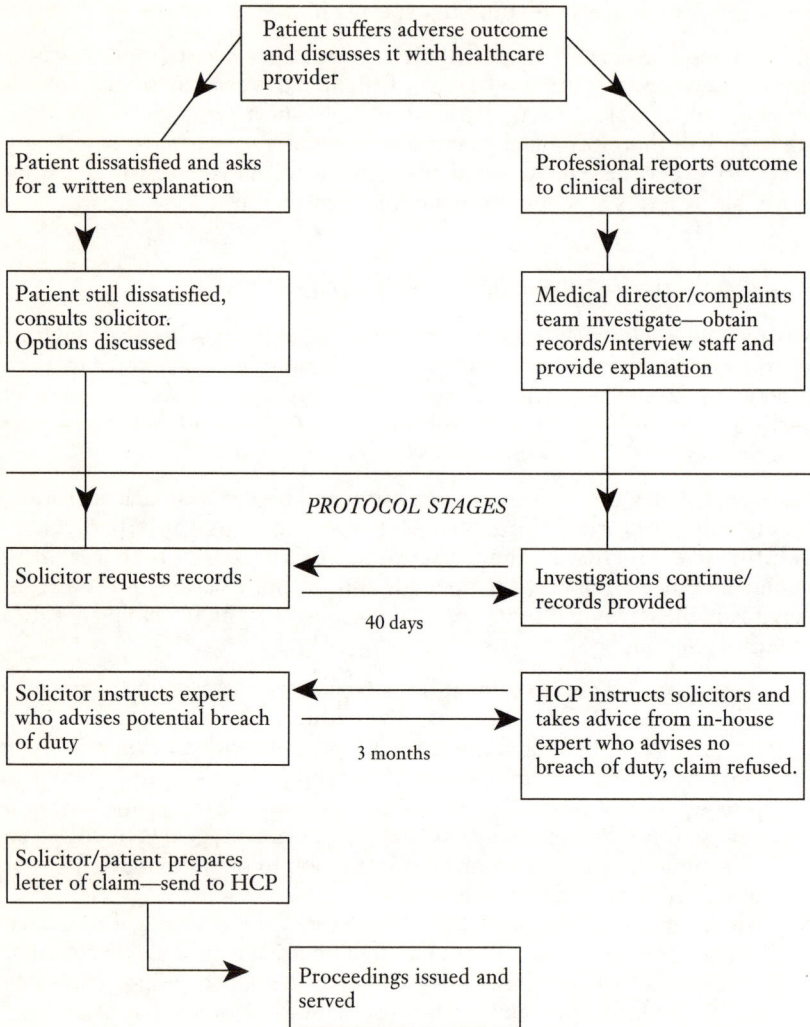

Patient suffers adverse outcome and discusses it with healthcare provider

Patient dissatisfied and asks for a written explanation

Professional reports outcome to clinical director

Patient still dissatisfied, consults solicitor. Options discussed

Medical director/complaints team investigate—obtain records/interview staff and provide explanation

PROTOCOL STAGES

Solicitor requests records

Investigations continue/ records provided

40 days

Solicitor instructs expert who advises potential breach of duty

HCP instructs solicitors and takes advice from in-house expert who advises no breach of duty, claim refused.

3 months

Solicitor/patient prepares letter of claim—send to HCP

Proceedings issued and served

Annex B   Medical negligence and personal injury claims: a Protocol for obtaining hospital medical records

Law Society Civil Litigation Committee—revised edition June 1998

APPLICATION ON BEHALF OF A PATIENT FOR HOSPITAL MEDICAL RECORDS FOR USE WHEN COURT PROCEEDINGS ARE CONTEMPLATED

Purpose of the forms

This application form and response forms have been prepared by a working party of the Law Society's Civil Litigation Committee and approved by the Department of Health for use in NHS and Trust hospitals.

The purpose of the forms is to standardise and streamline the disclosure of medical records to a patient's solicitors, who are investigating pursuing a personal injury claim against a third party, or a medical negligence claim against the hospital to which the application is addressed and/or other hospitals or general practitioners.

Use of the forms

Use of the forms is entirely voluntary and does not prejudice any party's right under the Access to Health Records Act 1990, the Data Protection Act 1984, or ss 33 and 34 of the Supreme Court Act 1981. However, it is Department of Health policy that patients be permitted to see what has been written about them, and that healthcare providers should make arrangements to allow patients to see all their records, not only those covered by the Access to Health Records Act 1990. The aim of the forms is to save time and costs for all concerned for the benefit of the patient and the hospital and in the interests of justice. Use of the forms should make it unnecessary in most cases for there to be exchanges of letters or other enquiries. If there is any unusual matter not covered by the form, the patient's solicitor may write a separate letter at the outset.

Charges for records

The Access to Health Records Act 1990 prescribes a maximum fee of £10. Photocopying and postage costs can be charged in addition. No other charges may be made.

The NHS Executive guidance makes it clear to healthcare providers that 'it is a perfectly proper use' of the 1990 Act to request records in that framework for the purpose of potential or actual litigation, whether against a third party or against the hospital or trust.

The 1990 Act does not permit differential rates of charges to be levied if the application is made by the patient, or by a solicitor on his or her behalf, or whether the response to the application is made by the healthcare provider directly (the medical records manager or a claims manager) or by a solicitor.

The NHS Executive guidance recommends that the same practice should be followed with regard to charges when the records are provided under a voluntary agreement as under the 1990 Act, except that in those circumstances the £10 access fee will not be appropriate.

The NHS Executive also advises—
- that the cost of photocopying may include 'the cost of staff time in making copies' and the costs of running the copier (but not costs of locating and sifting records);
- that the common practice of setting a standard rate for an application or charging an administration fee is not acceptable because there will be cases when this fails to comply with the 1990 Act.

Records: what might be included

X-rays and test results form part of the patient's records. Additional charges for copying X-rays are permissible. If there are large numbers of X-rays, the records officer should check with the patient/solicitor before arranging copying.

Reports on an 'adverse incident' and reports on the patient made for risk management and audit purposes may form part of the records and be disclosable: the exception will be any specific record or report made solely or mainly in connection with an actual or potential claim.

Records: quality standards

When copying records healthcare providers should ensure —
1. All documents are legible, and complete, if necessary by photocopying at less than 100% size.
2. Documents larger than A4 in the original, eg ITU charts, should be reproduced in A3, or reduced to A4 where this retains readability.
3. Documents are only copied on one side of paper, unless the original is two sided.
4. Documents should not be unnecessarily shuffled or bound and holes should not be made in the copied papers.

Enquiries/further information

Any enquiries about the forms should be made initially to the solicitors making the request. Comments on the use and content of the forms should be made to the Secretary, Civil Litigation Committee, The Law Society, 113 Chancery Lane, London WC2A 1PL, telephone 0207 320 5739, or to the NHS Management Executive, Quarry House, Quarry Hill, Leeds LS2 7UE.

The Law Society
May 1998

APPLICATION ON BEHALF OF A PATIENT FOR HOSPITAL MEDICAL RECORDS FOR USE WHEN COURT PROCEEDINGS ARE CONTEMPLATED

This should be completed as fully as possible

Insert

Hospital

Name

and

Address

| TO: Medical Records Officer |
| Hospital |

1
(a)   Full name of patient (including previous surnames)
(b)   Address now
(c)   Address at start of treatment
(d)   Date of birth (and death, if applicable)
(e)   Hospital ref no if available
(f)   NI number, if available

2. This application is made because the patient is considering
(a)   a claim against your hospital as detailed in para 7 overleaf YES/NO
(b)   pursuing an action against someone else   YES/NO

3 Department(s) where treatment was received

4 Name(s) of consultant(s) at your hospital in charge of the treatment

5 Whether treatment at your hospital was private or NHS, wholly or in part

6 A description of the treatment received, with approximate dates

7 If the answer to Q2(a) is 'Yes' details of
(a)   the likely nature of the claim
(b)   grounds for the claim
(c)   approximate dates of the events involved

8 If the answer to Q2(b) is 'Yes' insert
(a)   the names of the proposed defendants
(b)   whether legal proceedings yet begun   YES/NO
(c)   if appropriate, details of the claim and action number

9 We confirm we will pay reasonable copying charges

10 We request prior details of
a)   photocopying and administration charges for medical records YES/NO
b)   number of and cost of copying x-ray and scan films YES/NO

11 Any other relevant information, particular requirements, or any particular documents not required (eg copies of computerised records)

Signature of solicitor

Name
Address
Ref.

Telephone Number
Fax number

Please print name beneath each signature.

Signature by child over 12 but under

18 years also requires signature by parent

Signature of patient

Signature of parent or next friend if appropriate

Signature of personal representative where patient has died

FIRST RESPONSE TO APPLICATION FOR HOSPITAL RECORDS

NAME OF PATIENT

Our ref

Your ref

1 Date of receipt of patient's application

2 We intend that copy medical records will be dispatched within 6 weeks of that date   YES/NO

3 We require pre-payment of photocopying charges   YES/NO

4 If estimate of photocopying charges requested or pre-payment required the amount will be £   /notified to you

5 The cost of x-ray and scan films will be £   /notified to you

6 If there is any problem, we shall write to you within those 6 weeks YES/NO

7 Any other information

Please address further correspondence to
Signed
Direct telephone number
Direct fax number
Dated

SECOND RESPONSE ENCLOSING PATIENT'S HOSPITAL MEDICAL RECORDS

Address   Our Ref.

                                               Your Ref.

1   NAME OF PATIENT:

We confirm that the enclosed copy medical records are all those within the control of the hospital, relevant to the application which you have made to the best of our knowledge and belief, subject to paras 2–5 below

YES/NO

2   Details of any other documents which have not yet been located

3   Date by when it is expected that these will be supplied

4   Details of any records which we are not producing

5   The reasons for not doing so

6   An invoice for copying and administration charges is attached
YES/NO

Signed

Date

Annex C Templates for letters of claim and response

C1 Letter of claim

Essential Contents
1.   **Client's name, address, date of birth, etc.**
2.   **Dates of allegedly negligent treatment**
3.   **Events giving rise to the claim**:
     - an outline of what happened, including details of other relevant treatments to the client by other healthcare providers.
4.   **Allegation of negligence and causal link with injuries:**
     - an outline of the allegations or a more detailed list in a complex case;
     - an outline of the causal link between allegations and the injuries complained of.
5.   **The client's injuries, condition and future prognosis**
6.   **Request for clinical records (if not previously provided)**
     - use the Law Society form if appropriate or adapt;
     - specify the records require;
     - if other records are held by other providers, and may be relevant, say so;
     - state what investigations have been carried out to date, eg information from client and witnesses, any complaint and the

outcome, if any clinical records have been seen or experts advice obtained.

7. **The likely value of the claim**
   - an outline of the main heads of damage, or, in straightforward cases, the details of loss.

Optional information

What investigations have been carried out
An offer to settle without supporting evidence
Suggestions for obtaining expert evidence
Suggestions for meetings, negotiations, discussion or mediation

Possible enclosures
Chronology
Clinical records request form and client's authorisation
Expert report(s)
Schedules of loss and supporting evidence

C2 Letter of response

Essential Contents
1. Provide **requested records** and invoice for copying:
   - explain if records are incomplete or extensive records are held and ask for further instructions;
   - request additional records from third parties.
2. **Comments on events and/or chronology:**
   - if events are disputed or the healthcare provider has further information or documents on which they wish to rely, these should be provided, e.g. internal protocol;
   - details of any further information needed from the patient or a third party should be provided.
3. **If breach of duty and causation are accepted:**
   - suggestions might be made for resolving the claim and/or requests for further information;
   - a response should be made to any offer to settle.
4. **If breach of duty and/or causation are denied:**
   - a bare denial will not be sufficient. If the healthcare provider has other explanations for what happened, these should be given at least in outline;
   - suggestions might be made for the next steps, eg further investigations, obtaining expert evidence, meetings/ negotiations or mediation, or an invitation to issue proceedings.

Optional matters

An offer to settle if the patient has not made one, or a counter offer to the patient's with supporting evidence

Possible enclosures:
Clinical records

Annotated chronology
Expert reports

Annex D Lord Woolf's recommendations

1. Lord Woolf in his Access to Justice Report in July 1996, following a detailed review of the problems of medical negligence claims, identified that one of the major sources of **costs and delay** is **at the pre-litigation stage** because –
(a) Inadequate incident reporting and record keeping in hospitals, and mobility of staff, make it difficult to establish facts, often several years after the event.
(b) Claimants must incur the cost of an expert in order to establish whether they have a viable claim.
(c) There is often a long delay before a claim is made.
(d) Defendants do not have sufficient resources to carry out a full investigation of every incident, and do not consider it worthwhile to start an investigation as soon as they receive a request for records, because many cases do not proceed beyond that stage.
(e) Patients often give the defendant little or no notice of a firm intention to pursue a claim. Consequently, many incidents are not investigated by the defendants until after proceedings have started.
(f) Doctors and other clinical staff are traditionally reluctant to admit negligence or apologise to, or negotiate with, claimants for fear of damage to their professional reputations or career prospects.

2. Lord Woolf acknowledged that under the present arrangements **healthcare providers**, faced with possible medical negligence claims, have a number of **practical problems** to contend with –
(a) Difficulties of finding patients' records and tracing former staff, which can be exacerbated by late notification and by the health care provider's own failure to identify adverse incidents.
(b) The healthcare provider may have only treated the patient for a limited time or for a specific complaint: the patient's previous history may be relevant but the records may be in the possession of one of several other healthcare providers.
(c) The large number of potential claims which do not proceed beyond the stage of a request for medical records, or an explanation; and that it is difficult for healthcare providers to investigate fully every case whenever a patient asks to see the records.

Annex E How to contact the Forum

The Clinical Disputes Forum

Chairman
Dr Alastair Scotland
Director of Medical Education
Chelsea and Westminster Hospital

Secretary
Sarah Leigh
c/o Margaret Dangoor
3 Clydesdale Gardens

369 Fulham Road
London
SW1 9NH
(telephone: 0208 746 8000)

Richmond
Surrey
TW10 5EG
(telephone: 0208 408 1012)

APPENDIX D

Pre-action protocol for personal injury claims (December 1998)

1 Introduction

1.1 Lord Woolf in his final Access to Justice Report of July 1996 recommended the development of pre-action protocols: 'To build on and increase the benefits of early but well informed settlement which genuinely satisfy both parties to dispute.'

1.2 The aims of pre-action protocols are:
- more pre-action contact between the parties
- better and earlier exchange of information
- better pre-action investigation by both sides
- to put the parties in a position where they may be able to settle cases fairly and early without litigation
- to enable proceedings to run to the court's timetable and efficiently, if litigation does become necessary.

1.3 The concept of protocols is relevant to a range of initiatives for good litigation and pre-litigation practice, especially:
- predictability in the time needed for steps pre-proceedings
- standardisation of relevant information, including documents to be disclosed.

1.4 The Courts will be able to treat the standards set in protocols as the normal reasonable approach to pre-action conduct. If proceedings are issued, it will be for the court to decide whether non-compliance with a protocol should merit adverse consequences. Guidance on the court's likely approach will be given from time to time in practice directions.

1.5 If the court has to consider the question of compliance after proceedings have begun, it will not be concerned with minor infringements, e.g. failure by a short period to provide relevant information. One minor breach will not exempt the 'innocent' party from following the protocol. The court will look at the effect of non-compliance on the other party when deciding whether to impose sanctions.

2 Notes of guidance

2.1 The protocol has been kept deliberately simple to promote ease of use and general acceptability. The notes of guidance which follow relate particularly to issues which arose during the piloting of the protocol.

Scope of the Protocol

2.2 This protocol is intended to apply to all claims which include a claim for personal injury and to the entirety of those claims: not only to the personal injury element of a claim which also includes, for instance, property damage.

2.3 This protocol is primarily designed for those road traffic, tripping and slipping and accident at work cases which include an element of personal injury with a value of less than £15,000 which are likely to be allocated to the fast track. This is because time will be of the essence, after proceedings are issued, especially for the defendant, if a case is to be ready for trial within 30 weeks of allocation. Also, proportionality of work and costs to the value of what is in dispute is particularly important in lower value claims. For some claims within the value 'scope' of the fast track some flexibility in the timescale of the protocol may be necessary, see also paragraph 3.8.

2.4 However, the 'cards on the table' approach advocated by the protocol is equally appropriate to some higher value claims. The spirit, if not the letter of the protocol, should still be followed for multi-track type claims. In accordance with the sense of the civil justice reforms, the court will expect to see the spirit of reasonable pre-action behaviour applied in all cases, regardless of the existence of a specific protocol.

2.5 The timetable and the arrangements for disclosing documents and obtaining expert evidence may need to be varied to suit the circumstances of the case. Where one or both parties consider the detail of the protocol is not appropriate to the case, and proceedings are subsequently issued, the court will expect an explanation as to why the protocol has not been followed, or has been varied.

Early notification

2.6 The claimant's legal representative may wish to notify the defendant and/or his insurer as soon as they know a claim is likely to be made, but before they are able to send a detailed letter of claim, particularly for instance, when the defendant has no or limited knowledge of the incident giving rise to the claim or where the claimant is incurring significant expenditure as a result of the accident which he hopes the defendant might pay for, in whole or in part. If the claimant's representative chooses to do this, it will not start the timetable for responding.

The letter of claim

2.7 The specimen letter of claim at Annex A will usually be sent to the individual defendant. In practice, he/she may have no personal financial interest in the financial outcome of the claim/dispute because he/she is insured. Court imposed sanctions for non-compliance with the protocol may be ineffective against an insured. This is why the protocol emphasises the importance of passing the letter of claim to the insurer and the possibility that the insurance cover might be affected. If an insurer receives the letter of claim only after some delay by the insured, it would not be unreasonable for the insurer to ask the claimant for additional time to respond.

Reasons for early issue

2.8 The protocol recommends that a defendant be given three months to investigate and respond to a claim before proceedings are issued. This may not always be possible, particularly where a claimant only consults a solicitor close to the end of any relevant limitation period. In these circumstances, the claimant's solicitor should give as much notice of the intention to issue proceedings as is practicable and the parties should consider whether the court might be invited to extend time for service of the claimant's supporting documents and for service of any defence, or alternatively, to stay the proceedings while the recommended steps in the protocol are followed.

Status of letters of claim and response

2.9 Letters of claim and response are not intended to have the same status as a statement of case in proceedings. Matters may come to light as a result of investigation after the letter of claim has been sent, or after the defendant has responded, particularly if disclosure of documents takes place outside the recommended three-month period. These circumstances could mean that the 'pleaded' case of one or both parties is presented slightly differently than in the letter of claim and response. It would not be consistent with the spirit of the protocol for a party to 'take a point' on this in the proceedings, provided that there was no obvious intention by the party who changed their position to mislead the other party.

Disclosure of documents

2.10 The aim of the early disclosure of documents by the defendant is not to encourage 'fishing expeditions' by the claimant, but to promote an early exchange of relevant information to help in clarifying or resolving issues in dispute. The claimant's solicitor can assist by identifying in the letter of claim or in a subsequent letter the particular categories of documents which they consider are relevant.

Experts

2.11 The protocol encourages joint selection of, and access to, experts. Most frequently this will apply to the medical expert, but on occasions also to liability experts, eg engineers. The protocol promotes the practice of the claimant obtaining a medical report, disclosing it to the defendant who then asks questions and/or agrees it and does not obtain his own report. But it maintains the flexibility for each party to obtain their own expert's report, if necessary after proceedings have commenced, with the leave of the court. It would also be for the court to decide whether the costs of more than one expert's report should be recoverable.

2.12 Some solicitors choose to obtain medical reports through medical agencies, rather than directly from a specific doctor or hospital. The defendant's prior consent to the action should be sought and, if the defendant so requests, the agency should be asked to provide in advance the names of the doctor(s) whom they are considering instructing.

Negotiations/settlement

2.13 Parties and their legal representatives are encouraged to enter into discussions and/or negotiations prior to starting proceedings. The protocol does not specify when or how this might be done but parties should bear in mind that the courts increasingly take the view that litigation should be a last resort, and that claims should not be issued prematurely when a settlement is in reasonable prospect.

Stocktake

2.14 Where a claim is not resolved when the protocol has been followed, the parties might wish to carry out a 'stocktake' of the issues in dispute, and the evidence that the court is likely to need to decide those issues, before proceedings are started. Where the defendant is insured and the pre-action steps have been conducted by the insurer, the insurer would normally be expected to nominate solicitors to act in the proceedings and the claimant's solicitor is recommended to invite the insurer to nominate solicitors to act in the proceedings and do so 7–14 days before the intended issue date.

3 The Protocol

Letter of claim

3.1 The claimant shall send to the proposed defendant two copies of a letter of claim, immediately sufficient information is available to substantiate a realistic claim and before issues of quantum are addressed in detail. One copy of the letter is for the defendants, the second for passing on to his insurers.

3.2 The letter shall contain **a clear summary of the facts** on which the claim is based together with an indication of the **nature of any injuries** suffered and of **any financial loss incurred**. In cases of road traffic accidents, the letter should provide the name and address of the hospital where treatment has been obtained and the claimant's hospital reference number.

3.3 Solicitors are recommended to use a **standard format** for such a letter— an example is at Annex A: this can be amended to suit the particular case.

3.4 The letter should ask for **details of the insurer** and that a copy should be sent by the proposed defendant to the insurer where appropriate. If the insurer is known, a copy shall be sent directly to the insurer. Details of the claimant's National Insurance number and date of birth should be supplied to the defendant's insurer once the Defendant has responded to the letter of claim and confirmed the identity of the insurer. This information should not be supplied in the letter of claim.

3.5 **Sufficient information** should be given in order to enable the defendant's insurer/solicitor to commence investigations and at least put a broad valuation on the 'risk'.

3.6 The **defendant should reply within 21 calendar days** of the date of posting of the letter identifying the insurer (if any). If there has been no reply by the defendant or insurer within 21 days, the claimant will be entitled to issue proceedings.

3.7 The **defendant**('s insurers) will have a **maximum of three months** from the date of acknowledgment of the claim **to investigate.** No later than the end of that period the defendant (insurer) shall reply, stating whether liability is denied and, if so, giving reasons for their denial of liability.

3.8 Where the accident occurred outside England and Wales and/or where the defendant is outside the jurisdiction, the time periods of 21 days and three months may reasonably be extended up to 42 days and six months.

3.9 Where **liability is admitted,** the presumption is that the defendant will be bound by this admission for all claims with a total value of up to £15,000.

Documents

3.10 If the **defendant denies liability**, he should enclose with the letter of reply, **documents** in his possession which are **material to the issues** between the parties, and which would be likely to be ordered to be disclosed by the court, either on an application for pre-action disclosure, or on disclosure during proceedings.

3.11 Attached at Annex B are **specimen**, but non-exhaustive, **lists** of documents likely to be material in different types of claim. Where the claimant's investigation of the case is well advanced, the letter of claim could indicate which classes of documents are considered relevant for early disclosure. Alternatively these could be identified at a later stage.

3.12 Where the defendant admits primary liability, but alleges contributory negligence by the claimant, the defendant should give reasons supporting those allegations and disclose those documents from Annex B which are relevant to the issues in dispute. The claimant should respond to the allegations of contributory negligence before proceedings are issued.

Special damages

3.13 The claimant will send to the defendant as soon as practicable a Schedule of Special Damages with supporting documents, particularly where the defendant has admitted liability.

Experts

3.14 Before any party instructs an expert he should give the other party a list of the **name**(s) of **one or more experts** in the relevant speciality whom he considers are suitable to instruct.

3.15 Where a medical expert is to be instructed the claimant's solicitor will organise access to relevant medical records—see specimen letter of instruction at Annex C.

3.16 **Within 14 days** the other party may indicate **an objection** to one or more of the named experts. The first party should then instruct a mutually acceptable expert.

3.17 If the second party objects to all the listed experts, the parties may then instruct **experts of their own choice**. It would be for the court to decide subsequently, if proceedings are issued, whether either party had acted unreasonably.

3.18 If the **second party does not object to an expert nominated**, he shall not be entitled to rely on his own expert evidence within that particular speciality unless:
(a)   the first party agrees,
(b)   the court so directs, or
(c)   the first party's expert report has been amended and the first party is not prepared to disclose the original report.

3.19 **Either party may send to an agreed expert written questions** on the report, relevant to the issues, via the first party's solicitors. The expert should send answers to the questions separately and directly to each party.

3.20 The cost of a report from an agreed expert will usually be paid by the instructing first party: the costs of the expert replying to questions will usually be borne by the party which asks the questions.

3.21 Where the defendant admits liability in whole or in part, before proceedings are issued, any medical report obtained by agreement under this protocol should be disclosed to the other party. The claimant should delay issuing proceedings for 21 days from disclosure of the report, to enable the parties to consider whether the claim is capable of settlement. The Civil Procedure Rules Part 36 permit claimants and defendants to make offers to settle pre-proceedings.

Annex A Letter of claim

To

Defendant

Dear Sirs

> ### <u>Re:</u>   <u>Claimant's full name</u>
> ### <u>Claimant's full address</u>
> ### <u>Claimant's Clock or Works Number</u>
> ### <u>Claimant's Employer (name and address)</u>

We are instructed by the above named to claim damages in connection with an *accident at work/ road traffic accident / tripping accident* on   day of   *(year)* at *(place of accident which must be sufficiently detailed to establish location)*

Please confirm the identity of your insurers. Please note that the insurers will need to see this letter as soon as possible and it may affect your insurance cover and/or the conduct of any subsequent legal proceedings if you do not send this letter to them.

The circumstances of the accident are:

(brief outline)

The reason why we are alleging fault is:

(simple explanation eg defective machine, broken ground)

A description of our clients' injuries is as follows:-

(brief outline)

(In cases of road traffic accidents)

Our client (state hospital reference number) received treatment for the injuries at name and address of hospital).

He is employed as *(occupation)* and has had the following time off work *(dates of absence)*. His approximate weekly income is *(insert if known)*.

If you are our client's employers, please provide us with the usual earnings details which will enable us to calculate his financial loss.

We are obtaining a police report and will let you have a copy of the same upon your undertaking to meet half the fee.

We have also sent a letter of claim to *(name and address)* and a copy of that letter is attached. We understand their insurers are *(name, address and claims number if known)*.

At this stage of our enquiries we would expect the documents contained in parts *(insert appropriate parts of standard disclosure list)* to be relevant to this action.

A copy of this letter is attached for you to send to your insurers. Finally we expect an acknowledgment of this letter within 21 days by yourselves or your insurers.

Yours faithfully

Annex B Pre-action personal injury protocol—standard disclosure lists

Fast track disclosure

RTA CASES

SECTION A

In all cases where liability is at issue—
(i) Documents identifying nature, extent and location of damage to defendant's vehicle where there is any dispute about point of impact.
(ii) MOT certificate where relevant.
(iii) Maintenance records where vehicle defect is alleged or it is alleged by defendant that there was an unforeseen defect which caused or contributed to the accident.

SECTION B

Accident involving commercial vehicle as potential defendant—
(i) Tachograph charts or entry from individual control book.
(ii) Maintenance and repair records required for operators' licence where vehicle defect is alleged or it is alleged by defendants that there was an unforeseen defect which caused or contributed to the accident.

SECTION C

Cases against local authorities where highway design defect is alleged.
(i) Documents produced to comply with Section 39 of the Road Traffic Act 1988 in respect of the duty designed to promote road safety to include studies into road accidents in the relevant area and documents relating to measures recommended to prevent accidents in the relevant area.

HIGHWAY TRIPPING CLAIMS

Documents from Highway Authority for a period of 12 months prior to the accident—
(i) Records of inspection for the relevant stretch of highway.
(ii) Maintenance records including records of independent contractors working in relevant area.
(iii) Records of the minutes of Highway Authority meetings where maintenance or repair policy has been discussed or decided.
(iv) Records of complaints about the state of highways.
(v) Records of other accidents which have occurred on the relevant stretch of highway.

WORKPLACE CLAIMS
(i) Accident book entry.
(ii) First aider report.
(iii) Surgery record.
(iv) Foreman/supervisor accident report.
(v) Safety representatives accident report.

(vi) RIDDOR report to HSE.

(vii) Other communications between defendants and HSE.

(viii) Minutes of Health and Safety Committee meeting(s) where accident/matter considered.

(ix) Report to DSS.

(x) Documents listed above relative to any previous accident/matter identified by the claimant and relied upon as proof of negligence.

(xi) Earnings information where defendant is employer.

Documents produced to comply with requirements of the Management of Health and Safety at Work Regulations 1992—

(i) Pre-accident Risk Assessment required by Regulation 3.

(ii) Post-accident Re-Assessment required by Regulation 3.

(iii) Accident Investigation Report prepared in implementing the requirements of Regulations 4, 6 and 9.

(iv) Health Surveillance Records in appropriate cases required by Regulation 5.

(v) Information provided to employees under Regulation 8.

(vi) Documents relating to the employees health and safety training required by Regulation 11.

WORKPLACE CLAIMS—DISCLOSURE WHERE SPECIFIC REGULATIONS APPLY

SECTION A—WORKPLACE (HEALTH SAFETY AND WELFARE) REGULATIONS 1992

(i) Repair and maintenance records required by Regulation 5.

(ii) Housekeeping records to comply with the requirements of Regulation 9.

(iii) Hazard warning signs or notices to comply with Regulation 17 (Traffic Routes).

SECTION B—PROVISION AND USE OF WORK EQUIPMENT REGULATIONS 1992

(i) Manufacturers' specifications and instructions in respect of relevant work equipment establishing its suitability to comply with Regulation 5.

(ii) Maintenance log/maintenance records required to comply with Regulation 6.

(iii) Documents providing information and instructions to employees to comply with Regulation 8.

(iv) Documents provided to the employee in respect of training for use to comply with Regulation 9.

(v) Any notice, sign or document relied upon as a defence to alleged breaches of Regulations 14 to 18 dealing with controls and control systems.

(vi) Instruction/training documents issued to comply with the requirements of Regulation 22 insofar as it deals with maintenance operations where the machinery is not shut down.

(vii) Copies of markings required to comply with Regulation 23.

(viii) Copies of warnings required to comply with Regulation 24.

SECTION C—PERSONAL PROTECTIVE EQUIPMENT AT WORK REGULATIONS 1992

(i) Documents relating to the assessment of the Personal Protective Equipment to comply with Regulation 6.

(ii) Documents relating to the maintenance and replacement of Personal Protective Equipment to comply with Regulation 7.

(iii) Record of maintenance procedures for Personal Protective Equipment to comply with Regulation 7.

(iv) Records of tests and examinations of Personal Protective Equipment to comply with Regulation 7.

(v) Documents providing information, instruction and training in relation to the Personal Protective Equipment to comply with Regulation 9.

(vi) Instructions for use of Personal Protective Equipment to include the manufacturers' instructions to comply with Regulation 10.

SECTION D—MANUAL HANDLING OPERATIONS REGULATIONS 1992

(i) Manual Handling Risk Assessment carried out to comply with the requirements of Regulation 4(1)(b)(i).

(ii) Re-assessment carried out post-accident to comply with requirements of Regulation 4(1)(b)(i).

(iii) Documents showing the information provided to the employee to give general indications related to the load and precise indications on the weight of the load and the heaviest side of the load if the centre of gravity was not positioned centrally to comply with Regulation 4(1)(b)(iii).

(iv) Documents relating to training in respect of manual handling operations and training records.

SECTION E—HEALTH AND SAFETY (DISPLAY SCREEN EQUIPMENT) REGULATIONS 1992

(i) Analysis of work stations to assess and reduce risks carried out to comply with the requirements of Regulation 2.

(ii) Re-assessment of analysis of work stations to assess and reduce risks following development of symptoms by the claimant.

(iii) Documents detailing the provision of training including training records to comply with the requirements of Regulation 6.

(iv) Documents providing information to employees to comply with the requirements of Regulation 7.

SECTION F—CONTROL OF SUBSTANCES HAZARDOUS TO HEALTH REGULATIONS 1988

(i) Risk assessment carried out to comply with the requirements of Regulation 6.

(ii) Reviewed risk assessment carried out to comply with the requirements of Regulation 6.

(iii) Copy labels from containers used for storage handling and disposal of carcinogenics to comply with the requirements of Regulation 7(2A)(h).

(iv) Warning signs identifying designation of areas and installations which may be contaminated by carcinogenics to comply with the requirements of Regulation 7(2A)(h).

(v)   Documents relating to the assessment of the Personal Protective Equipment to comply with Regulation 7(3A).

(vi) Documents relating to the maintenance and replacement of Personal Protective Equipment to comply with Regulation 7(3A).

(vii) Record of maintenance procedures for Personal Protective Equipment to comply with Regulation 7(3A).

(viii)Records of tests and examinations of Personal Protective Equipment to comply with Regulation 7(3A).

(ix) Documents providing information, instruction and training in relation to the Personal Protective Equipment to comply with Regulation 7(3A).

(x)   Instructions for use of Personal Protective Equipment to include the manufacturers' instructions to comply with Regulation 7(3A).

(xi) Air monitoring records for substances assigned a maximum exposure limit or occupational exposure standard to comply with the requirements of Regulation 7.

(xii) Maintenance examination and test of control measures records to comply with Regulation 9.

(xiii)Monitoring records to comply with the requirements of Regulation 10.

(xiv) Health surveillance records to comply with the requirements of Regulation 11.

(xv) Documents detailing information, instruction and training including training records for employees to comply with the requirements of Regulation 12.

(xvi) Labels and Health and Safety data sheets supplied to the employers to comply with the CHIP Regulations.

SECTION G—CONSTRUCTION (DESIGN AND MANAGEMENT) REGULATIONS 1994

(i)   Notification of a project form (HSE F10) to comply with the requirements of Regulation 7.

(ii) Health and Safety Plan to comply with requirements of Regulation 15.

(iii) Health and Safety file to comply with the requirements of Regulations 12 and 14.

(iv) Information and training records provided to comply with the requirements of Regulation 17.

(v)   Records of advice from and views of persons at work to comply with the requirements of Regulation 18.

SECTION H—PRESSURE SYSTEMS AND TRANSPORTABLE GAS CONTAINERS REGULATIONS 1989

(i)   Information and specimen markings provided to comply with the requirements of Regulation 5.

(ii) Written statements specifying the safe operating limits of a system to comply with the requirements of Regulation 7.

(iii) Copy of the written scheme of examination required to comply with the requirements of Regulation 8.

(iv) Examination records required to comply with the requirements of Regulation 9.

(v)   Instructions provided for the use of operator to comply with Regulation 11.

(vi) Records kept to comply with the requirements of Regulation 13.

(vii) Records kept to comply with the requirements of Regulation 22.

SECTION I—LIFTING PLANT AND EQUIPMENT (RECORDS OF TEST AND EXAMINATION ETC.) REGULATIONS 1992

(i) Record kept to comply with the requirements of Regulation 6.

SECTION J—THE NOISE AT WORK REGULATIONS 1989

(i) Any risk assessment records required to comply with the requirements of Regulations 4 and 5.

(ii) Manufacturers' literature in respect of all ear protection made available to claimant to comply with the requirements of Regulation 8.

(iii) All documents provided to the employee for the provision of information to comply with Regulation 11.

SECTION K—CONSTRUCTION (HEAD PROTECTION) REGULATIONS 1989

(i) Pre-accident assessment of head protection required to comply with Regulation 3(4).

(ii) Post-accident re-assessment required to comply with Regulation 3(5).

SECTION L—THE CONSTRUCTION (GENERAL PROVISIONS) REGULATIONS 1961

(i) Report prepared following inspections and examinations of excavations etc. to comply with the requirements of Regulation 9.

(ii) Report prepared following inspections and examinations of work in cofferdams and caissons to comply with the requirements of Regulations 17 and 18.

NB Further Standard Discovery lists will be required prior to full implementation.

Annex C Letter of instruction to a medical expert

Dear Sir,

Re: (**Name and Address**)

D.O.B. –

Telephone No. –

Date of Accident –

We are acting for the above named in connection with injuries received in an accident which occurred on the above date. The main injuries appear to have been (**main injuries**).

We should be obliged if you would examine our Client and let us have a full and detailed report dealing with any relevant pre-accident medical history, the injuries sustained, treatment received and present condition, dealing in particular with the capacity for work and giving a prognosis.

It is central to our assessment of the extent of our Client's injuries to establish the extent and duration of any continuing disability. Accordingly, in the prognosis section we would ask you to specifically comment on any areas of continuing complaint or disability or impact on daily living. If there is such continuing disability you should comment upon the level of suffering or inconvenience caused and, if you are able, give your view as to when or if the complaint or disability is likely to resolve.

Please send our Client an appointment direct for this purpose. Should you be able to offer a cancellation appointment please contact our Client direct. We confirm we will be responsible for your reasonable fees.

We are obtaining the notes and records from our Client's GP and Hospitals attended and will forward them to you when they are to hand/or please request the GP and Hospital records direct and advise that any invoice for the provision of these records should be forwarded to us.

In order to comply with Court Rules we would be grateful if you would insert above your signature a statement that the contents are true to the best of your knowledge and belief.

In order to avoid further correspondence we can confirm that on the evidence we have there is no reason to suspect we may be pursuing a claim against the hospital or its staff.

We look forward to receiving your report within _____ weeks. If you will not be able to prepare your report within this period please telephone us upon receipt of these instructions.

When acknowledging these instructions it would assist if you could give an estimate as to the likely time scale for the provision of your report and also an indication as to your fee.

Yours faithfully

APPENDIX E

Practice Direction—Protocols

General

1.1 This Practice Direction applies to the pre-action protocols which have been approved by the Head of Civil Justice.

1.2 The pre-action protocols which have been approved are specified in the Schedule to this Practice Direction. Other pre-action protocols may subsequently be added.

1.3 Pre-action protocols outline the steps parties should take to seek information from and to provide information to each other about a prospective legal claim.

1.4 The objectives of pre-action protocols are:
(1) to encourage the exchange of early and full information about the prospective legal claim,
(2) to enable parties to avoid litigation by agreeing a settlement of the claim before the commencement of proceedings,
(3) to support the efficient management of proceedings where litigation cannot be avoided.

Compliance with protocols

2.1 The Civil Procedure Rules enable the court to take into account compliance or non-compliance with an applicable protocol when giving directions for the management of proceedings (see CPR rules 3.1(4) and (5) and 3.9(e)) and when making orders for costs (see CPR rule 44.3(5)(a)).

2.2 The court will expect all parties to have complied in substance with the terms of an approved protocol.

2.3 If, in the opinion of the court, non-compliance has led to the commencement of proceedings which might otherwise not have needed to be commenced, or has led to costs being incurred in the proceedings that might otherwise not have been incurred, the orders the court may make include:
(1) an order that the party at fault pay the costs of the proceedings, or part of those costs, of the other party or parties;

(2)　an order that the party at fault pay those costs on an indemnity basis;

(3)　if the party at fault is a claimant in whose favour an order for the payment of damages or some specified sum is subsequently made, an order depriving that party of interest on such sum and in respect of such period as may be specified, and/or awarding interest at a lower rate than that at which interest would otherwise have been awarded;

(4)　if the party at fault is a defendant and an order for the payment of damages or some specified sum is subsequently made in favour of the claimant, an order awarding interest on such sum and in respect of such period as may be specified at a higher rate, not exceeding 10% above base rate (cf CPR rule 36.21(2)), than the rate at which interest would otherwise have been awarded.

2.4 The court will exercise its powers under paragraphs 2.1 and 2.3 with the object of placing the innocent party in no worse a position than he would have been in if the protocol had been complied with.

3.1 A claimant may be found to have failed to comply with a protocol by, for example:

(a)　not having provided sufficient information to the defendant, or

(b)　not having followed the procedure required by the protocol to be followed (eg not having followed the medical expert instruction procedure set out in the Personal Injury Protocol).

3.2 A defendant may be found to have failed to comply with a protocol by, for example:

(a)　not making a preliminary response to the letter of claim within the time fixed for that purpose by the relevant protocol (21 days under the Personal Injury Protocol, 14 days under the Clinical Negligence Protocol),

(b)　not making a full response within the time fixed for that purpose by the relevant protocol (3 months of the letter of claim under the Clinical Negligence Protocol, 3 months from the date of acknowledgement of the letter of claim under the Personal Injury Protocol),

(c)　not disclosing documents required to be disclosed by the relevant protocol.

Pre-action behaviour in other cases

4 In cases not covered by any approved protocol, the court will expect the parties, in accordance with the overriding objective and the matters referred to in CPR 1.1(2)(a), (b) and (c), to act reasonably in exchanging information and documents relevant to the claim and generally in trying to avoid the necessity for the start of proceedings.

Commencement

5.1 Compliance or non-compliance, as the case may be, with the protocols specified in the Schedule will be taken into account by the court in dealing with any proceedings commenced after 26 April 1999 but will not be taken into account by the court in dealing with proceedings started before that date.

5.2 Where, in respect of proceedings commenced after 26 April 1999, the parties have by work done before that date substantially achieved the object designed to be achieved by steps to be taken under a protocol, the parties need not take those steps and their failure to do so will not be treated, for the purposes of paragraphs 2 and 3, as non-compliance.

5.3 Where, in respect of proceedings commenced after 26 April 1999, the parties have not had time since the publication of the protocols in January 1999 to comply with the applicable provisions, their failure to have done so will not be treated, for the purposes of paragraphs 2 and 3, as non-compliance.

5.4 As and when an additional protocol is approved, a Practice Direction will specify the date after which compliance or non-compliance with that protocol will be taken into account by the court.

Schedule
1   Personal Injury Protocol
2   Clinical Negligence Protocol

APPENDIX F

Types of ADR

Mediation

Often used interchangeably with the term ADR. It is the most commonly used ADR procedure and has been increasingly used since the implementation of the Civil Procedure Rules 1998. Mediation can be either:

(a) *Facilitative*—a neutral intermediary encourages the parties to reach settlement which can then be reduced to a binding and enforceable agreement. The tactic of 'shuttle diplomacy' is often used by the mediator to bring about a settlement. He focuses on the parties' interests rather than their legal rights and if possible tries to achieve a creative solution which may recognise, for example, the parties' ongoing business relationship. The emphasis is on a 'win-win' solution.

(b) *Evaluative*—less common but the intermediary may give the parties a non-binding opinion to assist the parties in reaching a settlement.

Conciliation

Similar to mediation but the conciliator plays a more proactive or evaluative role and suggests settlement terms, makes recommendations and evaluates the legal merits of the case.

Negotiation

Directly between the parties.

Early neutral evaluation

Procedure available through the Commercial Court and the Technology and Construction Court (it has also been used in the USA). A judge is appointed to hear the case put by each of the parties. The judge may give directions as to the preparatory steps he would like the parties to take for the evaluation and the form which it is to take. He delivers an initial evaluation in the light of the submissions made to him giving the parties an early indication of the merits of the case and the likely outcome were the matter to proceed to trial. This may encourage the parties to enter into settlement discussions earlier than they might otherwise have done. If settlement is not reached and the matter proceeds to trial the early neutral evaluation judge will not try the matter.

Judicial appraisal

A variation of early neutral evaluation. A retired judge will sit for a fee and give an appraisal of a case, usually based on written submissions from the parties. The parties are free to agree whether or not his view is binding on them or merely indicative for the future. They can also agree in what form they would like the retired judge to express his view. Again this has been used quite frequently in the USA and it was used extensively in the settlement of the Lloyd's litigation.

Expert determination

The parties jointly appoint an agreed expert to report on a particular issue in dispute. Used commonly where the dispute is of a technical nature, for example, on a valuation of shares or property.

Mini-trial/ executive tribunal

The parties present their case in outline to a panel comprising a senior executive from each party and a neutral adviser. Witness evidence is rarely given although experts may be required to give their views. The tribunal then considers the submissions and gives its opinion which may lead to a successful settlement.

Non-binding/binding arbitration

Held in private and less formal than court proceedings. The parties control the range of issues to be determined and whether or not they will be bound by the decision given by the arbitrator.

A combination

The parties may agree to use any combination of the above. Mediation/ arbitration has become increasingly common. The parties mediate under the threat of an imposition of an award by an arbitrator. It is also becoming more common to find ADR/ arbitration clauses in contracts.

APPENDIX G

Key steps in a multi-track action*

(* For key steps in an action in the Commercial Court, see Appendix H)

Pre-action steps
- Comply with relevant pre-action protocol or, in its absence, practice direction to protocols.
- Consider ADR.
- Consider making offer to settle (CPR Part 36).
- Consider pre-action disclosure (CPR 31.16).

Issue proceedings—CPR Part 7
- On standard claim form (Form N1) (CPR 7.3). Claims above £15,000 (and £50,000 for personal injury cases) can be issued in the High Court.
- Contents of claim form specified in CPR 16.2.
- Statement of value to be included in claim form (CPR 16.3).
- Claim form (or particulars of claim) must be verified by statement of truth (CPR Part 22).
- The court may order that the claim continue without any other statements of case (CPR 16.8).
- Alternative procedure for claims—Part 8.

Serve proceedings—CPR Part 6
- Within four months of issue (within six months of issue if service is outside the jurisdiction) (CPR 7.5).
- Application by claimant for an extension of time for service of claim form (CPR 7.6).
- Application by defendant for service of claim form where claim form is issued but not yet served on defendant (CPR 7.7).

File particulars of claim—CPR Part 7

- Particulars of Claim should be contained in or served with the claim form, alternatively be served within 14 days after service of the claim form (CPR 7.4).
- Content of particulars of claim specified in CPR 16.4 and 16.5 and CPR 16 PD. (See also Chancery Guide—Appendix 1 for Chancery cases.)
- Particulars of Claim must be verified by a statement of truth if not contained in the claim form (CPR Part 22).
- Particulars of Claim must be accompanied with forms for defending or admitting the claim or for acknowledging service (CPR 7.8).

File acknowledgement of service—CPR Part 10

- May be filed (Form N9) within 14 days after service of claim form (if includes particulars of claim) or where particulars of claim served separately, 14 days after service of particulars of claim where defendant is unable to file defence within 14 days after service of particulars of claim or if defendant wishes to challenge the court's jurisdiction (CPR 10.1 and 10.3).
- Contents of acknowledgement of service specified in CPR 10.5 and CPR Part 10 PD.

File defence—CPR Part 15

- Within 14 days of service of particulars of claim or if the defendant files an acknowledgement of service under Part 10 within 28 days after service of particulars of claim (CPR 15.4).
- The parties may agree one extension of time of up to 28 days (CPR 15.5).
- Contents of defence specified in CPR 16.5 and CPR Part 16 PD.
- Defence must be verified by a statement of truth (CPR Part 22).

Counterclaim—CPR Part 20

- Serve at the same time as the defendant files the defence if without court's permission or at any other time with court's permission (CPR 20.4).

Reply

- May be filed when the claimant files his allocation questionnaire (CPR 15.8). (Chancery Guide para 4.9 suggests that if possible for Chancery cases the reply should be served before filing the allocation questionnaire.)
- Must be verified by a statement of truth (CPR Part 22).
- The claimant must serve his reply (CPR 15.8(b)).

Allocation to appropriate track—CPR Part 26

- When a defendant files a defence, the court will serve an allocation questionnaire on each party (CPR 26.3) to be completed by a specified date.
- The court may order a stay (of its own initiative or at the parties request) of one month (or such longer period as it considers appropriate) to enable the parties to attempt to settle the case (CPR 26.4).
- Cases will be allocated to a track in accordance with the principles set out in CPR 26.5–26.8 (generally, to small claims track if less than £5,000, to fast track if less than £15,000, or multi track if over £15,000 or for remedies other than damages). An allocation hearing may be held if necessary (Para.6 PD).

Case management on multi track—CPR Part 29: Case Management Conference

- Where case is allocated to multi-track, the court will (a) give directions for the management of the case, set a timetable for the steps between giving directions and trial, or (b) fix (i) a case management conference or (ii) a pre-trial review or (iii) both. A trial date or trial 'window' will be fixed as soon as practicable (CPR 29.2).

Interim remedies—CPR Part 25

- The court may grant interim remedies prior to or after the commencement of proceedings. Full details of the various remedies available, including interim injunctive relief, are set out in CPR 25.1.

Summary judgment—CPR Part 24

- Summary judgment is now available to both plaintiff and defendant or at the court's own initiative.
- The court may give summary judgment if a claim/defence or particular issue has 'no realistic prospect of success' and there is no other reason why the case or issue should be disposed of at trial. (CPR 24.2).
- The respondent should be given at least 14 days' notice of the date fixed for the hearing (CPR 24.4(3)) together with a copy of the evidence filed in support.
- Any written evidence the respondent wishes to rely on must be filed at least 7 days before the summary judgment hearing (CPR 24.5(1)).
- Any written evidence the applicant wishes to rely on must be filed at least 3 days before the summary judgment hearing (CPR 24.5(2)).
- Where the hearing is at the court's initiative any party who wishes to rely on written evidence at the hearing should file it at least 7 days before the hearing, and file any evidence in reply at least 3 days before the hearing (CPR 24.5(3)).
- When determining a summary judgment application the court may give directions as to filing and service of the defence or give further case management directions (CPR 24.6).

Offers to settle/payments into court—CPR Part 36

[Note: the provisions relating to offers and payments are complex and reference should be made to the provisions of Part 36 in full]

- A claimant or a defendant may make a pre-action offer to settle (CPR 36.10). If the offeror is a defendant to a money claim, he must pay an equivalent amount into court within 14 days of service of the claim form. The court will take a pre-action offer to settle into account when making any order as to costs (CPR 35.10).

- A claimant may make a Part 36 offer, and a defendant may make a Part 36 offer or payment, at any time after proceedings have commenced. It must comply with the formal requirements set out in CPR 36.5.
- Where a defendant fails to beat a claimant's Part 36 offer he may be ordered to pay interest on the damages awarded at a rate not exceeding 10% over base from the latest date when he could have accepted the offer without the permission of the court. The court may also award the claimant indemnity costs (plus interest not exceeding 10% above base) for the same period (CPR 36.21).
- Where a claimant fails to match a defendant's Part 36 offer or payment at trial, he may be ordered to pay the defendant's costs incurred after the time for acceptance of the offer has expired (CPR 36.20).

Disclosure—CPR Part 31

- No set time limit for giving disclosure—will depend on the case.
- Disclosure is usually restricted to standard disclosure (CPR 31.5, as defined in CPR 31.6), unless the court orders or the parties have agreed in writing, and that it be dispensed with or otherwise limited. (See also Chancery Guide para 6.2 for Chancery cases.)
- A party has a duty to disclose documents which are or have been in his control (CPR 31.8).
- Unless agreed otherwise by the parties, each party is required to list documents indicating which documents are no longer in the party's control and what has happened to those documents (CPR 31.10).
- A party is required to make a reasonable search for documents (CPR 31.7) when giving standard disclosure and to include in his list of documents a disclosure statement which sets out the extent of the search he has made to locate documents which he is required to disclose (CPR 31.10(6) and CPR Part 31 practice direction, para 4.2).
- The court may make an order for specific disclosure or inspection (CPR 31.12).
- There is an obligation on the parties to notify other parties immediately of any documents which come to a party's notice (CPR 31.11).

Witness evidence—CPR Part 32

- The court may control evidence (CPR 32.1).
- No set time limit for preparation of witness evidence—will depend on the case.
- Form and content of witness statements specified in CPR 32.8 and PD paras 17–20. (For Chancery cases, see also Chancery Guide Appendix 4.)
- A witness statement must be verified by a statement of truth (CPR Part 22)
- The court may give directions as to the order in which witness statements are to be served and whether or not statements are to be filed (CPR 32.4(3)).
- Witness summaries are permissible where it is not possible to obtain a signed witness statement although permission is required from the court to serve a witness summary (CPR 32.9).
- A witness must give oral evidence at trial except in certain prescribed circumstances (CPR 32.2, 32.5).
- A witness giving oral evidence at trial may amplify his statement or raise new matters if the court considers there is good reason to do so (CPR 32.5(3) and (4)). For Chancery cases a supplemental witness statement should be prepared where practicable (see Chancery Guide, para 9.12).

Expert evidence—CPR Part 35

- The court has a duty to restrict expert evidence to that which is reasonably required to resolve the proceedings (CPR 35.1).
- No set time limit for preparation of expert evidence—will depend on the case.
- The expert has an overriding duty to the court (CPR 35.3). (See also Chancery Guide, paras 6.8 and 6.9 for Chancery cases.)
- No party may call an expert or put in evidence an expert's report without the court's permission (CPR 35.4).
- The court may direct that evidence be given by a single joint expert (CPR 35.7).
- The court may require a party who has access to information which is not available to the other party, to prepare and file a report and serve a copy of that report on the other party (CPR 35.9).
- Form and content of the expert's report specified in CPR 35.10 and PD paras.1.1 and 1.2.
- Expert's report must be verified by a statement of truth (CPR Part 22).
- Written questions may be put to an expert (CPR 35.6) (See also Chancery Guide, para 6.19 for Chancery cases.)
- The court may direct discussions between experts requiring them to identify the issues in the proceedings and where possible reach

agreement on those issues and subsequently prepare a statement for the court showing the issues on which they agree and issues on which they disagree and a summary of their reasons for disagreeing (CPR 35.12). (See also Chancery Guide, para 6.16 for Chancery cases.)

- The court may appoint an assessor to prepare a report on any matter at issue in the proceedings (CPR 35.15).

Listing questionnaire—CPR Part 29.6

- A listing questionnaire may be sent to the parties for completion and returned by a specified date (CPR 29.6(1)). The court may convene a listing hearing to determine what directions are appropriate (CPR 29.6(3)).

Pre-trial review—CPR Part 29.7

- A pre-trial review may be convened by the court (if required), notice of which must be served at least 7 days before the hearing (CPR 29.7).
- As soon as practicable after the completion of the listing questionnaire, the listing hearing or the pre-trial review, the court will set a timetable for trial or a trial date (CPR 29.8).

Trial

- Unless the trial judge otherwise directs, the trial will be conducted in accordance with any orders previously made.

Note: This chart summarises the key steps in an action on the multi-track as set out in the Civil Procedure Rules. For full details of the relevant provisions, reference should be made to the text of the rules.

APPENDIX H

Key steps in a Commercial Court case

Note This chart highlights the key procedural steps and differences in Commercial Court cases set out in the Commercial Court Guide. In the Commercial Court, all actions will proceed as if allocated to the multi-track. The CPR in relation to track allocation will not apply.

Pre-action steps
- Comply with relevant pre-action protocol or, in its absence, practice direction to protocols.
- Consider ADR.
- Consider making offer to settle (CPR Part 36).
- Consider pre-action disclosure (CPR 31.16).

Issue proceedings—CPR Part 7 (Paras B2–B3)
- On standard claim form (Form N1(CC)) (B3.1).
- Contents of claim form specified in CPR 16.2.
- No statement of value required (B3.3).
- Claim form must be verified by a statement of truth (B3.7).
- Claim form must be served with forms for defending or admitting the claim or acknowledging service (B3.6).
- Alternative procedure for claims—Part 8.

Serve proceedings—(Paras B5–B6)
- Within four months of issue (within six months of issue if service is outside the jurisdiction) (CPR 7.5).
- Application by claimant for an extension of time for service of claim form (CPR 7.6).
- Service of the claim form must be by the claimant (B5).
- Application by defendant for service of claim form where claim form is issued but not yet served on defendant (CPR 7.7).

(Early case management conference, if appropriate)
(paras D7.3–7.4)

File acknowledgment of service (Para B7)
- An acknowledgment of service (Form N9(CC)) should be filed in every case usually within 14 days after service of the claim form (or longer if claim form is served out of the jurisdiction (B7.3 and 7.4).

Serve and file particulars of claim if not already done so
(Paras C1–C2 and Appendix 4)
- Particulars of claim should be served 28 days after the acknowledgement of service has been filed.
- Parties may agree extensions of time for serving particulars of claim. It must be evidenced in writing and notified to the court. If agreed extension exceeds six weeks, reasons must be specified (C2.4).
- Contents of particulars of claim set out in CPR 16.4 and 16.5, CPR Part 16 PD, C1.2 and Appendix 4.
- Particulars of claim must be verified by a statement of truth (CPR Part 22 and C1.7–1.8).
- Where particulars of claim exceed 25 pages a summary must be prepared (C1.3).
- Particulars of claim must be served and filed by the claimant (C1.9).
- Trial may be ordered without service or filing of particulars of claim or defence or other statements of case (B3.8).

Serve and file defence (Paras C1, C3 and Appendix 4)

- Defendant must serve and file defence generally, 28 days after service of particulars of claim (C3.2 and 3.7).
- Extensions of time for service of defence may be agreed between the parties exceeding 28 days. The agreement must be evidenced in writing and notified to the court.
- If the agreed extension exceeds six weeks, reasons must be specified (C3.4–3.5).
- Contents of defence specified in CPR 16.5, CPR Part 16 PD, and C1.2 and Appendix 4.
- Where the defence exceeds 25 pages a summary must be prepared (C1.3).
- Defence must be verified by a statement of truth (CPR Part 22).

Counterclaim (see CPR Part 20)

- Serve at the same time as the defendant files the defence if without court's permission or at any other time with court's permission (CPR 20.4 and D7.24).

Reply (Paras C1, C4 and Appendix 4))

- A reply may be filed and served 21 days after service of the defence, or later if granted by the court (C4.2–4.3).
- Must be verified by a statement of truth.

Preparation for case management conference

Prepare case memorandum (Para D4)

- The case memorandum should contain a short and uncontroversial description of what the case is about and a very short and uncontroversial summary of the material procedural history of the case since it was commenced.

Prepare list of issues (Para D5)
- This should include both issues of fact and law. A separate section of the document should list what is common ground between the parties.

Prepare case management bundle (Para D6 and Appendix 11)
- The case management bundle should be provided to the court at least 7 days before the case management conference.
- The case management bundle should contain the claim form, case memorandum, list of issues, pre-trial timetable (or case management information sheet where no pre-trial timetable has been ordered at the relevant time), statements of case subsequent to the claim form, the principal orders made in the case and any agreement in writing made by the parties to disclose documents without making a list or any agreement in writing that disclosure shall take place in stages.

Prepare provisional estimate of trial length (Para D12.1 and Appendix 6)

Lodge and serve case management information sheet (Para D7.10 and Appendix 6)
- Each party must provide this to the court (and copies to other parties) at least 7 days before the case management conference.
- It should refer to all applications which the parties want to make at the case management conference.

Case management conference
- The case management conference is mandatory under the Commercial Court Guide.
- Generally the Commercial Court case management procedure set out in Section D of the Commercial Court Guide takes the place of CPR 29 and the Practice Direction supplementing that part.
- Generally clients need not attend, but the Commercial Court does have power to require attendance.

Interim remedies
(Same procedure as in multi-track flowchart)

↓

Summary judgment
(Same procedure as in multi-track flowchart)

↓

Offers to settle/Payments into court
(Same procedure as in multi-track flowchart)

↓

Disclosure (Para E)
- Usually considered at the case management conference (E2.1).
- No set time limit for giving disclosure—will depend on the case.
- In the Commercial Court parties can expect to be required to give disclosure beyond standard disclosure, in relation to the case as a whole or at least for particular issues in the case (E1.2).
- A party has a duty to disclose documents which are or have been in his control (CPR 31.8).
- The parties may agree in writing to give disclosure without listing documents. However the court may still require each party to make a disclosure statement (E2.2).
- A party is required to make a reasonable search for documents (CPR 31.7) when giving standard disclosure and to include in his list of documents a disclosure statement which sets out the extent of the search he has made to locate documents which he is required to disclose (CPR 31.10(6) and CPR Part 31 practice direction, para 4.2).
- The disclosure statement must conclude with a certification that the duty of disclosure has been understood and carried out and that the list is complete. The court may also order that the disclosure statement be verified by affidavit or witness statement. (E3.7).
- Specific disclosure may be required to be verified at any stage by affidavit or witness statement (E4.4).
- A 'special disclosure order' may be made in appropriate cases (E.5 and Appendix 9).
- There is an obligation on the parties to notify other parties immediately of any documents which come to a party's notice (CPR 31.11)

↓

Witness evidence (Para H)

- The court may control evidence (CPR 32.1).
- Usually considered at the case management conference.
- No set time limit for preparation of witness evidence—will depend on the case.
- Form and content of witness statement specified in CPR 32.8 and CPR Part 32 PD paras 17–20 and H1.3.
- A witness statement (and supplemental statement) must be verified by a statement of truth (CPR Part 22).
- Generally simultaneous exchange of witness statements—there is no requirement to file (Appendix 8).
- A supplemental witness statement should be served where the witness proposes materially to add to or alter his statement (H1.8).
- A witness must give oral evidence at trial except in certain prescribed circumstances (CPR 32.2, 32.5).

Expert evidence (Para H)

- The court has a duty to restrict expert evidence to that which is reasonably required to resolve the proceedings (CPR 35.1).
- Usually considered at the case management conference.
- No set time limit for preparation of expert evidence—will depend on the case .
- The expert witness has an overriding duty to the court (CPR 35.3 and Appendix 12).
- No party may call an expert or put in evidence an expert's report without the court's permission (CPR 35.4).
- No presumption in favour of a single joint expert (H2.4).
- Form and content of expert's report specified in CPR Part 35, PD paras 1.1 and 1.2 and H2.11–2.15 and Appendix 12.
- Expert's report must be verified by a statement of truth (H2.14).
- Generally simultaneous exchange of expert reports (H2.18 and Appendix 8) although sequential exchange may also be ordered.
- Written questions may be put to an expert (H2.27–2.28).

Lodge and serve progress monitoring information sheet (Paras D8.2–8.3 and Appendix 13)

- This must be sent to the Listing Office at least 3 clear days before the progress monitoring date.
- The information sheet confirms (i) whether the parties have complied with the pre-trial timetable (ii) if not, the respects in which they have not (iii) whether they will be ready for a trial

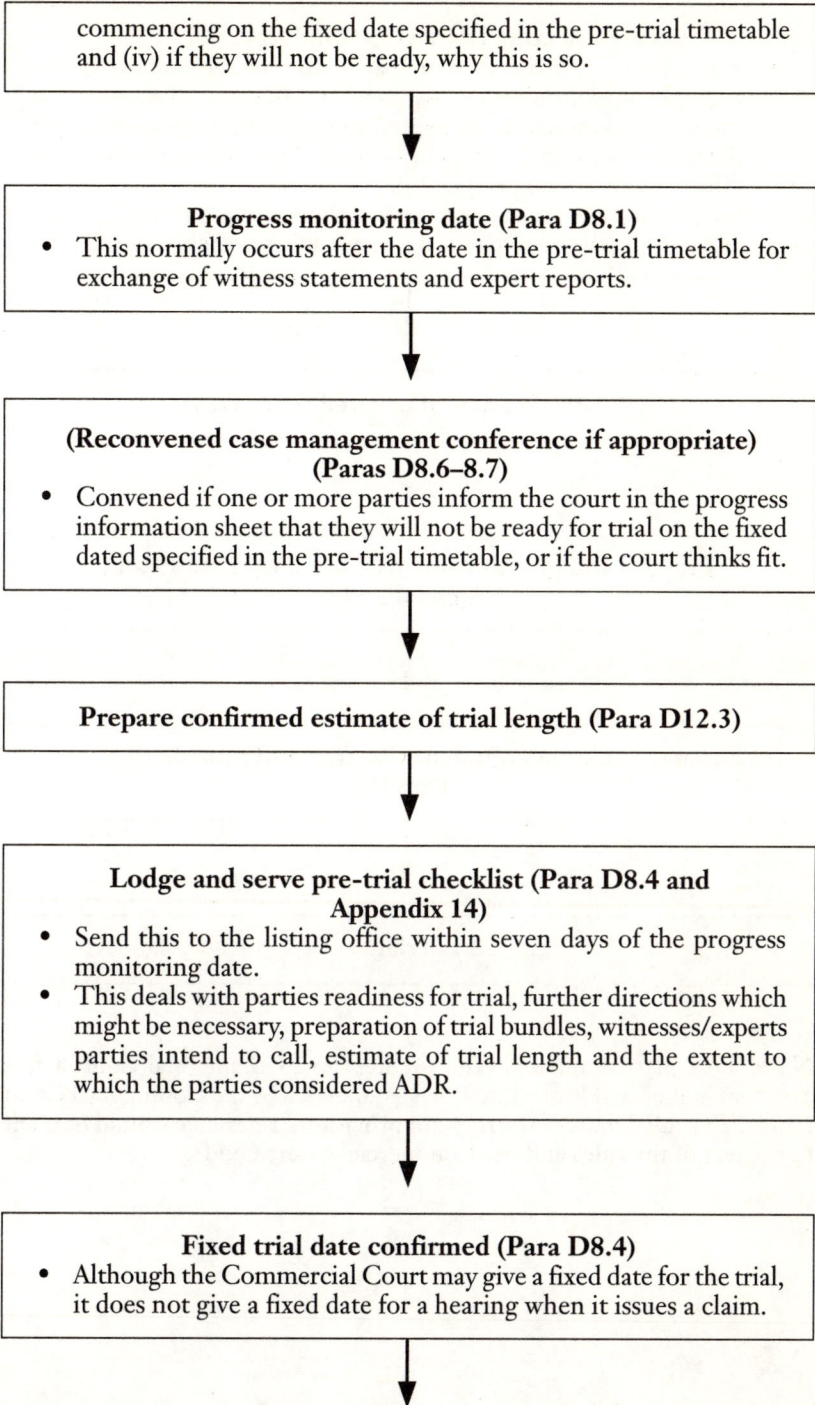

commencing on the fixed date specified in the pre-trial timetable and (iv) if they will not be ready, why this is so.

↓

Progress monitoring date (Para D8.1)
- This normally occurs after the date in the pre-trial timetable for exchange of witness statements and expert reports.

↓

(Reconvened case management conference if appropriate) (Paras D8.6–8.7)
- Convened if one or more parties inform the court in the progress information sheet that they will not be ready for trial on the fixed dated specified in the pre-trial timetable, or if the court thinks fit.

↓

Prepare confirmed estimate of trial length (Para D12.3)

↓

Lodge and serve pre-trial checklist (Para D8.4 and Appendix 14)
- Send this to the listing office within seven days of the progress monitoring date.
- This deals with parties readiness for trial, further directions which might be necessary, preparation of trial bundles, witnesses/experts parties intend to call, estimate of trial length and the extent to which the parties considered ADR.

↓

Fixed trial date confirmed (Para D8.4)
- Although the Commercial Court may give a fixed date for the trial, it does not give a fixed date for a hearing when it issues a claim.

↓

Experts meeting (Para H2.19 and Appendix 12)
- The experts are required to prepare a joint memorandum for the court recording the expert issues which they have discussed, the expert issues on which they agree and the expert issues on which there is a difference of opinion and a summary of what that difference of opinion is (H2.24).
- Each expert may also prepare a short supplemental report highlighting the reasons why the expert adheres to his view (H2.26).

(Pre-trial review, if ordered (Para D13))

Prepare and give to court trial bundles (Para I3 and Appendix 11)

Exchange skeleton arguments for trial and provide to court (Para I6)

Trial

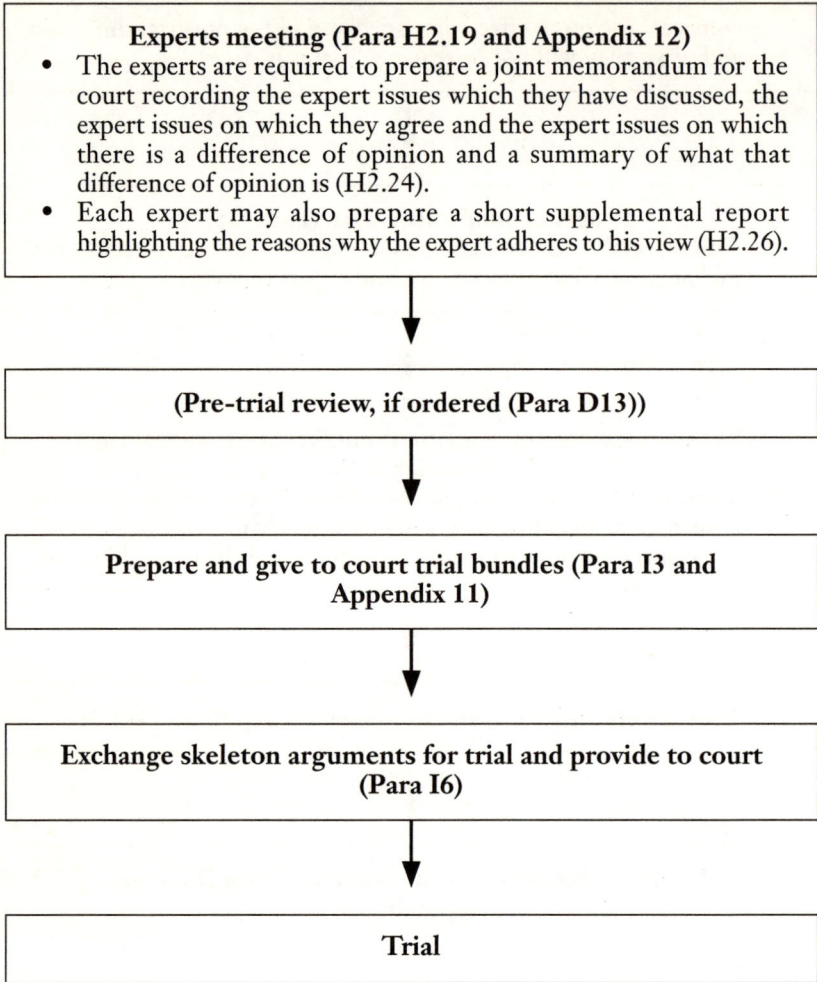

Note: This chart summarises the key steps in a Commercial Court action as set out in the Civil Procedure Rules as amended by the Commercial Court Guide. For full details of the relevant provisions, reference should be made to the text of the rules and the Commercial Court Guide.

APPENDIX I

Pro forma list of documents: standard disclosure

Notes:

* The rules relating to standard disclosure are contained in Part 31 of the Civil Procedure Rules and Section E of the Commercial Court Guide.
* Documents to be included under standard disclosure are contained in Rule 31.6
* A document has or will have been in your control if you have or have had possession, or a right of possession, of it **or** a right to inspect or take copies of it.

In the	
Claim No.	
Claimant(s) (including ref)	
Defendant(s) (including ref)	
Date	

Disclosure Statement

1. I state that I have carried out a reasonable and proportionate search to locate all the documents which I am required to disclose under the order made by the court on (*insert date*)

(I did not search for documents-

1. pre-dating
2. located elsewhere than
3. in categories other than

)

I certify that I understand the duty of disclosure and to the best of my knowledge I have carried out that duty. I further certify that the list of documents set out in or attached to this form, is a complete list of all documents which are or have been in my control and which I am obliged under the order to disclose.

I understand that I must inform the court and the other parties immediately if any further document required to be disclosed by Rule 31.6 comes into my control at any time before the conclusion of the case.

(I have not permitted inspection of documents within the category or class of documents (as set out below) required to be disclosed under Rule 31(6)(b) or (c) on the grounds that to do so would be disproportionate to the issues in the case.)

Signed _____   **Date** _____

(Claimant)(Defendant)('s litigation friend)

Position or office held (*if signing on behalf of firm or company*)
Please state why you are the appropriate person to make the disclosure statement.

List of documents: continued overleaf

219

List and number here, in a convenient order, the documents (or bundles of documents, if of the same nature, e.g. invoices) in your control, which you do not object to being inspected. Give a short description of each document or bundle so that it can be identified, and say if it is kept elsewhere, i.e. with a bank or solicitor

I have control of the documents numbered and listed here. I do not object to you inspecting them/producing copies.

List and number here, as above, the documents in your control which you object to being inspected. (Rule 31.19)

I have control of the documents numbered and listed here, but I object to you inspecting them:

Say what your objections are

I object to you inspecting these documents because:

List and number here, the documents you once had in your control, but which you no longer have. For each document listed, say when it was last in your control and where it is now.

I have had the documents numbered and listed below, but they are no longer in my control.

APPENDIX J

Pro forma list of documents: standard disclosure (Commercial Court)

Notes:

* The rules relating to standard disclosure are contained in Part 31 of the Civil Procedure Rules and Section E of the Commercial Court Guide.
* Documents to be included under standard disclosure are contained in Rule 31.6
* A document has or will have been in your control if you have or have had possession, or a right of possession, or it or a right to inspect or take copies of it.

In the	High Court of Justice Queen's Bench Division Commercial Court Royal Courts of Justice
Claim No.	
Claimant(s) (including ref)	
Defendant(s) (including ref)	
Date	
Party returning this form	

Disclosure Statement of (Claimant)(Defendant)

1. (I/We), (name(s)) state that (I/we) have carried out a reasonable search to locate all the documents which (I am *or* ....*here name the party* is) required to disclose under (the order made by the court or the agreement in writing made between the parties on) (*insert date*)

2. The extent of the search that (I/we) made to locate documents that (I am *or here name the party* is) required to disclose was as follows:

3. (I/We) limited the search in the following respects:-

    a. (I/We) did not search for documents

    1. pre-dating

    2. located in the following places

    3. in the following categories or classes

    b. (*Other limits, if any, e.g. documents post-dating*

4. The facts considered in arriving at the decision that it was reasonable to limit the search in the respects identified above were as follows (*the facts must be set out in detail: see paragraph E3.6 of the Commercial Court Guide*):

5. (I/We) certify that (I/we) understand the duty of disclosure and to the best of (my/our) knowledge (I have*or here name the party* has) carried out that duty. (I/We) further certify that the list above is a complete list of all documents which are or have been in (my *or here name the party's*) control which (I am *or here name the party* is obliged under (the said order *or* the said agreement in writing) to disclose.

6. (I *or here name the party*) understand(s) that (I *or here name the party*) must inform the court and the other parties immediately if any further documents required to be disclosed by Rule 31.6 comes into (my *or here name the party's*) control at any time before the conclusion of the case.

7. ((I *or here name the party*) (have/has) not permitted inspection of documents within the category or class of documents (as set out below) required to be disclosed under Rule 31(6)(b) or (c) on the grounds that to do so would be disproportionate to the issues in the case.)

Signed _____ **Date** _____

Name(s) _____

Position or office held _____

Please state why you are the appropriate person(s) to make the disclosure statement

List and number here, in a convenient order, the documents (or bundles of documents, if of the same nature, e.g. invoices) in your/the claimant's/the defendant's control, which you/the claimant/ the defendant do/does not object to being inspected. Give a short description of each document or bundle so that it can be identified, and say if it is kept elsewhere, i.e. with a bank or solicitor

A. (I)(The claimant)(The defendant) (have/has) control of the documents numbered and listed here. (I)(The claimant)(The defendant) (do not)(does not) object to you inspecting them/producing copies.

List and number here, as above, the documents in the claimant's/the defendant's control which the claimant/the defendant objects to being inspected. (Rule 31.19)

B. (I)(The claimant)(The defendant) (have)(has) control of the documents numbered and listed here, but (I)(the claimant)(the defendant) (object)(objects) to you inspecting them:

Say what the claimant's/ the defendant's objections are

(I)(The claimant)(The defendant) (object)(objects) to you inspecting these documents because:

List and number here, the documents the claimant/the defendant once had in his/her/its control, but which the claimant/the defendant no longer has. For each document listed, say when it was last in the claimant's/the defendant's control and where it is now.

C. (I)(The claimant)(The defendant)(have)(had) the documents numbered and listed below, but they are no longer in (my)(the claimant's)(the defendant's) control.

APPENDIX K

Appendix 9 to the Commercial Court Guide—draft special disclosure order

Appendix 9

Draft Special Disclosure Order

Draft special disclosure order This is considered at CPR 31.12

It is ordered that :
(1) On or before [*] each party shall carry out a thorough search for all documents relevant to [the issues listed in the Schedule to this order/the issues in the case], including (for avoidance of doubt) all documents which may lead to a train of inquiry enabling a party to advance his own case or damage that of his opponent.
(2) On or before [*] each party shall disclose [by list]:
    (a) any documents located as a result of the search by that party under (1) above, and
    (b) any other documents relevant to [the issues listed in the schedule to this order/the issues in the case] that were once but are no longer in his control (as defined by CPR 31.8(2)).
(3) The parties remain under a continuing obligation until the proceedings are concluded to disclose documents described in (1) above.
(4) Each party is at liberty to apply to the Court, on notice to all other parties, for further directions in relation to the carrying out of this order.
(5) Costs in the case.

APPENDIX L

Pro forma witness statement

IN THE HIGH COURT OF JUSTICE
[20[ ]   Folio No   ]
[QUEEN'S BENCH DIVISION]
[COMMERCIAL COURT]

BETWEEN

[CLAIMANT]

Claimant

-and-

[DEFENDANT]

Defendant

[SUPPLEMENTAL] WITNESS STATEMENT OF
[JOHN HENRY BROWN]

INTRODUCTION[1]

I [**JOHN HENRY BROWN**[2]] of [place of residence at work/address] will say:[3]

1. I am [give job description or explain relationship with party/to proceedings. Explain relationship to other witnesses where relevant].
2. [Short paragraph summarising witness' role/outlining nature of his evidence].
3. [Refer to previous statements, if any, and explain why additional evidence is necessary eg to update previous statement.]

---

1   Headings used for ease of reference only—not for insertion in statement (although headings may be used in body of statement to break down evidence by issue, etc).
2   Set out name in full.
3   The statement should 'be in the intended witness's own words'.

4.   [Identify the source of documents referred to in the statement (eg documents prefixed 'C' are from Claimant's list and documents prefixed 'D' are from Defendant's list) or attach paginated copies and refer to relevant pages in parenthesis. To comply with the rules, you should give in the margin the reference to any document or documents[4]].

5.   [Indicate which statements are made from the witnesses own knowledge and which are matters of information or belief, and the source for any matters of information or belief].

6.   [If the statement refers to exhibits it should state 'I refer to the (description of exhibit) marked.............'.

BACKGROUND FACTS

[   ]

FACTUAL EVIDENCE

[   ]

[Present events in chronological order or by issue. Cross-refer to relevant documents. Document references should appear in the margin.

Use short numbered paragraphs with sub-headings to divide up issues.

Use short sentences stating simple facts where possible.

All numbers including dates should be in figures.]

STATEMENT OF TRUTH

I believe that the facts stated in this witness statement are true.

Signed[5]...

JOHN HENRY BROWN

Dated this   day of   20[ ].

---

4   PD19.1(7).
5   The witness should sign or initial each page of the statement as well as the final page, to confirm that it accurately sets out his evidence.

IN THE HIGH COURT OF JUSTICE
[QUEEN'S BENCH DIVISION]
[COMMERCIAL COURT]

BETWEEN

[CLAIMANT]

Claimant

-and-

[DEFENDANT]

Defendant

**[SUPPLEMENTAL] WITNESS STATEMENT OF
JOHN HENRY BROWN**

NAME OF SOLICITORS
ADDRESS
TELEPHONE NUMBER
Ref: [   ]
SOLICITORS FOR THE [CLAIMANTS]

IN THE HIGH COURT OF JUSTICE
[QUEEN'S BENCH DIVISION]
[COMMERCIAL COURT]

BETWEEN

[CLAIMANT]

Claimant

-and-

[DEFENDANT]

Defendant

**EXHIBIT [JHB [1]] REFERRED TO IN THE
[SUPPLEMENTAL] WITNESS STATEMENT OF
[JOHN HENRY BROWN]**

. . . .

JOHN HENRY BROWN[6]

Dated the   day of   20[ ]

---

6   Where copy documents are attached, witness should review them and sign the attached
frontsheet to confirm correct versions are attached. The documents should be paginated.

APPENDIX M

Draft letter of instruction to expert adviser

Confidential

[The Expert Adviser]
[Address]

[Date]

Dear *[Expert Adviser]*

[Matter Heading]

Thank you for agreeing to act as an expert adviser in this matter.

This letter is to confirm the basis of your retainer in this case on behalf of our client, *[state name of client]*. I set out below your terms of engagement and general scope of work, and the position on confidentiality and privilege. I should be grateful if you would confirm that these terms are acceptable to you.

Background

State, in outline, the principal known issues in the case and broad description of expert advice required (eg process engineering, banking practice etc.).

If relevant at this stage, refer to (and enclose) the key documents for consideration by the expert at this stage (normally copies of relevant contracts, etc).

Scope of instructions and timing

You are aware of the parties to this dispute *[set out in full]* and you have indicated that you do not have a conflict of interest in acting for *[client]* in this matter. Please confirm that this is the case.

Please also provide details of any publications (including articles, books, seminar materials or research papers) you have produced which are relevant to the issues in dispute.

[The present engagement is not for the purposes of acting as an expert witness in court proceedings. However, there is a possibility that our client may wish to instruct you at some later date to act as an independent expert witness in any [subsequent] court proceedings which are commenced relating to the issues in dispute and in respect of which you have currently been retained to advise. If you are appointed as an independent expert witness to give or prepare evidence for the purpose of court proceedings you will have a duty to help the court on matters within your expertise and this duty will override any obligation which you have to our client. In addition, the Commercial Court has set out certain detailed requirements in the Commercial Court Guide in relation to expert witness evidence to be given to the Commercial Court. While this guidance has been issued specifically in relation to the Commercial Court, we consider that it applies to an expert witness in *all* cases. A copy of the guidance is enclosed by way of appendix to this letter. *You may also wish to include a copy of the revised draft code of guidance for experts by way of appendix to this letter.*

[In the event that you are appointed to act as an independent expert witness you will cease to advise our client in an advisory capacity.] You will also be given new instructions by way of separate letter which will set out the basis of your appointment as expert witness and confirm your duties to the court.]

Team and fees

We understand that your team will consist of [*state members of team*] and that you agree to notify us in advance of any changes or additions to the team.

We understand that your daily rates are as follows:

[*Set out rates for each member of the team*].

[*State any special arrangements in relation to travel or other expenses*].

[*State whether fees are to be paid by a third party*].

Invoices should be submitted on a [*monthly*] basis direct to [*client*]. The payment terms agreed are [*payment within x days*].

You have indicated that [the likely fee for the team's services will be [£   ], [the estimated time which is likely to be required for this matter is [hours]].

Privilege and confidentiality

This matter is strictly confidential. No information relating in any way to this matter, or your work for it, is to be disclosed to any third party (other than those who we have confirmed are assisting us or our clients in connection with this case) without the client's prior written consent.

All correspondence and all preparatory papers for your report are legally privileged, as they are being prepared in contemplation of litigation, and in the provision of legal advice. Please therefore, ensure that all papers, memoranda, correspondence and other materials are clearly headed 'Strictly Privileged and Confidential—prepared for the purpose of advising on the issues in dispute' and that they are circulated through us (addressed to (*state relevant member of team*)). These materials should not be circulated within your organisation (beyond the members of your team) and without prior discussion with us to ensure that appropriate steps are taken to retain privilege.

You must ensure that all necessary internal procedural steps are taken to ensure that these obligations are met.

Our team dealing with this matter is [*partner*] who has overall responsibility for the case, [*assistant/s*] who have responsibility for [*set out roles*] and [*name other members of team where relevant*]. Your primary contact will be [*name relevant asssistant/s*]. If you have any questions on any of the matters detailed above, please contact [*state relevant member of team*].

Their contact details are [phone/ fax/ email]

Please confirm your acceptance of this retainer on these terms.

Yours sincerely

Appendix

(i)   It is the duty of an expert to help the court on the matters within his expertise. This duty is paramount and overrides any obligation to the person from whom he has received instructions or by whom he is paid.

(ii) Expert evidence presented to the court should be, and should be seen to be, the independent product of the expert uninfluenced by the exigencies of litigation.

(iii) An expert witness should provide independent assistance to the court by way of objective unbiased opinion in relation to matters within his expertise. An expert witness should never assume the role of an advocate.

(iv) An expert witness should not omit to consider material facts which could detract from his concluded opinion.

(v)   An expert witness should make it clear when a particular question or issue falls outside his expertise.

(vi) If an expert's opinion is not properly researched because he considers that insufficient data is available, then this must be stated with an indication that the opinion is no more than a provisional one.

(vii) In a case where an expert witness who has prepared a report could not assert that the report contained the truth, the whole truth and nothing but the truth without some qualification, that qualification should be stated in the report.

(viii)If, after exchange of reports, an expert witness changes his view on any material matter having read another expert's report or for any other reason, such change of view should be communicated in writing (through legal representatives) to the other side without delay, and when appropriate to the court.

An expert appointed to give evidence to the Commercial Court is specifically required to comply with these requirements at all stages of his involvement in the case and must confirm in his report that he has done so.

APPENDIX N

Draft letter of instruction to expert witness

[*The Expert Witness*]
[*Address*]

[*Date*]

Dear [*Expert Witness*]

[*Court Heading*]

Thank you for agreeing to act as an independent expert witness to give and/ or prepare evidence for the purpose of the above court proceedings.

This letter is to confirm the basis on which our client [*state name of client*] has retained you for this purpose. I set out below your terms of engagement and general scope of work, and the position on confidentiality and privilege. I should be grateful if you would confirm that these terms are acceptable to you.

Background

State, in outline, the principal issues in the case based on the case summary produced pursuant to CPR Part 29, practice direction, paragraph 5.7.

If relevant at this stage, refer to (and enclose) the key documents for consideration by the expert at this stage (normally the statements of case, the case summary, copies of relevant contracts, etc). You should keep a clear record of all documents disclosed to the expert.

Scope of instructions and timing

You are aware of the parties to this dispute [*set out in full*] and you have indicated that you do not have a conflict of interest in acting for [*client*] in this matter. [Please confirm that this is the case.]

You are requested to provide expert evidence to the court, and to prepare such report/s as may be required from time to time on the issues set out below.

In summary, you have been asked to consider:

[*Set out issues to be considered and reported on by expert by reference to the issues identified for consideration by the experts at the Case Management Conference*].

[*Where an expert witness has previously been retained by the client as expert adviser, any instructions which have previously been given to the expert in his capacity as expert adviser **and which are necessary** for the expert to give or prepare evidence for the Court in his capacity as expert witness should be repeated in full without cross reference to the previous instructions. If appropriate it should also be emphasised to the expert witness that he will no longer continue to act as expert adviser*].

This letter sets out your instructions for the purpose of preparing your expert evidence to the Court. However as this matter proceeds, further instructions may be given to you. Such instructions will be in writing.

You are to be assisted by [*set out details of any other experts appointed and outline their responsibilities*].

The timetable to which we are currently working will require experts reports to be exchanged by [*date*]. Following exchange of reports, we will require your assistance in reviewing expert evidence served by the other parties, and [possibly providing one or more supplemental reports in reply. The current timetable for exchange of any supplemental reports is [*date*]].

In addition, at any stage in the proceedings, you may be asked by the Court to hold discussions [or meetings in Commercial Court cases] with the other parties' expert witnesses to identify the issues in the proceedings and where possible, reach agreement on those issues. Following such discussions or meetings, the Court may require you to prepare, in conjunction with the other parties' expert witnesses, a statement for the Court identifying the issues on which you agree and those issues on which you disagree together with a summary of your reasons for disagreeing. [This will be mandatory in Commercial Court cases].

You may also be asked (once only) to respond to written questions which may be put to you by another party to the proceedings within 28 days of service of your report, but only for clarification of your report.

If the matter proceeds to trial, you and/or members of your team may have to present oral evidence in Court and attend when the other parties' expert witnesses give their evidence. We would expect the trial to take place during [*state approximate date*].

Role of an expert witness

As an expert witness appointed to give or prepare evidence for the purpose of Court proceedings, you will have a duty to help the Court on matters within your expertise and this duty overrides any obligation you have to our client. In addition, the Commercial Court has set out certain detailed requirements in the Commercial Court Guide in relation to expert witness evidence to be given to the Commercial Court. While this guidance has been issued specifically in relation to the Commercial Court, we consider that it applies to an expert witnesses in *all* cases. The guidance is as follows:

(i)   It is the duty of an expert to help the court on the matters within his expertise. This duty is paramount and overrides any obligation to the person from whom he has received instructions or by whom he is paid.

(ii)   Expert evidence presented to the court should be, and should be seen to be, the independent product of the expert uninfluenced by the exigencies of litigation.

(iii) An expert witness should provide independent assistance to the court by way of objective unbiased opinion in relation to matters within his expertise. An expert witness should never assume the role of an advocate.

(iv)   An expert witness should not omit to consider material facts which could detract from his concluded opinion.

(v)   An expert witness should make it clear when a particular question or issue falls outside his expertise.

(vi)   If an expert's opinion is not properly researched because he considers that insufficient data is available, then this must be stated with an indication that the opinion is no more than a provisional one.

(vii) In a case where an expert witness who has prepared a report could not assert that the report contained the truth, the whole truth and nothing but the truth without some qualification, that qualification should be stated in the report.

(viii) If, after exchange of reports, an expert witness changes his view on any material matter having read another expert's report or for any other reason, such change of view should be communicated in writing (through legal representatives) to the other side without delay, and when appropriate to the court.

An expert appointed to give evidence to the Commercial Court is specifically required to comply with these requirements at all stages of his involvement in the case and must confirm in his report that he has done so.

Please find enclosed an extract from the Civil Procedure Rules (CPR Part 35 and accompanying practice direction), an extract from the Commercial Court Guide (appendix 12 as set above and section H2) and the revised draft code of guidance for experts which set out the relevant provisions relating to expert witnesses.

Team and fees

We understand that your team will consist of [*state members of team*] and that you agree to notify us in advance of any changes or additions to the team.

We understand that your daily rates are as follows:

[*Set out rates for each member of the team*].

[*State any special arrangements in relation to travel or other expenses including any rates for attendance at court and provisions for payment on late notice of cancellation of a court hearing*].

[*State the arrangements for providing for the costs of dealing with questions for experts and discussions between experts*].

[*State whether fees are to be paid by a third party*].

Invoices should be submitted on a [*monthly*] basis direct to [*client*]. The payment terms agreed are [*payment within x days*].

You have indicated that [the likely fee for the team's services will be [£   ]], [the estimated time which is likely to be required for this matter is [   ] hours].

Privilege and confidentiality

This matter is strictly confidential. Save where ordered by the court, no information relating in any way to this matter, or your work for it, is to be disclosed to any third party (other than those who we have confirmed are assisting us or our clients in connection with this case) without the client's prior written consent.

Although material instructions given to you for the purpose of preparing your report, whether written or oral are not privileged and the substance of those instructions must be summarised in your report, you should not disclose these instructions to anyone without our consent or unless ordered to do so by the court.

You must ensure that all necessary internal procedural steps are taken to ensure that these obligations are met.

Our team dealing with this matter is [*partner*] who has overall responsibility for the case, [*assistant/s*] who have responsibility for [*set out roles*] and [*name other members of team where relevant*]. Your primary contact will be [*name relevant assistant/s*]. If you have any questions on any of the matters detailed above, please contact [*state relevant member of team*].

Their contact details are [phone/ fax/ email].

Please confirm your acceptance of this retainer on these terms.

Yours sincerely

APPENDIX O

Form of wording of statement of truth to be included in expert's report

Pro forma wording for inclusion at end of report

- I [the expert] understand my duty to the court and confirm that I have complied with that duty (CPR 35.10(2)).
- I believe that the facts I have stated in this report are true and that the opinions I have expressed are correct.

Pro forma wording for inclusion at end of expert's report prepared for Commercial Court case

- I [the expert] have read and understood Appendix 12 to the Commercial Court Guide.
- I [the expert] have complied with and will continue to comply with Appendix 12 at all stages of my involvement in the case.
- The assumptions upon which my opinion is based are not in my opinion unreasonable or unlikely assumptions (*or, where in the expert's opinion any assumption is unreasonable or unlikely, this must be clearly stated*).
- The facts stated in my report that are facts within my own direct knowledge have been identified as such and are true.
- The opinions in my report represent my true professional opinion.

INDEX

Alternative dispute resolution
commercial contracts, ADR
    clauses, inclusion in, 28
Commercial Court, early neutral
    evaluation procedure, 23, 202,
    203
key features under CPR, 17
overriding objective, compliance
    with, 18, 27
Part 36 offers, use of in relation to,
    79
pre-trial review, consideration
    during, 22
process management, role of in-
    house and external lawyer,
    28–31
professional negligence claims, use
    in, 162, 164
stay of proceedings to facilitate use
    of, 19–21
suitability, client-based screening
    procedure, 28
types of, 202, 203
use in high value commercial
    disputes, 19, 26, 27
use pre-action, 16
Woolf Report, recommendations
    on, 17

Case management
See also **Case management
    conference**
appeals, effect of introducing
    permission requirement, 94
determination of preliminary
    issues, Court of Appeal
    waiting times, 90
evidence, late service, applicable
    penalties, 92
multi-track cases, allocation on
    basis of questionnaire
    response, 84
role of court in, 81, 82

Case management—*contd*
striking out, penalty for failure to
    comply, 92–94
summary judgment, applicable
    test, 90, 91
trial preparation timetables, cost
    implications, 89
use of in multi-track cases, 82, 83
Woolf Report, recommendations
    on, 81

Case management conference
Alternative dispute resolution,
    investigation of use at (*See also*
    **Alternative dispute
    resolution**), 22
Commercial Court, attendance by
    advocate, 88
documentary requirements, 85, 86
legal representative, need for
    knowledge of case, 87, 88
operation during transitional
    phase, 84
reading lists and time estimates, 86

Civil justice reforms
Commercial Court cases, key steps
    under, 211–218
implementation, effect on
    commercial litigation, 1
multi-track action, key steps under,
    204–210
transitional phase, overview of, 2, 3

Conditional fee agreements
action funded under, summary
    assessment of costs, 45
changes under Access to Justice
    Act 1999, 39, 40
effect of use in commercial
    cases, 43
expert witnesses, use of by, 142
implications for corporate
    defendants, 43, 44